HATEMONGER

HATE MONGER

STEPHEN MILLER, DONALD TRUMP, AND THE WHITE NATIONALIST AGENDA

———

JEAN GUERRERO

WM

WILLIAM MORROW

An Imprint of HarperCollinsPublishers

HarperCollins books may be purchased for educational, business, or sales promotional use. For information, please email the Special Markets Department at SPsales@harpercollins.com.

FIRST EDITION

Designed by Kyle O'Brien

Library of Congress Cataloging-in-Publication Data has been applied for.

ISBN 978-0-06-298671-9

20 21 22 23 24 LSC 10 9 8 7 6 5 4 3 2 1

For Armando "Mando" Montaño
Who died young, and lives on

CONTENTS

HATEMONGER

PROLOGUE

STEPHEN MILLER WAS CENTER STAGE. He grinned at the sea of red baseball caps in the San Diego Convention Center on May 27, 2016. In a slim suit with a pocket square, he adjusted the podium microphone and told spectators that his boss—the man who would "save" the country—was about to come out. The crowd erupted. "Are you ready to secure that border?" Miller asked, lifting a finger in the air. "Are you ready to stop Islamic terrorism? And are you ready to make sure that American children are given their birthright in their own country?"

Miller could hardly contain himself. He rocked back and forth on his heels. He swung side to side. Long dismissed as a sideshow, the svelte pale thirty-year-old was months from becoming one of the most powerful people in the US government. He coaxed cheers from thousands in his home state of California, where once he had faced hisses and boos. "I want you to shout so loud that all the people who betrayed you can hear you!" he cried. "Every single person who's beaten you down, and ignored you, and said that you were wrong, and mocked and demeaned and scorned you, every person who's lectured you sanctimoniously while living the high life in DC—shout so loud that their conference tables will shake!"

Outside the convention center, more than a thousand people had gathered to protest Trump's campaign as xenophobic, racist and sexist. They waved signs exclaiming BULLY and BIGOT. They were upset about Trump's characterizations of Mexicans as "rapists" and "criminals" and his call for "a total and complete shutdown of Muslims entering the United States." Trump's fans confronted his critics, ready to brawl. A white man spat the N-word in a black man's face. Someone screamed "Hitler!" A paunchy Trump supporter with a bullhorn told black men they were going to Hell. "You hate Trump! You despise God!" he said. One responded: "God is black!" The white man replied, *"God's not black!"* He continued, "When God puts you in Hell, you're not gonna play the race card with him." He added, mockingly, "I'm just a minority member! I'm just a minority member!"

Trump took the stage. He called his rally a "lovefest." He said people protesting were "thugs." The magnate lamented all of the "young children killed by illegal immigrants." He had hired Miller as a speechwriter and senior policy advisor a few months before. The California native helped craft Trump's attacks on Mexicans and Muslims, drawing from dubious sources, such as research bankrolled by eugenicists and white nationalist websites and texts. He was inspired in part by *The Camp of the Saints,* a virulently racist book by French author Jean Raspail that depicted "the end of the white world" after it was overrun by the Third World, with refugees described as "a single, solid mass, like some gigantic beast with a million legs."[1] The title of the novel comes from the Christian Bible's Book of Revelation, in which Satan and his armies "marched up over the broad plain of the earth and surrounded the camp of the saints," God's beloved city, "but fire came down from heaven and consumed them."

Outside, the racially charged tension and vitriol reached fever pitch. People threw punches. They lit rags on fire. Objects flew.

Police showed up in riot gear, wielding batons, and declared an un-lawful assembly. "If you refuse to move, chemical agents and other weapons will be used," authorities declared in Spanish and English. Helicopters buzzed overhead, the skies turned from blue to gray. People linked arms, determined to stay. By the time the sun set over the bay, dozens of people were handcuffed and jailed.

It's impossible to understand the Trump era, with its unparalleled polarization, without tracing Miller's journey to the White House. Miller is the architect of Trump's border and immigration policies. Prematurely balding and with a penchant for bespoke suits, he has long, articulate fingers that fit a man often depicted as a behind-the-scenes puppeteer. Many are baffled at how someone so young, with little policy or legal expertise, gained so much power— outlasting and overtaking his mentor, Stephen K. Bannon, Trump's former chief strategist. Before joining Trump, Miller was communications director for Senator Jefferson Beauregard Sessions III. He had little other work experience. But it's no accident that a public relations flack guides Trump's central agenda. Trump has long derived power from mythmakers. Author Tony Schwartz made him an American business icon in *The Art of the Deal*. Producer Mark Burnett turned him into a reality TV star in *The Apprentice*. Bannon turned him into an alt-right hero on the blog Breitbart. Miller helped make him president.

In a White House where people are frequently forced out, Miller has survived. Revered by towering figures on the far right— such as radio host Rush Limbaugh—he has been vilified by the left, compared to Nazi propaganda minister Joseph Goebbels and the fictional cave-dwelling creature Gollum. Despite calls for his resignation, he has clung to his office in the West Wing.

He grasps Trump's grudges and goals. Both are showmen. Both enjoy Las Vegas casinos. They owe early affluence to fathers in real estate. Miller flexes loyalty to Trump on TV, attacking critics with a ferocious barrage of verbiage that emerges in complete paragraphs. Both have publicly relished the thought of causing pain and death to criminals. When five black and Latino youth were falsely accused of beating and raping a white woman in Central Park in 1989, Trump paid for full-page ads prior to their wrongful conviction, calling for the "crazed misfits" to be executed. "I want to hate these muggers and murderers," he wrote. At Duke University in 2005, Miller wrote in favor of the death penalty, saying he'd take rapists apart "piece by piece" by hand.[2] Both men have a taste for the morbid.

From the campaign trail to the White House, Miller helped Trump conjure an "invasion" of "animals" come to steal American jobs and spill American blood. He repeatedly beat the drum about the gang Mara Salvatrucha (MS-13), casting the border crisis as a battle between good and evil. Many MS-13 members had tattoos of devil horns and the calling code for El Salvador, 503, on their biceps and backs. The gang formed in Miller's home county of Los Angeles. They comprised less than one percent of gang members in America, but Miller was obsessed with them. The young men partook in the bloodshed of dark fairy tales, luring victims into the forest and using blunt weapons. Miller wrote them into his boss's speeches again and again. From Long Island to DC to the West Coast, Trump invoked their horror-movie crimes. He said, "They butcher those little girls. They kidnap, they extort, they rape and they rob. They prey on children. They shouldn't be here. They stomp on their victims. They beat them with clubs. They slash them with machetes, and they stab them with knives . . . They're animals."

The demonization of migrants is to Miller what the border wall is to Trump: a tool with which to mobilize the base. With it, he sold cruelty and castigation toward brown youths: separating migrant children from parents; revoking protections for people brought to the US as children; incarcerating teenagers with tenuous ties to MS-13; and more. Trump said "alien minors" were "a great cost to life." The nation stomached invisible barricades against families who broke no laws: the suspension of travel from Muslim-majority countries; slashing refugee admissions, mostly from African and Asian countries; cutting off Central American access to US asylum; restricting green cards to the poor. Collectively, those actions choked off legal entries of non-white people and torched America's reputation as a haven for the persecuted. Miller narrowed the focus of the Department of Homeland Security, with its mandate to protect America from cyber threats and terrorism, to sift out the desperate and the destitute.

Miller and Trump are masters of messaging. But like sorcerers who lost control of their spells, they denied any role in the rising tide of white rage. They were not directing Patrick Crusius as he allegedly walked into a Walmart in El Paso with an assault rifle, imagining he was saving the United States from "a Hispanic invasion," and massacred twenty-two people. They did not tell Robert Bowers to murder eleven people at a synagogue in Pittsburgh, one of the federal hate crimes a grand jury has accused him of committing. They did not suggest James Fields Jr. crash his Dodge Challenger into liberal protestors in Charlottesville, Virginia, killing an innocent woman, shattering bones and bloodying dozens of bystanders.

But the duo packaged the hate that fuels white terrorism and sold it like cotton candy at an amusement park. Right-wing militias stocked up on weapons, preparing for revolution. In the midst of an impeachment inquiry, Trump retweeted a pastor's warning of an impending "civil war–like fracture." As early as 2017, Trump's former advisor Roger Stone said, "Try to impeach him. Just try it. You will have a spasm of violence in this country—an insurrection like you've never seen."

———

THE ENTIRE IDEOLOGICAL ARC OF Miller's life can be understood as a quest to save the country after he, too, became convinced it was under threat. He saw America as a damsel in distress: penetrated, invaded, besieged. As a youth, he referred to the US as a female "with a beating heart." Miller was bewitched by right-wing talk radio. The voice of Rush Limbaugh beamed into his hometown of Santa Monica from the state capital, telling him everything he identified with was under attack by liberals, "feminazis," the media and multiculturalism.[3]

These days, California leads the charge against Trump, though the ideas that vaulted Trump to the White House were once mainstream in Miller's home state. When Miller was a boy, Republican governor Pete Wilson invoked an "invasion" of migrants, blaming them for California's fiscal problems. State leaders pushed narratives of migrants as subhuman welfare guzzlers. They circulated a mocking poem in broken English: "We have a hobby, it's called breeding. Welfare pay for baby feeding."[4] Hostility toward migrants became so intense, California passed a proposition to deny public services to the undocumented, including education for their kids. (It was found unconstitutional.)

As a teenager, Miller was courted by a bespectacled, hoarse-voiced ex-Marxist on a mission: to give the weapons of the counterculture 1960s civil rights left to the right. David Horowitz was leading a campaign to defend young conservatives in trouble due to allegations of racism, sexism and homophobia. In 1993, he helped reinstate a university fraternity suspended for circulating flyers honoring a hate song about a "hot fucking, cock-sucking, Mexican whore" named Lupe, a pre–pubescent girl described as becoming so ravenous for sex that she will "suck out your guts," her maggot-filled corpse crying out for more after she mysteriously winds up dead.[5]

The Studio City resident groomed teenagers like Miller through what became his School for Political Warfare. Horowitz told them radical leftists were collaborating with foreign enemies to destroy the US, and that they had to fight viciously to stop them. It was a war of light versus dark forces, and Christian America was at stake. Horowitz taught them to use the language of civil rights to attack civil rights. Wielding the shield of free speech and wearing the armor of oppressed minorities, his acolytes attacked minorities for their perceived assault on the purity of Western heritage. Waving the lance of equality, they pierced equality—an imagined war on self-determination. Miller learned to invert and deflect criticism under his guidance. Horowitz would play a significant role in Trump's campaign, with Miller as his vehicle.

It may strike some as ironic that one of the nation's currently bluest states bred Trump's supporting cast. Other key players were California natives or spent significant time in the state: from Bannon, who produced right-wing documentaries in Hollywood, to Julia Hahn, a Breitbart editor turned special assistant to the president who grew up in Beverly Hills. But there's a logic to California's role. California is the state of Hollywood and Silicon Valley, of reality television and virtual reality—of make-believe. Here in the Golden State on the coast, mythic identity is the main commodity: the glorified antihero; the dream of minds made into eternal algorithms; the obsession with sealing the border in the name of "Western heritage." What these ideas express is not an excess of imagination but the opposite: the mind overtaken by a single fantasy.

Reality bends to such fantasy. American essayist Rebecca Solnit describes a right-wing ideology of isolation that stems from fantastical notions of virility, embodied by the gun-toting cowboys of the Western.[6] This vision stems from a fear of penetration, and can yield homophobia, misogyny, xenophobia and Trump's immigration policy.

Trump knew how to hatemonger before he met Miller. He'd been doing it for decades. But when their paths collided, there was an alchemy. Trump's riches, marketing instinct and emotional racism merged with Miller's fanatical ideology, work ethic and strategic thinking. America's flesh-and-bones reality as a nation of immigrants strained under the weight of Miller's conviction, Trump's populism and their instincts for doubling down.

Miller sought to deter flows of brown and black people into the United States by plugging "loopholes" and sending a tough message. It didn't work. Border apprehensions rose to their highest level in more than a decade. Unable to enter legally through Trump-tightened ports of entry, families climbed the border fencing. Children were teargassed. The surge continued, a steady increase since Trump's first year in office. Thousands of Central American families marched to the border, images of their tired masses reaching fans of *The Camp of the Saints* like the fulfillment of a fantasy. Miller blamed the Deep State and the Democrats. He purged DHS leadership. When a career official derided as an Obama holdover was given a chance at the helm in 2019, that official stemmed the migrant influx through diplomacy in Central America.

Miller repeatedly harnessed crises to boost Trump's popularity with the base and promote delusions of a plot to ruin America. As the president faced impeachment for abuse of power and obstruction of Congress, Miller turned that trouble into a doomsday pitch for reelection, helping his boss draft a long, dramatic letter to House Speaker Nancy Pelosi, accusing her of endangering democracy. "Your egregious conduct threatens to destroy that which our Founders pledged their very lives to build," it read. The letter cited the threat of "open borders."

This is the story of how Miller grabbed control of one of the most important issues of our time. Every fiction begins with us versus them, with the separation of one from another. Miller's story is

America's story: a microcosm for our path to the present. His child-hood reveals the roots of Trump's white nationalist agenda and the rupture at the heart of our country. As a boy, Miller waged an ideo-logical war on his dark-skinned classmates and their supporters. He learned to speak in terms of heritage and culture rather than race and skin color. Later, he fought to revive a racially exclusionary im-migration system. He and Trump identify as nationalists, not white nationalists. But their brand of nationalism—politically incorrect, full of dog whistles for white supremacists, built from white nation-alist ideas—deliberately energized and enraged white men across the nation. Miller and Trump rode that rage to the White House, where they began to change the ethnic flows into the United States and will continue to do so for as long as they can.

"Are you ready to show them who's still in charge?" Miller asked the mostly white male crowd in San Diego. He savored the roars. They validated his extremism, validated a vision that was transforming the country and the world. "Are you ready to do something they will write about for a thousand years?"

CHAPTER ONE

"BROWN ANIMALS"

STEPHEN GREW UP IN AN apocalyptic decade of Los Angeles. Earthquakes shook the city. An inferno reddened the skies and tore through the verdant seaside mountains near his home in Santa Monica, devouring hundreds of houses. In 1992, several miles east of him, thousands of people rioted when a jury decided that four policemen who had brutally beaten Rodney King, a black man, were not guilty. Sixty-three people were killed, thousands were injured, businesses were looted and burned. On televisions across the nation people watched a white truck driver as he was pulled from his rig and beaten nearly to death. His name, Reginald Denny, would echo through white homes in Southern California to justify racist anxieties for decades.

While Stephen played with his siblings in Santa Monica, the demographics of his home state were changing. *Time* ran a cover story about the "browning" of America, and California was ground zero.[1] President Reagan had signed the Immigration Reform and Control Act in 1986, offering amnesty to millions in exchange for sanctions against employers who knowingly hire anyone in the country without legal permission. But the workplace enforcement provisions were rarely enforced and easy to evade; companies kept hiring the undocumented. Illegal entries continued unabated, especially through Southern California.

California was in the midst of a recession due in part to a battering by nature—earthquakes, fires, floods—triggering an exodus of people out of the state.[2] Governor Pete Wilson, a former San Diego mayor, saw an opportunity. He won reelection in 1994 by blaming the migrant "invasion" for the state's fiscal problems.[3] He ran television advertisements showing parents running across the border from Mexico through the San Ysidro Port of Entry in California, clutching their children. "They keep coming," an ominous voice said over the footage.[4]

Dozens of people were dying in highway traffic collisions as they raced into the country, desperate for the American dream. Officials erected yellow "Caution" signs along Interstate 5, like deer-crossing traffic signs, depicting silhouettes of sprinting families.

When Stephen was five years old, hundreds of families with Spanish surnames received a letter in their mailboxes from the Santa Monica–Malibu Unified School District headquarters. Whoever sent the letter used the district's bulk-mail permit number and address labels. It looked official. When the families opened it, they found a typed, one-page hate screed.[5] It opened with a reference to a drive-by shooting at Santa Monica High School, which Stephen would attend in a few years. The author said Mexicans were making the community unsafe and using up welfare. It called Mexicans "brown animals" and read: "We'll gas you like Hitler gassed the Jews."

The screed denied the existence of racism among white people and accused Mexicans of being "the real racists." It singled out Mexican American alumnus Oscar de la Torre, alleging that he had been elected student body president of the high school the previous year because he was Mexican. "De la Torre isn't smart enough to be ASB [Associate Student Body] janitor," the letter read. "Why should there be a double standard for these wild beasts?" It called for a boycott of Mexican celebrations such as Cinco de Mayo, and of the student group MEChA, the Chicano Student Movement of Aztlán. The text said Mexicans "infest our community with gays and lesbians." It encouraged them to put on bulletproof vests and get ready for the gun battle.

De la Torre was nineteen. His family received a copy of the letter, which appeared under the letterhead of a "Samohi Assn. for the Advancement of Conservative White Americans"—Samohi is a nickname for Santa Monica High School. With dimples and thick, arched black eyebrows, de la Torre was the son of immigrants from Jalisco, Mexico, and would dedicate his life to advocating for low-income youth of color. He called for a thorough investigation of the hate crime. Police said they suspected someone in the school was responsible.[6] "It was an inside job," de la Torre says.[7] "It was someone who had access to the high school databases. Every Latino, every Spanish surnamed person in the school."

Police retained a copy of the letter for fingerprints, but the hate crime remains unsolved as of this writing. A public records request turned up a single police report.[8] De la Torre says the lack of a resolution is indicative of how Santa Monica leaders felt, and feel, about racism. "Put it under the rug, let's not talk about it," he says.[9]

A couple of years later, a Republican in the California Assembly circulated a poem depicting migrants as parasitic: "We have a hobby, it's called breeding. Welfare pay for baby feeding . . . We think America damn good place. Too damn good for white man race."[10] The racist narrative disregarded the fact that migrants disproportionately take jobs requiring rigorous physical labor, such as construction, agriculture and meatpacking. But it gave people someone to blame. By focusing on "criminals," and "illegals," the state's leaders could insist that they were worried about people breaking the law and deny allegations of racism. They could accuse their critics of political correctness. "In the past, coded language has usually been a way for the oppressed to disguise their criticism of those in power," wrote local historian Rodolfo F. Acuña in 1996.[11] "Today, it is part of the ideological strategy of Euroamerican elites, serving to justify their domination of communities of color while disguising openly racist sentiments (*criminal* instead of *mexican*)."

California's right-wing politicians, in collaboration with far-right think tanks, websites and media personalities, launched a coded assault on non-white identity as a threat to public safety and prosperity. Slowly, the state was shaping the rhetoric that would one day vault Donald J. Trump to the White House. California conservatives blamed Mexicans for crime, congestion and plunging real estate values. Los Angeles was becoming a "third world cesspool," according to protest signs.[12] The San Fernando Valley had gone from ninety-two percent white in 1960 to only fifty-eight percent white in 1990. "Anglo anxiety in the face of demographic change was rampant," wrote Acuña. White supremacists spread their ideas online, forming new groups, splintering, multiplying. They began cloaking racist ideologies in the language of heritage and culture for new recruits. In 1993, federal agents in Los Angeles broke up a white terrorist plot to attack a black church and start a race war. Former Ku Klux Klan leader Tom Metzger called Southern California the "breeding ground" for white separatism.[13] Vigilantes stopped brown people on the street and asked for green cards. Militias gathered at the border.

Wilson sued the Clinton administration for the costs of incarcerating the "aliens." He sent California National Guard troops to the border. Wilson, who had been lagging in the polls, won reelection. Others took note. Democratic leader Dianne Feinstein told CBS's *Face the Nation* that "illegal aliens" were devouring state services—taking housing, classroom space and Medicaid. She proposed charging a $1 toll for legal border crossers to pay for more border guards. President Bill Clinton launched Operation Gatekeeper in California, beefing up border security through floodlights, surveillance cameras, ground sensors, helicopters and steel barriers.

Pat Buchanan ran for president parroting Wilson's rhetoric about an invasion, and urged that Western heritage stop being "dumped onto some landfill called multiculturalism." Whites, he said, were fleeing "Mexifornia." Buchanan lost. Later, experts attributed his failed bid to the fact that social media—which rewards the incendiary with virality—had yet to take off.[14]

But in California, the ideas spread far and wide. In 1994, the state passed Prop 187, a proposition to deny non-emergency social services to people who were in the country illegally. The brown community was spurred to action, organizing massive student walkouts and protests. The most controversial aspect of the bill was that it hurt migrant children, barring them from schools. "Providing public education for illegal alien children was by far the largest single cost factor," says one of the Prop 187 drafters, former US attorney Pete Nuñez. "How could you leave [public education] out, if your argument was that illegal immigration costs taxpayers?"[15]

It provoked a backlash. University MEChA groups linked up with high school students. They worked to speed up the naturalization of their loved ones. The mobilization would turn California deep blue, and Prop 187 was ruled unconstitutional. In 1982, the US Supreme Court had guaranteed access to public schools, citing the Fourteenth Amendment, which says no state can "deny to any person within its jurisdiction the equal protection of the laws." The Court also found there is no rational basis to deny education to migrant children, given that doing so would harm the greater society. "By denying these children a basic education," the Court explained, "we deny them the ability to live within the structure of our civic institutions, and foreclose any realistic possibility that they will contribute in even the smallest way to the progress of our Nation." The Court also stated that punishing children for the actions of their parents "does not comport with fundamental conceptions of justice."

Anti-immigrant sentiments remained mainstream, though. Slurs like "wetbacks" and "beaners" were common schoolyard taunts. The word "Mexican" became an insult.

California Mexicans preferred to call themselves "Hispanic." Some looked down on new arrivals as "indios." In Latin America, racism and white supremacy are widespread, as in the US. In Mexico, the criticism "malinchista" refers to someone who prefers white foreigners to her own dark people. It comes from the legend of Malinche, an indigenous woman who helped the Spaniards defeat the natives (a controversial insult now, as feminists point out that Malinche was enslaved and had no choice). The ruling elites across Latin America are often lighter skinned than the majority, prioritizing foreign interests in exchange for favors.

Euroamerican identification is catalyzed among immigrants in the United States through saturation in the culture. "It is more than a cliché that many Mexicans and Latinos want to be white, or at least consider fairer skin better. The innocuous praise of relatives and friends for a newborn child '*Qué bonita pero prietita!*' ('How pretty she is, but a little dark!') thus takes on special meaning: darkness has many connotations, most of them negative," wrote Acuña. In the nineties, many Mexicans in California advertised their food as "Spanish." They bragged about European ancestors. They told their offspring: You're *American*. Many second-generation immigrants grew up contemptuous of their parents' flawed English. Assimilation often meant self-loathing.

Stephen grew up knowing Mexico and Mexicans. His family crossed the border to go on vacations. He noticed that people there wore American blue jeans and played American music. They loved the electric guitar. One December, people in Mexico wished him "Merry Christmas." He was pleased by their imitation, and later wrote that he "appreciated the spirit and kindness of the gesture and the genuine atmosphere of warmth it created."[16] He had no problems with Mexicans and other ethnicities, so long as they acted like him. Miller was Jewish, but he felt American above all. He saw Christmas as an expression of American culture. "Plus, we make up only 2 percent of the country's population," he wrote of Jews, explaining the importance of non-Jewish holidays to him.

He was growing up on right-wing talk radio, which was on the rise. The most notorious host, Rush Limbaugh, broadcast out of California's state capital. In 1992, he published a book called *The Way Things Ought to Be*—one of Miller's most formative books. "It was like a page-turning thriller to me. Every page was like some new revelation," Stephen later said.[17] Limbaugh railed against multiculturalism, "feminazis" and anyone who tried to make white men feel guilty. "I'm tired of hearing [Christopher Columbus] trashed," he wrote. "I don't give a hoot that he gave some Indians a disease that they didn't have immunity against . . . We're the best country on earth and I'm sick and tired of people trying to change history so as to portray this country as an instrument of evil. I'm sick and tired of hearing Western culture constantly disparaged."[18]

In Limbaugh's world, wealthy white men were the aggrieved ones. Anyone else who complained lacked self-reliance. He complained about an "out of touch" liberal media, Hollywood "elites" and school administrators, "We're teaching kids about tribal Africa instead of Aristotle." Women created feminism to "terrorize" men. Anita Hill was guilty of "one of the most heinous, malevolent attempts at character assassination." He belittled sexual harassment claims by women and said, "I love the women's movement . . . when I am walking behind it." He peddled conspiracy theories. He expressed contempt for the poor. "The poor in this country are the biggest piglets at the mother pig and her nipples," Limbaugh wrote. "The poor feed off of the largesse of this government and they give nothing back. Nothing. They're the ones who get all the benefits in this country. They're the ones that are always pandered to."

Miller was growing up in a world in which everything he identified with was under attack, according to Limbaugh. Miller's father, meanwhile, was waging his own battles on the home and business front. In 1991, Michael Miller sued his former law firm, claiming he had been forced out in violation of their partnership agreement and that they owed him $750,000, according to court documents. His old partners denied the allegations.[19] They said Michael had stopped showing up, billing time or generating clients for years—in other words, resigned. They pointed to a statement he himself had submitted to the Stanford Law School: "In 1987, I left the practice of law to pursue full time employment in real estate." Their court documents described Michael as "a masterpiece of evasion and manipulation," stating that he pressured the firm's legal clients to invest in his real estate ventures and refused to answer questions about his plans—making it difficult for the firm to operate. Michael denied the allegations, according to court documents, and argued that the firm owed much of its success to his family name.[20]

"Michael was very combative," recalls his former law partner David Stern, who said he harbors no hard feelings and even testified on his behalf in a subsequent case.[21] "It's just that some people, when confronted with a problem, try to resolve it. Others, like our president, like Stephen Miller, double and quadruple down. Michael definitely comes from the double- and quadruple-down school." In a court statement, Stern wrote: "Michael did not always operate rationally and sometimes let ego and selfishness, rather than fairness and good sense, guide him."

In 1992, Stephen's father's business began to experience cash flow problems in the midst of proceedings against his former law firm and a broader real estate recession.[22] The banks demanded payment on millions of dollars in loans. Michael didn't have the money, according to court documents.[23] They show that Michael filed for bankruptcy on multiple real estate partnerships. The Miller family faced the prospect of having to move out of the wealthy neighborhood North of Montana, where they lived in a five-bedroom house worth more than a million dollars. And then, on January 17, 1994, Stephen's sense of security was utterly rocked.

Just before dawn, a buried thrust fault slipped in the bowels of the earth, about eleven miles underground. Los Angeles shook hard, for the fourth time in Stephen's life. The 6.7-magnitude quake lasted less than twenty seconds, but in that span of time freeways snapped like twigs. Buildings and freeway bridges collapsed. Drivers crashed into the crumbling infrastructure. Gas from ruptured lines erupted into fires, consuming more construction.

The Northridge earthquake killed dozens of people and destroyed about twenty billion dollars in property. The Millers survived, but Cordary, Inc., properties were damaged. The company lost millions of dollars in equity, according to court documents. A few months later, in the case against his former law firm, the judge sided with the defendants, ordering Michael to pay nearly $275,000 in attorneys' fees for his former partners. He had lost the fight. "They had a rapid descent after a great deal of success," says Stephen's maternal uncle David Glosser.[24] "It was a time of great tension and anxiety."

Stephen's mom, Miriam, joined Michael at Cordary, Inc., as executive vice president. They hired Latin American housekeepers to cook meals and clean up after the children. Stephen was not a fan. He told a boy he hung out with, Taylor Brinckerhoff, that one housekeeper was "kind of emotionally abusive." He said his parents fired her after she stole a checkbook and tried to forge a check.[25]

Meanwhile, Miriam brought a new flair to the family real estate company. Decades later, the properties boasted about a "multicultural environment" and showcased fun activities: "fried chicken Friday"; pajama breakfasts ("Get out your flannel jammies and silly onesies . . . for pancakes, pastries and more! Photo station will be available!"); a wine and cheese party; a "Howl & Growl Halloween" featuring a dog costume contest; free AMC movie tickets for children who bring in ticket stubs proving they watched the civil rights film *Selma*; and a meeting with a nature expert who brought live tarantulas, snakes and Madagascar hissing cockroaches.[26]

When one resident complained about unrelated cockroaches in an online review, Miriam wrote: "We agree cockroaches are yucky and no one wants to have them . . . we baited and then sprayed your apartment . . . sorry you had a bad experience."[27]

In Stephen's third-grade class picture at Franklin Elementary School, he looks dazed and disheveled. Most of the other children are smiling and groomed. Later, his third-grade teacher, Nikki Fiske, would say he "was off by himself all the time." His desk was a mess, with "stuff mashed up," and he would pour glue on his body, then peel it off and eat it.[28] Fiske compared him to the Peanuts comic character Pig Pen, "with the dust cloud and crumbs flying all around him." Miller shared a desk with John Muller, a blond-haired boy with large glasses. "Along the midpoint of our desk, Stephen laid down a piece of white masking tape, explaining that it marked the boundary of our sides and that I was not to cross it," Muller later wrote, puzzled.[29] "I was a fairly neat kid . . . Stephen, meanwhile, could not have been much messier: his side of the desk was sticky and peeling, littered with scraps of paper, misshapen erasers and pencil nubs."

Jason Islas, a Mexican American boy in the class, was also having a hard time. In the class photo he has a glint in his eyes, wearing knee-high socks and brown boots with red shoelaces. His working-class parents were struggling with cocaine addiction and domestic violence.[30] They lived mid-city in a one-bedroom apartment; Islas slept in the living room with his brother. As their problems escalated, his parents decided to temporarily relocate to Kauai, to rebuild a hurricane-damaged house that belonged to his stepdad's father. Islas left Santa Monica in the middle of third grade to deal with the disaster. Miller stayed and confronted the earthquake. Soon, the boys would become friends.

SOUTH OF THE BORDER, IN Mexico, small farmers, known as campesinos, were also experiencing a cataclysmic shift in fortune. When the North American Free Trade Agreement (NAFTA) went into effect in 1994, they found themselves unable to compete with heavily subsidized US agriculture. Prices plummeted. They fled north to find jobs.[31] Their abandoned coffee and maize fields were turned into opium poppy fields. The new illegal trade led to violence, fueling the exodus.[32]

The Clinton administration launched Prevention Through Deterrence. By boosting resources for Border Patrol and new barriers, the government predicted that "illegal traffic will be deterred, or forced over more hostile terrain," where migrants will be in "mortal danger."[33] The strategy pushed the exiles into the desert, where hundreds began to bake or freeze to death.

The lopsided treaty that set them on a fatal path had been negotiated by US president George H. W. Bush, Canadian prime minister Brian Mulroney and Mexican president Carlos Salinas de Gortari. As a child, Salinas had fatally shot his twelve-year-old servant, Manuela, with his father's .22-caliber rifle, according to the Mexican newspaper *El Universal*.[34] He had been playing a game with his brother and neighbor. "I killed her with one shot, I'm a hero," he allegedly bragged to a reporter.[35]

The bullet struck Manuela's cheekbone at an upward angle and penetrated her skull. The boy's family told police they had just hired her and didn't know her last name or where she was from. The incident was ruled an accident; nobody was charged; copies of newspapers reporting the incident disappeared from libraries in Mexico for years. Salinas became one of the most powerful men, reviled by many in Mexico as a malinchista. And while he brought Mexico into the era of free trade and industrial manufacturing, he did it with a death sentence for the campo, forcing poor rural families to migrate north just as the US built a wall that pushed them into the desert, where thousands would die, forgotten, like Manuela.

STEPHEN'S FAMILY SOLD THEIR HOME in North of Montana. They purchased a home south of the 10 Freeway, near the largely Latin American neighborhood of Pico, in 1998. This house was smaller: a four-bedroom two-story house, peach-painted.

Some Kias, Lexuses and a Ford Mustang are parked on the street. There are fewer lawns than in North of Montana, as residents have replaced grass with drought-friendly succulents promoted by city subsidies. The harsh crowing of ravens punctures the birdsong and wind chimes. Some neighbors have box-shaped homes, built for Douglas Aircraft employees around World War II. One has a notice of intent to demolish. Several have been replaced by what some residents call "monster mansions." A building crew at one of them was recently harassed by a belligerent white man. He shouted the lyrics of "La Cucaracha," a Spanish folk song about a cockroach missing its legs. He chanted "Donald Trump," and said, "Hey beaners, this is not your country. Go back to Mexico." Neighbors exchanged concerned emails about it.[36]

Residents say the Millers keep to themselves. One says they cycle through housekeepers. "A new maid comes, and another maid comes. So it must be quite difficult," says the resident.[37] I knock on the door of the Miller home. A fifty-nine-year-old Peruvian woman, Gladys Quispe, opens the door. She says she can't speak about her employers without violating their privacy. But she agrees to tell me her story.

Quispe is a warm, vivid storyteller.[38] She was twenty-six when the streets of Peru were filled with bombs and bullets as President Alan García cracked down on Marxist guerrillas. When her son, Joshua, was an infant, she left his father, who was abusive. She had been raised by a single mother who taught her independence, so she thought she could raise her son on her own. Quispe even completed her certification as a nursing assistant. But the instability made it impossible to earn a living. She heard about people going to the US. A smuggler told her he could get her there, but it was too dangerous to take her son—he was too young.

She kissed Joshua and promised to come back for him, leaving him with her mother for now. She flew to Mexico City, then to Tijuana, where she met the smugglers nicknamed "coyotes." She recalled their whistle to cross, how she ran across a field, how the full moon illuminated her and the others like a lamp. Her heart drummed in her chest. She was the only woman in the group of crossers, her hair braided and pinned against her head. A Border Patrol vehicle rolled up to them in the dark. The coyotes sprinted down a canyon and led them into a ditch. Hissed at them to get down. "I didn't even breathe because I was so scared," she says in Spanish. Her face pressed against the earth, she lay still, cactus thorns digging into her flesh. They stood after more than an hour. The coyotes told them to close their eyes and hold on to each other.

She smelled something. They entered a tunnel and her feet became wet in a mush. They descended deeper into the sewage: suffocating, revolting, acidic. The thought of her son kept her going; she was shaking; she feared she'd drown. But then she saw rays of sunlight through her closed lids. They exited. She fell to her knees and sobbed. The men around her wept like boys. "I will never forget how I came to this country," she says.

The coyotes watched them, then took them to a stream where they could wash off. They placed her in the trunk of a car to Los Angeles. Once there, she got to work. She was able to repay the smuggler and send money to her mother and son. She saw baby Joshua grow up through photos, footprints and handprints on paper, letters. She spoke to him on the phone, listening to his voice change. She longed to visit, but it took until 1998—more than a decade—to acquire legal status. She immediately visited him and arranged for him to immigrate. They were reunited in 2002. After years of dedicating her life to cleaning the homes of the rich, she could live alongside her son. He was so handsome; his grandmother raised him well, with values and a work ethic. He finished school and started working in construction. Less than two years later, as they sat at home in South Central Los Angeles, happily, she told Joshua she didn't plan to clean houses forever. She wanted to do something to help those less fortunate: a community development project. "You can count on me to help," said her son. They were worried about the violence in their neighborhood. So many youths had gotten involved in gangs due to the lack of opportunity. They hadn't had a strong guide like Quispe's mother. Joshua told her he was going to the beach. He borrowed her car. While driving back to have dinner, he was fatally shot by members of a gang. "If God created man in his image," Quispe says, in tears, "why would we just live and cease to exist after death? It makes no sense. I analyze it and it makes no sense."

The crime was never solved. She has nobody to blame. Sometimes, in her grief, she blames herself. But she knows everything she did was out of love for Joshua, and she believes that she will see him again when she departs this world. Even if she could look his killer in the face, she says, she would feel sorrow for him. "We are all born innocent," she says. She doesn't understand why some people are so hell-bent on vilifying groups of people, as if some are inherently good and others inherently bad. "I truly believe that every human being has a right to have joy, to have a plate of food, to have an education, to be clothed, to be loved," she says.

The Miller house is a short walk from an underpass with a mural depicting the history of the Pico neighborhood. It was painted in 1983, depicting how the construction of the Santa Monica Freeway destroyed the homes of people of color: running through a cracked house, by a burning home on the beach, through brown hands.

STEPHEN WAS COMING OF AGE in the nineties, as people found like-minded strangers in chat rooms and forums on the World Wide Web. Antigovernment conspiracy theories were breeding online, with references to globalist elites plotting a New World Order.[39] Extremists calling themselves "Patriots" interpreted patriotism as the fight to dismantle the "evil" government and scale back civil rights. White terrorists bombed a federal building in Oklahoma City, killing 168 people, ranting about a socialist takeover.

In middle school, Stephen bought himself a subscription to *Guns & Ammo* during a magazine drive. From the cover, it looked more interesting than the other magazines offered.[40] He read a column by Charlton Heston, an actor turned gun-rights activist. It led him to *Guns, Crimes, and Freedom* by Wayne LaPierre, the leader of the National Rifle Association (NRA). The book argues that the founders wrote the Second Amendment to protect Americans' freedom. "This is about freedom. Not crime, not hunting, not recreation. Freedom," he wrote.

Stephen had a black cowboy hat he often wore.[41] He took pleasure in the writings of these men, whose tough voices filled his head and kept him company when his parents were busy. His father worked late. Playing at the house of his companion Taylor Brinckerhoff, Stephen told him he didn't want to sleep over because he wanted to see his dad and he hadn't seen him in a while. Stephen repeatedly told Taylor a story about going to an amusement park with his father.[42] When it turned out Stephen wasn't tall enough for one of the roller coasters, his dad stuffed his shoes with napkins to increase his perceived height. Stephen seemed amused by his father's ingenuity.

Stephen asked Taylor what he thought the worst punishment was. "The worst punishment is when my parents tell me I can't watch TV or that I'm grounded," Taylor said. "No, the worst punishment is the silent treatment," Stephen said. "What's the silent treatment?" Taylor asked. "It's when they just don't talk to you," Stephen said.

Stephen's father was fighting with his brother, according to court documents.[43] William Miller, who was eight years older than Michael and had a PhD in psychology, had invested money in Cordary, Inc., and leased offices for his counseling practice. William began to believe his brother, Michael, and father, Jay, who had become increasingly close through the business, were not being honest about how investments were being managed. In 1996, William sued for money allegedly owed to him by Cordary, Inc. In a statement, he wrote that Jay told him: "I won't pay. I know how to manipulate the law and the courts." Michael countersued, accusing his older brother of slander.

While engaged in that court dispute, two Miller property partnerships filed voluntary petitions for bankruptcy. A Citibank assignee sued Cordary, Inc., accusing Michael and Jay of withholding tens of thousands of dollars in security deposits owed to them, and of "intentionally and willfully" making false statements about transferring the money.[44] Michael and Jay filed a cross-complaint against the banks, brokers and more. The petitions for bankruptcy were dismissed. Cordary, Inc., lost several multimillion-dollar properties. The parties reached a settlement in 1999. Michael also reached a settlement with his brother.

It's unclear to what degree Stephen was aware of his father's battles. But surely he felt the tension, which may have informed his growing contrarian stance toward the world.

During a religious class Miller attended at temple, students were having a talk about ethics. The rabbi asked if it was ethical to pluck a few grapes from a grocery store counter and eat them. The students agreed that doing so was unethical, a form of stealing. Miller took the opposing position. It seemed to a participant that he was trying to get attention.[45] Another time, during a Hebrew class, pupils discussed how to fairly split up a slice of pizza. Miller reached forward and rested his palm on it—cutting off the debate about how to ethically share it.[46]

In 2000, Jay and his wife, Freya, wrote a will giving one-third of their multimillion-dollar estate to each of their children: William, Suzanne and Michael, with $5,000 for each of the grandkids and numerous donations, according to court records.[47] The estate included their Malibu coast home, Picasso artwork, a Chagall print, Freya's paintings, jewelry and a stock portfolio consisting of hundreds of stock shares in aircraft companies, banks and more. They left money to Jewish Family Service, the Anti-Defamation League, the Malibu Jewish Center and Synagogue and other Jewish organizations.

Around this time, Michael began prohibiting his older brother from attending family and holiday parties, according to court documents filed by William. His attorneys argued that Michael threatened "to disallow his parents from seeing their grandchildren" if William was included in events. In 2003, their parents amended their will so that Michael and his sister Suzanne would receive half of their estate each, with the exception of just $100,000 for William. When their father died in 2005, Freya ceded her rights as executor to Michael. William contested the amendments as "void and unenforceable" due to "undue influence and/or duress." His attorneys wrote, "Michael threatened and yelled at his parents whenever they or either of them evinced a willingness to include William in any family gatherings . . . these acts cumulatively over the years caused the Contestant's parents to treat Contestant not as an equal child, but as a less deserving child."

William alleged that Michael took advantage of their father's "lack of capacity stemming from his physical/emotional deterioration after 2000." He said his psychological credentials substantiated his contentions. Michael denied all of his brother's allegations. William dropped the suit. He was unwilling to put his mother "through the trauma of a deposition and testifying in Court," according to court documents, "because [he] was concerned that if Freya was compelled to testify, her relations with Michael and his sister Suzanne would be greatly compromised."

Freya wrote William a series of letters, which he brought to the court after her death in 2015. "Jay and I loved William very much and I wanted him to be treated equally," she wrote in 2005. "I Freya B Miller want my share of the survivor's trust to be left to my son William Miller to equalize the disparity," she wrote in 2007. "Jay and I wanted my (our) 3 children to be treated equally," she wrote in 2008.

Michael learned about the letters, and Freya revoked them in formal amendments. Michael's attorneys wrote: "Despite it being clear that the trustors jointly decided to treat William differently than their other children, William, by means of deception, fraud, and undue influence, caused Freya to execute multiple handwritten documents."

The family reached a settlement. Michael agreed to give William $200,000. William agreed to "withdraw all allegations made by him." Michael included a draft no-contact clause, stating that William "shall forever cease and desist from making any attempts to contact" him or his sister. But Michael wanted the settlement to have "teeth," according to court documents. He expanded the no-contact clause to include spouses, children and grandchildren. William contested the clause, unwilling to be permanently separated from his nieces, nephews and other family. Michael's attorneys wrote, "Petitioner only wants to prolong this decades long dispute with his family because the only contact he has with them is through litigation."

When it became clear he had to sign the agreement or risk losing the settlement money, William signed. He would never speak to his closest relatives again.

AS MICHAEL WENT TO WAR with his brother and the banks, Stephen was going through puberty. He had a collection of political speeches by George Washington, Thomas Jefferson and more.[48] He broke into pedantic and performative arguments. He was the outspoken middle child. His sister, Alexis, was confident but less provocative. Jacob was quiet. All were studious.[49]

Stephen watched the original *Star Trek* series. He liked following William Shatner's Captain Kirk on his galactic quest "to boldly go where no man has gone before." His classmate Jason Islas, meanwhile, was in Kauai exploring nature. "All you needed was a tree and an empty field and you were good for hours," Islas says. Papaya trees and hibiscus grew in the backyard. Sugarcane rose nearby. The hurricane-damaged house his family was fixing was a studio with a half partition where the children slept. The family hiked and spent days on the beach. His mother and stepfather went to individual therapy and family therapy with the children. "They were really trying to make a difference and better themselves," he says.

When Jason's family decided to return to Santa Monica, having had their fill of the island, Islas entered seventh grade at Lincoln Middle School, his skin browned by the sun. He and Miller became friends. The boys had a mutual love of space travel. Islas wanted to be an astronaut, and even went to the Oahu Challenger center for a space travel simulation. Miller talked excitedly about *Star Trek* episodes on the phone. In one, Captain Kirk admonishes his crew for seeking to blast an alien ship. He says, "The greatest danger facing us is ourselves, and irrational fear of the unknown. There's no such thing as the unknown, only things temporarily hidden, temporarily not understood." The alien ship threatens to blow them up. Spock tells Captain Kirk that they're doomed. "Checkmate." Captain Kirk replies, "Not chess, Mister Spock. Poker." He broadcasts a bluff to the hostile ship: the Enterprise is shielded by "corbomite," which would cause any attack to backfire. It works. They're spared and survive. Islas hadn't watched *Star Trek,* but he liked imagining the dramas Miller described on the phone, back when dialup was an issue and children had to compete with siblings who wanted to chat on AOL. "I spent a lot of time listening to him, more than talking," Islas says. "It was sort of a lopsided relationship . . . He was confident, and I'm sure that's what drew me to him. He expressed his opinions. He seemed comfortable in his skin. He was very much himself, whoever he was."

Islas, on the other hand, did not. The radio beamed negative commentary about Mexicans across the state. But he loved his Mexican roots. His mother's charming and ornery *bisabuela,* Grandma Bama, spoke Spanish and made sweet tamales with cinnamon. She wrapped warm homemade tortillas in cloth and placed them in wicker baskets. His biological father, whom he hadn't seen in Kauai, drove him to Tijuana, Mexico, for a day trip and bought an Aztec sunstone sculpture. Islas studied the complex hieroglyphs on the solar calendar—the serpent, coatl; the lizard, cuetzpalin; the flint knife, tecpatl—and felt a sense of pride.

"I really got into my Latino heritage," Islas says. His seventh-grade teacher assigned a "Who Am I" project. They had to fill a binder with research about their identity. Islas investigated his ancestors and began to take Spanish classes. He learned his paternal great-grandfather had fled Mexico during the revolution in the early 1900s. The nation's new leaders were scapegoating priests and other religious leaders. "He was somehow associated with the church, so the story goes that his mom basically said you gotta go, they're gonna kill you."

Islas, Miller and their friend Chris Moritz ate lunch together. Moritz, born in Santa Monica like the others, carried himself like a New Englander. He wore casual Nantucket gear and spoke formally, evoking the original Santa Monica beach boy of the fifties. The boys had special things in common. They listened to Frank Sinatra, not pop music. They geeked out on history and science fiction. Miller's hairline was receding slightly, and he said he was proud of it because it made him look distinguished. "He had a strange way of taking things other people would have been insecure about and turning them into strengths."

Miller made comments about his Latin American housekeeper that made Islas uncomfortable. He said he hated that she dropped him off at school in her "junky" car, which made him "look poor." Islas felt the discomfort of his class. He wanted to defend the poor woman, but he was nervous. "It made me feel bad about myself, so I just kept quiet," he says.

Islas became anxious about his wardrobe. He asked his mother to buy him a suit for Miller's bar mitzvah. His mother was barely scraping by, but she bought him one at Nordstrom. Then Islas had a confirmation party that was also a baptism and First Communion; he had never undergone those rituals until he decided to reconnect with his Mexican heritage. He recalled worrying that Miller would judge him for his modest party.

"Stephen's bar mitzvah [celebration] was on the beach in Malibu at a beautiful restaurant. And my confirmation party was in my uncle's backyard. We had a bounce house for the kids because there were lots of kids—we were a big family—and a grill for the carne asada. And my aunts and uncles sitting around on plastic furniture, you know, outdoor yard furniture, drinking beers, having a great time. In retrospect I'm like, that's the party I want to be at. Not the one where I have to worry about whether or not I'm wearing the right suit."

The summer after middle school, Islas called Miller and left a voicemail. Weeks went by without a response. "I have a vague recollection of worrying how I was gonna manage to be friends with him in high school . . . I wanted to branch out." A few days before high school started, he got a call back. Miller launched into a speech that would remain seared in Islas's memory. He told him they couldn't be friends anymore because of Islas's Latino heritage and a list of other attributes. "What he targeted was, looking back, an impressive feat of understanding what I didn't like about myself . . . It was the opposite of empathy, where you're able to tune into someone's emotional space and then hurt them because you're emotionally aware enough to know what hurts them," Islas said. "He talked about my height—I'm five foot four, I've always been a small kid, shorter on average for most of my life, still am. He talked about my skin—I didn't have great skin." He attacked his lack of confidence, "all the things I had doubts about. And then he topped it off with the whole Latino thing . . . The conversation was remarkably calm. He expressed hatred for me in a calm, cool, matter-of-fact way."

Jason felt numb, then relieved. He found friends who didn't judge him for where he came from. After a time, he says, his mother and stepfather's old habits returned. Islas says his mother came to him with a black eye and asked for advice. If she left his stepfather, she wouldn't be able to afford housing in Santa Monica, with its well-funded schools. "It's the type of decision human beings shouldn't ever have to make—do I stay in this bad situation in the hopes that my kids get a shot at living a better life than I do, or do I leave and risk their future?" His mother chose to stay. Islas balked when he rode his bicycle and saw lawn signs in the progressive beach city proclaiming "Everyone is welcome here."

He thought, "Yeah, if you can afford it . . . This is the inherent contradiction of wealthy liberal politics. There is no effort to make the city affordable to working people like my mom . . . meanwhile [the city] bans plastic straws." Islas became an activist for affordable housing, defeating a measure that would have required voter approval for high-rises.

When journalists reached out to Islas for the story about his falling-out with Miller, he wondered if it was appropriate to speak. "I really think people ought not to be judged for the rest of their lives by who they were in middle school," he says. "However, Stephen Miller's personality, it calcified into something pretty dark. And there's definitely a common thread."

Islas thinks he and Miller became conscious of the left's hypocrisy at the same time. They noticed how local progressives claimed common cause with the disadvantaged, while working to protect their own privileges. But they had opposite reactions to the hypocrisy. Islas fought it; Miller came to embody it. "His ideology is the shadow self of white, upper-middle-class liberal identity politics," Islas says. He recalls an original *Star Trek* episode, "Mirror, Mirror," which he watched years after his friendship with Miller. In it, a transporter malfunction swaps Captain Kirk and his crew with evil versions of themselves from a parallel universe. "In many ways I think that's a good metaphor," Islas says. "Given the choice between striving for our better selves, he went the dark way—the mirror image of the world he came from."

The world Stephen came from, the world his grandparents and ancestors came from, would indeed inform the person he became. The progressive ideology of this coastal enclave was an illusion—one in which Miller's family first thrived.

CHAPTER TWO

"RIDICULOUS LIBERAL ELITE"

BEFORE THE LAWSUITS AND FINANCIAL disasters, the Millers lived the California dream. Stephen's father, Michael, got along with the city's progressives. With deep-set blue eyes and a broad forehead, Michael held fundraisers and donated to the campaigns of Mel Levine and Howard Berman for Congress, leading Westside Democrats who were pro-Israel.[1]

Santa Monica was undergoing a political metamorphosis. Middle-class progressives had united to pass one of the strictest rent-control ordinances in the history of the United States in 1979. It stunned many onlookers and led to a new nickname for the city: the People's Republic of Santa Monica. Others called it "Santa Moronica."[2] CBS ran a *60 Minutes* special about the coastal city, "The radicals, or the progressives as they call themselves, haven't renamed Santa Monica Ho Chi Minh City, but if they did, the people who used to rule here—the conservatives, the landlords, the developers, the businesspeople—wouldn't be at all surprised."

The city had long drawn working-class families with dreams of a surf-and-turf life. An early real estate pamphlet calls Santa Monica "paradise," reading, "So equable and mild is the climate throughout the entire year that sea bathing may be indulged in 365 days."[3] In 1966, the Santa Monica Freeway linked the sleepy city with downtown Los Angeles. Professionals moved there in droves. Construction boomed. High-rises sprouted up, blocking ocean views and creating congestion. In the mid-seventies, the city placed limits on new construction to try to reverse the problem. But the slowed growth didn't stop demand. Housing costs rose.[4] Older tenants and younger radicals united. They passed the rent control ordinance. Apartments with relatively cheap rents—$650 monthly—had Rolls-Royces and other luxury cars parked in front.[5]

The middle-class radicals won control of the city council, the mayor's office, the city manager's office and more in 1981. Landlords and other critics said the activists were distracting from real problems. "Rent control for the rich! Help the needy, not the greedy!" chanted protestors outside City Hall in April 1989, as the city celebrated the ten-year anniversary of rent control. A World War II armored vehicle drove by and aimed its 20-millimeter turret gun at the building as progressives inside ate frosted desserts.[6]

On August 23, 1985, the Santa Monica Pier was old and bore the scars of two storms—a testament to the power of nature to destroy the man-made. Its tattered pilings creaked with the pressure of the water, which rushed east as Stephen was born. Michael Miller, a noted attorney, was tasked with providing counsel to the Pier Restoration Corporation.[7] The ocean had swept away the bait shop, the harbor patrol station and more. City officials were nostalgic for the pier's heyday before the Great Depression, when its attractions, such as a roller coaster and a funhouse, still operated. The plan was to make the pier fun again, not to mention safe and lasting.

The city's Pier Restoration Corporation, a nonprofit, needed a lawyer who could get along with the politically diverse board, including progressives. Board member Chris Harding says Michael was "compatible" with everyone.[8] He was known as a moderate Democrat. He was well-connected. He could be gruff, some would describe him as cocky or condescending, but he and his wife were a handsome couple, with their hazel-eyed, cherubic toddler daughter, Alexis, and their newborn, Stephen.

Michael would soon grow tired of the people in charge. He had a subversive streak that stretched back to his youth. Some still remember his campaign speech for student body president at Inglewood High School in 1967. Bob Wolfe, a former classmate, says the school then was a "throwback to the fifties" with beehive hairdos and sock hops.[9] Administrators enforced a stiff facade of moral purity. Michael enlisted the help of Wolfe and Paul Grossman to write his speech. "We really wanted Mike to make a big splash," says Grossman.[10] They were known for their humor, improvising stop animation comedy shticks. The three boys had created a James K. Polk Fan Club, jokingly praising the Mexican American War. "Without Polk's wisdom and foresight," Wolfe wrote then, "we would probably be speaking Spanish in California today."

Michael spoke before the student body in an auditorium, wearing a button-up shirt and tie. There was a sound effect of a phone ringing. He picked up a Princess phone. "Hello, yes, this is Michael Miller." Pause. "The administration?" His tone shifted toward exasperated: "Yes, I'll accept the charges." The joke implied that administrators were so cheap that they would call a student collect. The school's authorities were "intolerant of dissent of any kind," so the students ate it up. Grossman says tiny infractions (a skirt too short, sideburns too long) could get a student swatted with a wooden panel. The auditorium filled with laughter. The jab turned Michael into a hero. "It was the most mild rebuke," Grossman says. "But even a mild rebuke was like, revolutionary . . . In those days, you didn't make fun of teachers. You wouldn't *dream* of making fun of teachers or the principal." Classmates crowded around Miller, slapping him on the back. "That's great, Mike, you really gave it to them!" they said. "Mike Miller, he's not afraid of *anything,* man. He really gave it to the administration."

Miller became student body president. The yearbook read, "This year's second semester Student Council, under direction of Student Body President Michael Miller, did much to accomplish the desires and interests of students." He organized a basketball game with the Harlem Clowns. Noon movies. A school spirit competition. Body painting. A tissue-wrapping contest.[11]

Michael's performative impulses came, in part, from his parents. Jay and Freya were associate members of the Magic Castle, an invite-only clubhouse for the Academy of Magical Arts.[12] In showrooms, guests dine while gasping at coin tricks, card tricks, vanishing acts, gravity-defying acts, clairvoyance and other seeming miracles. The clubhouse has a strict dress code. According to the website: "All members and guests are required to dress in evening wear or business attire that is conservative, formal, and elegant . . . when in doubt, OVERDRESS."[13] The academy offers classes in magic: the study of illusions and principles underlying human perception to shock, fool and awe through careful manipulation and misdirection.

Michael's parents introduced him to magic, but also to history and other more serious subjects. Sharon Rifelli, Michael's cousin, says her uncle Jay had her study the Founding Fathers, "paragraph by paragraph and sentence by sentence."[14] He asked her to consider what they were thinking and feeling when they wrote those words. "He motivated me to think while studying, not just absorb information," she says. Jay understood the value of a good education. He smelled of cigars, which he smoked. Like his wife, Freya, who loved to dress up and dazzle people, he put on a suit to go to the Las Vegas casinos. He knew how to flatter the wealthy, remembering their names. "If you ever saw that man work a room, you would know why I idolized him—he had such a big personality," says Rifelli. "He would just go around the entire room as if the grand celebrity had just arrived, slapping everybody on the back, glad-handing, biggest smile you ever saw. He was amazing, absolutely amazing. No inhibition, no self-consciousness. He had that special something you just have to be born with."

Jay's father, Nison, had come from eastern Europe in 1904 during one of the largest emigrations in Jewish history, hundreds of thousands fleeing poverty and massacres called pogroms. They rode steamships across the Atlantic. In America, the rich were welcomed. Those in steerage—largely Jews—were interrogated. The nervous or inarticulate could be deemed mentally deficient or deranged. They were labeled with chalk and placed in cages for another look, along with those who looked diseased. But a majority, like Nison, were accepted.[15] He worked as a peddler, saved up, then sent for his wife and children. He applied for citizenship in 1928 in Detroit. A few years later, his petition was denied. The reason: "Ignorance." A black-and-white portrait shows him well-dressed, in a tie and jacket, with disheveled hair. In 1940, he applied for naturalization again, now a "paper stand owner." He was granted citizenship.[16]

Around that time is when Jay met Freya, an artistic girl with movie-star looks. With stained-red lips and big, bright eyes, Freya loved to dance and to paint. Her parents were self-made Jews from the Pale of Settlement, in western Imperial Russia. In Pittsburgh, they taught themselves to speak English while rolling cigars and bought a small grocery store, putting their daughter through design college. Freya and Jay got pregnant when he was a newly commissioned ensign to the Navy during World War II. Several years later, they traveled across the country to settle in West Los Angeles with two children. Michael, their third child, was born in 1950 in the Golden State.[17]

Michael grew up as his parents accrued wealth in Los Angeles. His father, Jay, launched a real estate business and went to law school. He became a leader in the Jewish community. Michael's mother, Freya, became a full-time artist. She had easels and live models come over to the house. Her studio was full of oil paint tubes. "The smell of oil paint—it was just intoxicating," says Rifelli. She gave her art to her family. The couple built a modernist ocean-front home with slanted ceilings and large windows facing the water, Freya's paintings on the walls. On their backyard deck, they enjoyed spectacular views of the sunlit horizon. They had achieved the American dream in one generation.

Michael decided to study law like his father. He attended the University of California, Santa Cruz. He told Bob Wolfe, who also went there, that his middle name, "Darrow," came from Clarence Darrow, an attorney of the American Civil Liberties Union who became famous in the early 1900s, successfully defending a black family against murder charges brought after they fought back against a violent white mob. "[T]he life of the Negro race has been a life of tragedy, of injustice, of oppression," Darrow told an all-white jury. "The law has made him equal, but man has not . . . I ask you, in the name of progress and of the human race, to return a verdict of not guilty in this case."

Wolfe and countless other students marched in San Francisco to protest the Vietnam War, sexism and racism. "People didn't come in as hippies, but they certainly developed that way. I never went to class in the spring after freshman year. We were on strike every spring," Wolfe says. He never saw Michael there, nor did Michael's ex-girlfriend, Margie Strimling. They lost track of him. Strimling had spent the fall of freshman year cooped up in the library with Miller. "He was a very hard worker," she says.[18] Their romance fizzled out. Neither Wolfe nor Strimling could believe it when they learned Michael was the father of Stephen Miller.

Strimling called Stephen "the most horrible man in the Trump administration."

California was a majority conservative state back then. Hollywood actor Ronald Reagan had launched his campaign for governor by attacking the universities, characterizing young liberal protesters as anti-American traitors. He said, "Get them out of there. Throw them out. They are spoiled and don't deserve the education they are getting." He wrote a letter expressing his contempt, "How far do we go in tolerating these people & this trash under the excuse of academic freedom & freedom of expression?" He conjured the trope of the "welfare queen." A master of the stage, he rallied support for himself as a hero battling dark forces. In 1964, Reagan summed up what he thought was at stake—what he thought the students did not understand. "We are faced with the most evil enemy mankind has known in his long climb from the swamp to the stars." The enemy, he said, was "the welfare state." [19]

Michael kept his nose in books. He got into Stanford University Law School. He honed his debating skills and won an award "for outstanding contributions to the life of the school." [20] He served as president of the Moot Court Board, for an oral practice seminar. Miller helped judge the performance of aspiring lawyers as they briefed and argued cases. [21] He moved back to Los Angeles, where he cofounded Stern & Miller, focusing on corporate and real estate law. He helped his father, Jay, with his real estate business, Cordary, Inc., and met the woman who would become his wife. Miriam Glosser was a graduate of the Columbia University School of Social Work and worked with troubled teenagers. Like Michael, she was the grandchild of eastern European Jews who escaped persecution. She was shy next to Michael, but with a similar fondness for the showy, decorating their walls with large art and bright red paints.

The family moved into their five-bedroom, two-story house in the North of Montana neighborhood. During a recent visit to the home the Millers were forced to leave, the block is full of what look like fenced-in mini villas with groomed lawns and curving stone pathways, adorned with roses and vines. The street is quiet, with the buzzing of dragonflies, the gentle flapping of American flags, the occasional drone of a military aircraft. Luxury automobiles line the street: Mercedes-Benzes, BMWs, a red Porsche, a silver Tesla Model S. Birds flit around. Monarchs flutter by. It has the air of an enchanted neighborhood. One house is so full of playthings they spill onto the lawn: a smiling stuffed lion and teddy bears, board games, tennis balls.

Laborers maintain this world. Dark-skinned nannies push the strollers of white babies on the sidewalks. Sweat drips from one brown man's face as he mows his employer's lawn. Three men detail a silver BMW. They play banda music and pull junk from the vehicle: an old DVD player, a beach umbrella, beach chairs. "Aqui está bien?" A Mexican man washes dead leaves from the sidewalk with a hose, sunlight glinting on its stream, enchanted like the neighborhood. He shapes and sculpts the garden. He plants olive trees, opening their branches to keep them from leaning. The nearby cross streets are Marguerita, Alta, San Vicente. It's been more than a century since these lands belonged to people who spoke their native language.

Miriam and Michael had their third and final child, Jacob, in 1989. While Stephen and his siblings were young, Miriam took a break from social work to raise them.[22] The Santa Monica Pier, reconstructed with Michael's help, today stretches over the Pacific Ocean on barnacle-encrusted steel girders, offering breathtaking views of the coast. Green mountains rise out of the mist. Golden cliffs cradle the beach. Palm trees sway in the breeze. The pier is a chorus of Spanish, English, Farsi, Chinese. Children laugh on the roller coaster and carousel, and play in the arcade. People buy churros, funnel cake, mollusks. At night, the pier is luminous. Electric colors from the Ferris wheel dance on the black water below.

Michael became more active in his father's real estate business, Cordary, Inc. His politics moved farther to the right. He served on the community relations committee of the Los Angeles Jewish Federation and as president of its western region. He traveled to the Soviet Union with California's lieutenant governor Leo McCarthy to meet refuseniks, Soviet Jews denied permission to emigrate to Israel. Miriam's brother David Glosser recalled: "[Michael] aspired to political office himself . . . Miriam had aspirations that Michael would achieve political influence and office."[23]

The nationwide New Left had been spurred by Tom Hayden, a Santa Monica leader whose politics were too far left for Michael. In 1982, Michael helped organize a debate between Hayden and Bill Hawkins, Hayden's opponent for the California Assembly seat.[24] Hayden had pushed the rent control opposed by many landlords and wrote the Port Huron Statement in the sixties—the manifesto of left-wing students. "We are people of this generation, bred in at least modest comfort, housed now in universities, looking uncomfortably to the world we inherit," it read. The movement proclaimed solidarity with Argentine revolutionary Che Guevara and Cuba's Fidel Castro. Hayden would later lament allowing the "fundamental issue of patriotic nationalism . . . to be controlled by conservatives."[25]

Hayden, who has since died, wrote an article in 2006 about a meeting with Michael Berman, the brother and chief operative of Congressman Howard Berman, whose campaign Michael Miller supported in the eighties. He said Berman looked him in the eye and said, "I represent the Israeli defense forces."[26] He led Hayden to believe he was "the gatekeeper protecting Los Angeles' Westside for Israel's political interests." Many Jewish Democrats in the district, where they represented a third of voters, were uncomfortable with the new left's sympathies for Palestinians—including Hayden's. Berman told him that if he promised to be "a good friend to Israel," the Jewish Federations would "rent" him the Assembly seat.

Michael Miller was a Zionist, one of the city's Jewish Federation leaders. He made real estate his primary business in 1987, taking over Cordary, Inc., which specialized in office buildings and apartment houses, from his father. But when his law firm admitted new shareholders, he threatened litigation, according to court documents. His former partner David Stern wrote him in 1988, "Michael, we have known each other for 15 years. There is no reason that the ending of our legal 'partnership' need be acrimonious. You have made the decision not to practice law and I respect your choice. You obviously enjoy the freedom and financial rewards in real estate . . . We can, if you choose, continue to have a relationship . . . the decision is yours." Michael wrote back that he had not resigned and had no intention of resigning. "Your letter fundamentally misstates and misrepresents the underlying factual situation," he replied.[27]

Michael soon found himself in court fighting multiple lawsuits—with his family, the banks and his former law partners. His friends stopped receiving invitations to Democratic fundraisers from Michael. Instead, he invited them to events for Republicans. "I remember thinking, gee, Michael must've changed his politics, I wonder why he thinks I changed mine," says Chris Harding, who was on the board of the Pier Restoration Corporation. Michael would later join the board of the Hebrew Union College, the main Jewish seminary in North America for the education of rabbis of Reform Judaism, which generally attracts the most left-leaning Jews. "He was interested in attempting to see to it that we would educate our rabbis in what he felt would be a more 'even-handed,' kind of manner," says Rabbi David Ellenson, president of the college at the time. He described Michael as "a staunch Republican."[28]

Miriam's brother David Glosser, a retired neuropsychologist, recalls his brother-in-law as "a traditional economic Republican who, over the years, became more and more embittered over regulation and what he felt was the intrusion into his personal and business affairs by what he called the 'ridiculous liberal elite of the West Coast around California.' . . . He was convinced that American universities and colleges were more or less dominated by the extreme left-wing political view of the world."[29] After one of Michael's tirades at a restaurant dinner with family, Glosser lost control of himself. "So what you're trying to say is the entire intellectual elite of the country disagrees with you?" he asked. Seemingly taken aback by ill-restrained laughter at the table, Michael argued that university faculties were not the intellectual elite.

"As far back as I can remember, Michael always wanted to argue with me about politics and policy," Glosser says. The two argued good-naturedly, but over time Glosser decided he was no longer interested in debating his sister's husband. "It was pointless. When the facts dictated that he, at least partially, concede a point he would change the subject rather than deal with the contradiction."

Over time, he noticed that Miriam was adopting Michael's perspectives. David and his sister had been raised in a liberal household—their parents were members of the American Civil Liberties Union and kept the *New Republic* on their coffee table. David volunteered with the Philadelphia chapter of the Hebrew Immigrant Aid Society (HIAS) and Physicians for Human Rights (PHR). It was surprising to David that she sided with Michael. He wasn't sure if his sister was simply trying to keep the peace or if she truly believed his ideas. But as much as David disagreed with their politics, he thought of Michael and Miriam as thoughtful and thoroughly decent parents.

STEPHEN'S EARLIEST YEARS WERE CHOREOGRAPHED
mostly by his mom, who took care of him and his siblings at home.
He learned to play percussion, including a marimba. They occasionally traveled to Miriam's hometown of Johnstown, Pennsylvania. They rode the Inclined Plane, a cable-traction funicular for
rescuing people from floods by carrying them up a large hill. Stephen learned his maternal family history. "He was inculcated in his
heritage and the story of his immigrant forebears," recalls Richard Burkert, president of the Johnstown Area Heritage Association
(JAHA).[30]

Decades before, Stephen's maternal grandmother, Ruth Glosser,
had decided to record the family history in a forty-seven-page document, completed in 1998, "A Precious Legacy." Ruth dedicated it
to Izzy, her husband and partner in crime, who taped relatives' rec-
ollections.[31] "Some may ask my reasons for devoting the time and
energy necessary to compile a family history. Why bother? Who
cares? . . . [Our family] survived the worst two anti-Jewish excesses
of the twentieth century—the pogroms which took place in the
Russian empire and Russian-held Poland, and the Holocaust which
exterminated six million Jews during World War II. They survived
because they emigrated . . . to remember is to defy the objectives of
the czarist regime and the Nazis."

She believed her generation was "the bridge between the past
and the future," and felt a responsibility to help her kids and grand-
kids remember their great-grandparents after they died: "The ones
who came to this country with virtually nothing but the clothes on
their backs . . . the generation who all their lives spoke English with
the trace of a Yiddish accent."

Wolf Glosser was Stephen Miller's maternal great-great-
grandfather. He was born in a town of marshes and forests, Antopol,

in what is now Belarus. He and his family lived in a small house with a thatched roof and a dirt floor, no plumbing. One of Wolf's daughters, Bella, recalled: "At night we used to follow around my mother and keep saying, 'Mom, we're hungry, we're hungry' . . . and I was always scared."[32]

The Jews were being scapegoated for political and economic instability in the region after the assassination of Tsar Alexander II. "Between 1903 and 1906, pogroms were perpetrated in 64 towns and 626 townlets and villages. Thousands of Jews were slaughtered," wrote Ruth. The Glossers lived in fear that they were next. Armed Cossacks galloped through on horseback, and peasants who visited the shtetls to conduct business expressed hostility, mimicking the Jews' speech, calling them "God killers," and siccing their dogs on the children. "Under the instigation of nationalist agitators or zealous local clergy, such confrontations would occasionally turn into public 'blood' accusations, collective attacks on Jewish shops, and, ultimately, full-fledged pogroms," wrote Ewa Morawska in her history of small-town Jews at the turn of the century, *Insecure Prosperity*.[33] Wolf asked the local rabbi for advice. According to Ruth: "[He] urged people '(with the help of God) to take things in their own hands' . . . and emigrate to America, 'Go . . . you will make a living there,' adding, 'Observe the Sabbath.' "

Wolf arrived at Ellis Island on January 7, 1903. He peddled bananas in New York City and changed his name to Louis. "One of the main things everybody wanted to do when they came to America was become Americanized," recalled his grandson Izzy.[34] Louis's oldest son, Nathan, came and found a small Pennsylvania town that appealed to him. Johnstown had been built on a floodplain at the fork of two rivers, where the banks had been narrowed for construction. In 1889, it had been ravaged by what was then the deadliest disaster in the nation's history, and which would remain the largest single day of civilian loss of life until September 11,

2001: more than two thousand people, including nearly four hundred children, were wiped out by a flood.

"Most of the people in Johnstown never saw the water coming; they only heard it; and those who lived to tell about it would for years after try to describe the sound of the thing as it rushed on them," wrote David McCullough in his book *The Johnstown Flood*. It had been caused by the failure of the South Fork Dam after millionaires manipulated the water flow for a private country club lake. Newspapers across the country covered the tragedy. There were accounts of corpses washing up for days, as well as miracles, "a blonde baby found in Verona . . . floating along in its cradle, having traveled almost eighty miles from Johnstown without suffering even a bruise."[35]

Hundreds left town, traumatized. But it was this place that would shape the fate of the Glosser family. Nathan found a job as a tailor, and soon bought the shop when a Jewish neighbor lent him money on a handshake; such acts of support were common among Jewish newcomers.[36]

Johnstown was becoming one of the nation's top steel producers. While most Jews from eastern Europe settled in large cities, the Glossers came to a small town as it was booming. Every day, the steel mills rained ash on the red-hued community, cradled between verdant hills and the Conemaugh and Little Conemaugh rivers. "The sky was often darkened by the products of the valley's industry," wrote David Glosser. "I didn't know for sure that the moon's natural color was not orange until reaching an age I'm embarrassed to admit . . . those dark skies meant good jobs, good paychecks, and good customers."[37]

The mills produced hundreds of thousands of steel tons for trains, railroads, skyscrapers, bridges, telegraph lines, hammers, engines. The product went for warships and weapons—the expression of America's might. Production spiked in the world wars, and Johnstown's economy thrived. Between 1880 and 1910, the population of the town grew from eight thousand to more than fifty thousand.[38]

Louis and Nathan expanded the store to sell secondhand clothing. They sent for Louis's wife, Bessie, and their unmarried children. By the 1920s, the family business became a full department store: Glosser Bros. It marketed itself as the "working man's friend" with the "lowest prices." They sold trunks, which migrants shipped full of gifts to loved ones in the Old World, including portraits of themselves in nice outfits, encouraging family migration.[39] Every afternoon when the mills closed, masses of dusty-faced men poured out in hard hats. Many stopped at the store.

Glosser Bros. was geared toward a mostly Christian clientele. It was decorated for Christmas, not Hanukkah. The business thrived even through the Depression. "Entertainment was almost as important as pricing in those dire times; people needed diversions to survive," wrote Robert Jeschonek, in a book about the business called *Long Live Glosser's*.[40] The Glossers were "masters of promotional gimmicks" and "retail ringmasters," he said. They offered free rabbits at Easter for boys who bought suits and chirping chicks to the children of other customers. They sponsored dances and a Bargain Circus. They held a monkey show; the creatures escaped and climbed the trees of Central Park. Hundreds of people lined up for the events, "which succeeded even when they failed (monkeys, anyone?) getting attention and boosting awareness of The Store," he wrote.

Most of the Glossers worked in the store, with forays. Sam, one of Louis's sons and Stephen's great-grandfather, tried joining the United States armed forces, but was rejected because of his blind left eye. When a Jewish Legion was organized in 1917 by Zionist leaders, Sam memorized the eye chart and enlisted to help the British seize Palestine. He traveled through the arid region, where Jews were setting up agricultural settlements. Sam started a friendship with David Ben-Gurion, the man who would later become the founding father of Israel. "Sam and Ben-Gurion stood guard duty together many times; according to family legend, they had been known to share a tent and became good friends," Jeschonek wrote. While in the service Sam met Pearl, the Palestine-born daughter of Russian Zionists. Ben-Gurion was at their wedding in 1919. The couple sailed back to the US. Izzy—Stephen Miller's maternal grandfather—was born three years later in Johnstown.

All their lives, the Glossers would strive to help the poor and persecuted. Louis donated relief for victims of pogroms back home. During the Depression, the Glossers left bags of free groceries on the doorsteps of the needy. Ruth wrote, "The misery, fear and economic deprivation of their earlier years were forever etched into their psyche. As a result, almost from the time of their arrival in the United States, and long before they had achieved financial stability they were already 'giving something back' . . . They had been on the receiving end of charity. And they never forgot this." They abided by the Jewish tradition of *tzedakah*, from the Hebrew word "justice." Unlike the Western concept of charity—to give out of a spontaneous desire to be kind—*tzedakah* is an ethical obligation to be just: to help the needy is to do what one must.

The family donated to an immigration organization, schools, hospitals, an orphans' asylum and more in the Old World. Louis gave to Zionist organizations in Palestine. Among the family's interests was establishing a Jewish homeland. They were ardent Zionists. "Although they died long before the State of Israel came into existence, the need for a Jewish homeland had been of paramount concern to them ever since the tragedy of brutal pogroms," Ruth wrote.

Stephen's mom, Miriam, grew up in Glosser Bros., a playground for her and her siblings. In her testimony to Jeschonek, she described her childhood as "a great adventure." She recalled "the wonderful aroma of hot roasted nuts that wafted through" the store. Her father, Izzy, had managed the toy department. "Checking out what was new on the [toy] shelves was always a highlight," she said. At closing, Izzy would let Miriam and her siblings "raid the candy department." She helped select each month's comic books, displayed near the colorfully decorated cigar boxes.

MIRIAM AND HER COUSINS LIVED on the same street, playing and drinking milkshakes on Sundays. They were a tight-knit group, naturally named "The Milkshake Club." They grew up learning about their refugee roots. Before leaving for Columbia University, Miriam worked in the Glosser Bros. lingerie department, and learned all about "excellent customer service," she told Jeschonek. Like her future husband, she had some prankster in her. "I remember, as preteens, my cousin Patti and I decided to print a weekly newspaper which primarily featured gossip (mostly made up) about our cousins and kids in our Sunday school classes," Miriam wrote. "That great opus was printed on the store mimeograph machine."[41]

She delighted in entertaining people. She was in her high school pep club. She starred as the main character in at least one play. A photograph of Miriam in dramatics class shows her kneeling at the feet of her fellow students as they pretend to stone her.[42] They were performing the classic Shirley Jackson short story "The Lottery." It describes a fictional American small town where the residents are convinced that to survive, they must select someone to be the annual sacrifice. Miriam played the scapegoat. Mouth agape, pretty face in profile, she held an arm up to protect herself. The other hand lay flat on the ground. She wore a skirt and a dark sweater. "It isn't fair," cried Miriam's character in the short story. Her classmates seemed bored and distracted as they feigned killing her. One girl fixed her hair and stared at the camera. In the narrative by Shirley Jackson, the victim's son participates. She screams, surrounded by her loved ones, "and then, they were upon her."

Glosser Bros. expanded to operate in three states and was listed on the American Stock Exchange. But in the mid-eighties, the company began to experience cash flow problems. It had been made private through a leveraged buyout. After decades of success, it filed for bankruptcy and was liquidated. "When they pulled out, they pulled the heart out of Johnstown," says Jack Roscetti, a hairstylist and longtime resident who counted many Glossers among his customers.[43]

The Glosser descendants spread out across the country. Ruth wrote, "Through the example of their lives [the Glossers] exemplified for their children and their children's children the importance of the values of tzedakah, a caring, harmonious family life, a personal commitment to make the world a better place . . . It is indeed a precious legacy." She concluded by listing the names of twenty-three families related to the Glossers who were killed in Antopol during the Holocaust. In 1924, as the eugenics movement gripped Americans with hatred of non-whites, legislation set quotas based on national origin, severely restricting the number of people who could come in from southern and eastern Europe, China, Italy, Japan and other areas. The Glossers' home in the Old World was obliterated by the Nazis and nearly all two thousand inhabitants who had stayed were murdered. "By the time Antopol was liberated in June of 1944 only seven Jews were still alive to bear witness to the massacre," wrote Ruth.

One of the Glossers went back to Antopol and paid to have a fence built around the cemetery and endowed maintenance for it. Burkert of the Johnstown Area Heritage Association says, "That's all that's left of the Glossers' ancestral village."

It was a memory the Glossers held on to, the memory of the annihilation. As Miriam raised Stephen and his siblings, it's unlikely she knew that the lesson her mother had tried to keep alive—about the dangers of demonization, about the value of those who came to the United States in rags, penniless and illiterate—would come under direct assault by her son.

CHAPTER THREE

"SPEAK ONLY ENGLISH"

STEPHEN STARTED AT SANTA MONICA High School in 1999. His father would refinance the house three times in the next four years.[1] (His younger brother, Jacob, would go to private school.) The year before, Santa Monica had experienced eight gang-related shootings within a couple of weeks, resulting in five deaths, including one across from the high school. The high school was experiencing what administrators called "a two-school phenomenon." One part went on to Ivy Leagues and top corporations, the other part dropped out.

A 2003 issue of the *Samohi* newspaper offered a snapshot.[2] The top story: "Grades Reflect Racial Discrepancies." Statistics showed half of the Fs that semester were earned by Latino students, who made up only a third of the total semester grades. The piece explored reasons for the achievement gap, including a lack of resources and the strict tardy policy that disproportionately affected children of the working class. One article featured "The Success Story of a Teen Mother at Samo," whose father disowned her due to her biracial relationship and who was able to get through school with the help of the on-campus teen parenting program, which included on-site childcare.

Despite racial harmony retreats and multicultural festivities, at lunch the quad divided. New immigrants hunched in corners and stairwells; other Latin American and black students hung out in the main quad; white and Asian students ate in the science quad, nicknamed "Disneyland." The groups were organized as in a Venn diagram, with some overlap. Miller spent time on the corner of the main quad, then the science quad. He hung out with Moritz and two Jewish boys. "Walter," a pseudonym, spoke to me about his years-long friendship with Miller on condition of anonymity, citing fears of professional retaliation.[3] Our first conversation was on the phone. He was visiting his parents, sitting in his old bedroom. "It's a little weird," he says. "Stephen has slept in this bedroom. There are probably photos of him somewhere in this house. The idea that someone could be friends with him for a lot of people probably seems insane. What kind of person could be friends with him . . . I'm that guy. What does it say about me?"

I meet Walter a few weeks later. He shows me pictures of himself with Miller: in a mall photo booth, at a sports game, on the beach, in Las Vegas. Walter was attracted to Stephen as a friend, he says, because Stephen was a fun guy. Both boys were athletic. Stephen could hold his breath for minutes and climb fences. He played tennis. He had "unexpected strength for his frame." They played sports, but weren't jocks. Neither got drunk nor partied much. Walter was interested in a few girls in his class but didn't go on many dates. Neither did Stephen.

Their socializing consisted of having lunch at school and hanging out on weekends: going to the movies, having dinner with each other's families, playing board games. They had sleepovers. They walked along Third Street Promenade and bumped into celebrities. "Whenever we would see a celebrity, [Stephen] would go up to them. And he would specifically try to say, 'I loved you in—' the most obscure, non-famous movie or TV show they'd been in, to endear himself to that person." At restaurants, Stephen engaged waiters in awkward conversations, interrogating them about their lives or the menu. Some found it hostile; others, amusing. "It was fun and outlandish—it's no different than a shock jock," Walter says. "He was funny. We enjoyed his antics. We thought he was interesting. He was creative, he was curious, and we'd go on adventures."

When it came to homework, Stephen was known to procrastinate. He stayed up until three or four in the morning. But he still had energy when he came into class every day. When Miller got his first car—a used beige Nissan, not a BMW or Audi like wealthier students—he didn't want to search for parking every morning. It was limited, with a lottery for seniors. So Stephen made a deal with the valets at the hotels across the street to park there.

After Miller moved away, the friends didn't see much of each other, hanging only during some holidays at home. "A lot of people like to characterize him as someone with no friends," Walter says. "He has friends. He probably has fewer now, because he hasn't nurtured those friendships like most people would." Stephen has become "mission-driven." Walter has seen him only twice since the Trump campaign. The media's stories about Miller aren't totally wrong, he says. "What they're saying about him, it's directionally accurate. I would just say, I think Stephen in reality is probably two-thirds of what you think of him in the media. If he's a ten in the media, on whatever scale you're thinking, in reality he's probably a six or seven," he says.

As a teenager, Stephen sometimes made comments that some interpreted as racist. "I believe that everyone is racist to a certain extent," Walter says. But, he says, Stephen never expressed hatred toward specific ethnicities. If any group provoked his ire, it was the Chicano Student Movement of Aztlán (MEChA). A 1999 MEChA document states: "We are a nationalist movement of Indigenous Gente that lay claim to the land that is ours by birthright. As a nationalist movement we seek to free our people from the exploitation of an oppressive society that occupies our land."

Miller interpreted this to mean MEChA wanted to reclaim California, an idea that was widely spreading on right-wing talk radio at the time.[4]

MEChA members, however, say the mission was to unite and empower Latin American youths. They didn't promote a takeover. Maria Vivanco was MEChA's president at the school. Stephen told her and her friends to "speak only English" when they crossed paths.[5] The girls spoke a hybrid of English and Spanish, Spanglish. Vivanco usually just laughed, seeing him as "a bizarre and lonely guy, a sad white kid who was disturbed." But one time she was chatting with her friends when Stephen came up to her and said, "Go back to your country!" Vivanco stared him down. "This *is* my country!" she replied. Vivanco was born in Santa Monica.

Occasionally, she saw him taunting new immigrants. He towered over them, talking at them aggressively and with unsettling confidence. "I don't remember what he was saying . . . but I remember they didn't know English. He was there screaming at them and I would physically go up to Stephen and say, 'Why don't you pick on someone your own size, and someone that can argue with you?' And he would walk away. And once or twice I told the administration, 'Hey, that guy is picking on those kids.' " Nearly two decades later, Miller complained that rather than engage in "spirited, open debate" his classmates wanted to tattle on him.[6] He said those challenges were "some of the toughest I faced in my life."[7]

Stephen wasn't afraid of the teachers, either. One Latin American teacher who spoke on condition of anonymity says anytime Stephen heard the teacher converse with the students in Spanish, he yelled at the teacher, too.[8] "This is America! We speak English!" he said.

While MEChA had meetings on campus, he occasionally passed by the open door and glared at Vivanco. She assumed he was trying to intimidate her. But, she says, "I never, ever felt intimidated by any white guy. First of all, I went to karate—since I was five years old. So at school, I was known as someone you couldn't fuck with, even with the Latino guys." Vivanco was bilingual. She was in Advanced Placement courses. She was in student government, did water polo, was on the swim team. Her mother, an immigrant from Oaxaca, Mexico, raised her to be proud of her indigenous roots. She told her never to let anyone talk down to or degrade her. "He was a joke to me. Looking back, I wish I'd been like, 'Hey, let's go have a coffee. Let's talk about this.' "

Stephen in the meantime had discovered conservative talk radio: *The Larry Elder Show.* Elder has a charismatic voice, a strong jaw and a broad smile. He calls himself the "Sage from South Central." In the nineties, he was a rising star, broadcast in the afternoons on KABC/790 across Los Angeles. A *Los Angeles Times* article described Elder as "a darling of white listeners who seemed to almost gush when they telephoned him on KABC talk radio, astonished to find a black man who not only wasn't going to chastise them, but who also often agreed with them."[9] In 2001, Elder published the book *The Ten Things You Can't Say in America.* In it, he argues that black people are more racist than white people, and that the problems of black people are due to a lack of self-determination.[10] Stephen read it with pleasure.[11]

Elder writes, "At American dinner tables all across the country, most parents urge their children to work hard, study hard, and prepare. But in black households, how much dinner table talk revolves around 'the white man done me wrong,' rather than focuses on grit, hard work, and preparation?" Like Limbaugh, Elder dedicated a chapter to media bias and belittled the idea of sexism, saying, "Smart women simply overlook boorish behavior by men."

Stephen called into his show and invited him to speak at his high school. Elder agreed. He came to campus and stood in front of a diverse crowd of Santa Monica High School students, including Stephen. He told them they had to learn how to pull themselves by the bootstraps and not use race as social capital. Vivanco thought about the racial harmony retreats she participated in, in which students and teachers got together to talk about race. They did an exercise called the "Privilege Walk." Everyone stood in a line and a facilitator asked questions: "If your parents own a home, take a step forward. If your parents read to you when you were a child, take a step forward." At the end, "we were able to see, wow . . . white students have a much higher advantage 'cause their parents have *means*. When people tell you we're all starting off on the same [foot], you have to remember that's not true. *We don't all have the bootstraps*."

Stephen seemed aroused by Elder's speech. Vivanco watched the pleasure in his face and felt herself getting really angry. She stood up and confronted her classmate. "You are a racist!" she said. Stephen shouted back, telling her she was wrong and didn't understand. In retrospect, she says, "I think looking back he didn't like to be confronted by a Latina girl, a teenage girl."

Vivanco was mentored by MEChAs from the University of California, Los Angeles, like other high schoolers during this period. They organized cultural events, such as a Día de Los Muertos (Day of the Dead) celebration. They led walkouts, including a protest about a *Toy Story 2* video game featuring a villain with a mustache and a sombrero who had to be fatally shot to advance to the next level. They held protests over evictions of black and brown students. Vivanco participated in a march organized by Dolores

Huerta, cofounder of the United Farm Workers, who led more than a hundred Santa Monica High School students to the Hilton-owned Doubletree next door, where brown and black workers were facing opposition to their unionizing efforts. The hotel was on school district–owned property; the students stood in solidarity with the workers.

Vivanco says the protesters were met by dozens of police in riot gear. A heavy police presence was not unusual around the school, across the street from the police department. But it was unusual for the police to meet them on school property in riot gear. "The police would come during lunch time and park off the main entrance, off Pico, and hang out in the main quad area. The main quad was primarily Latino, African American or black students." She says she saw a heavy presence of police in her neighborhood, too. "I saw folks like my brother and neighbors and classmates get arrested just 'cause they were being racially profiled," she says.

Classmate Kesha Ram, a year younger than Miller, recalls the same. She, too, was a target of Stephen's.[12] She organized events about climate change. Stephen found her and launched into speeches about how climate change was caused by volcanoes, not humans. "It was very jarring. Like, what are you talking about?" she says.

She wondered what drove him. "He would come up and start to pick a fight with you and his face would turn bright red," Ram says. "I don't know if it was passion or heated debate or he was just angry all the time, it was hard to tell. But he put on this real victimization attitude . . . It didn't feel particularly civil or curious." Stephen also argued with some white male progressive intellectuals in the journalism program. "[The liberal men] also had outsize opinions of themselves. I just remember thinking, I'll let them fight it out," Ram says. "Nobody really cares. People are dealing with gang violence and trying to put food on the table."

In the fall of 2001, Oscar de la Torre was a counselor at his old high school. He was the student who had been singled out by the hate letter sent a decade before to hundreds of Latin American families in Santa Monica, the one that called Mexicans "brown animals," threatened to gas them "like Hitler gassed the Jews," and insulted his intelligence. The Santa Monica–Malibu Unified School District had convened committees on topics such as class size and resources for a strategic plan. De la Torre co-chaired a committee on equality. Stephen showed up to one of the first meetings. Of all the committees, it was de la Torre's that drew his attention. Students, parents and city leaders gathered in the school library, with its earthy smell of old books. Miller listened as attendees talked about the need to provide opportunities for minority students. He seemed angry. Eventually, he shared his thoughts.

"Racism does not exist. It's in your imagination," he said. Stephen didn't "um" or "like" or meander like most teenagers. He had an ease with words and a passion for what he was saying. "A belief in racial oppression has become an article of faith, beyond question or reason," he later wrote, recalling his comments.[13] He said it was "incredibly damaging to put all this energy" into the idea that students were victims of discrimination; the school was "excusing black and Hispanic misbehavior by holding those students to a lower standard."

De la Torre studied the well-dressed teenager and guessed he'd grown up north of Montana Avenue, the dividing line between the city's affluent and everyone else. De la Torre recalled a game he used to play with his family there. His parents would drive him and his siblings to look at the palatial houses, daydreaming. The car filled with their voices: "That's my house!" "That's yours." "My house is better than yours!" De la Torre and six siblings lived in a two-bedroom apartment next to a cemetery in Pico, near a park that was built on a landfill.

He asked Stephen to tell him about himself. What middle

school had he attended? He said Lincoln Middle School. "That's mostly white," de la Torre said. "John Adams [Middle School] is mostly black and Latino. There is segregation."

Stephen said the segregation wasn't legally imposed, so it was irrelevant. He pointed to the civil rights movement as proof that racism was a thing of the past. De la Torre said people of color were still concentrated in poor neighborhoods. Stephen seemed annoyed, as if he'd already thought this through. "You had the opportunity to go to college, right?" he asked. The school counselor conceded that he'd gone to college. But, de la Torre said, "Most of the kids I grew up with—they're *dead.*" He remembered one neighbor he'd watched bleed to death only steps from his front door. Miller shook his head. If his friends were dead, he said, they were probably bad guys. "You can't blame society for that," he said.

De la Torre took a deep breath. The kid's words were outlandish. But he wanted to be patient with him. He tried to explain that youths turn to gangs for protection amid systemic oppression and lack of representation; that the US justice system is designed to accumulate convictions for people of color while permitting—even promoting—white impunity. Miller disagreed. The problem, he said, was de la Torre's people hadn't learned personal responsibility.

"One thing you gotta give him is he would do his homework," de la Torre says. "He knew all the right-wing commentators, whatever they were espousing—he knew the rhetoric." Miller became a regular at meetings for the district's strategic plan, often in a suit jacket and tie. He argued against bilingual education, Spanish-language announcements and multicultural activities such as Cinco de Mayo celebrations. He said the club for gay people was ruining the school. He attacked MEChA. "It was always a little shocking," says Julia Brownley, a Democratic congresswoman who was board president in 2002 and saw him at board meetings.[14] "He was clearly a very smart, articulate kid. But his opinions were pretty radical."

De la Torre thought it was strange that Miller wanted to spar about these subjects. "You'd think this guy's supposed to be happy—he's a teenager," he says. "But a part of me liked him because he had opinions. He was wrong in a lot of the shit he said, but at least he had some shit to say, you know what I'm saying? He was definitely there to get into a fight, and I kinda liked that about him."

Many were offended by Miller's comments and responded with hostility. At first, de la Torre intervened to make sure he had his say. But soon it struck him that he wasn't there to have a conversation. Sometimes, Miller just stood in the back, spoke his piece and swiftly departed. De la Torre says, "He didn't come with an open heart. He came with a shield and a sword. He was a master of feeling out the room and knowing how to elicit an emotional response. Once he got that anger, it was like, *that's right*. It was almost like, *gotcha*. He felt a sense of fulfillment. You could see it in his eyes. And it was just wicked. There's no other word to describe the feeling. It was *wickedness*. He was born with an ability to bring out anger from people, and he rejoiced in that, it made him powerful. He became important that way."

The echoes with the 1991 hate letter did not escape de la Torre: attacking MEChA, the gay club, alleged lower standards for minorities, de la Torre himself. The letter was still being circulated on campus, according to Lili Barsha, who visited the high school to pick up student writing samples for a Los Angeles–wide program of PEN America. When she went through the samples from Santa Monica High School, she found the racist tract from the mysterious "Samohi Assn. for the Advancement of Conservative White Americans." She asked her boss at PEN what to do about the tract and was advised to disregard it.

Miller carried the grievances into the meetings with de la Torre, personifying the nameless author who'd haunted de la Torre for years. But he stopped short of the death threats and animal references. "Stephen Miller did not invent that ideology," de la Torre says. "He learned it from somewhere. And the person who wrote that letter also learned it. These feelings that divide our country, they exist, they can morph, they can grow."

MILLER WAS INTO MOBSTER MOVIES. Growing up, the walls of his bedroom were decorated with framed posters of *Casino* and *Goodfellas*—two of his favorite films. "It wasn't that prototypical high school room that's covered in dozens or hundreds of things," Stephen's friend Walter says. "Not early nineties girls in bikinis or rock posters. It was more elegant than that."

The characters in the Martin Scorsese films are largely amoral, but they live by a code. In *Goodfellas*, Robert DeNiro's character summed it up, "Never rat on your friends, and always keep your mouth shut." Stephen occasionally styled himself after DeNiro's characters in those films. He wore a golden pinkie ring and slicked back his hair, polo shirts and button-downs with nice pants and a jacket—so he looked like a mobster. Classmate Jenness Hartley recalls, "He'd wear like a gold mafia-style ring on his finger. It was just bizarre. Everyone commented on his weird jewelry and I think he would wear a gold chain, too, occasionally."[15]

His favorite film, *Casino*, was based on the life of Frank Rosenthal, a former Las Vegas casino executive, handicapper and organized crime associate played by DeNiro as Sam "Ace" Rothstein. He and his violence-prone friends have a glitzy lifestyle. Rothstein opens the film: "[I] was a hell of a handicapper, I can tell you that. I was so good, that whenever I bet, I could change the odds for every bookmaker in the country. I had it down so cold that I was given paradise on earth. I was given one of the biggest casinos in Las Vegas." Ace smokes cigarettes, wears all-yellow and all-pink suits and always stays cool, even as others scream their heads off at him in irrational and emotional ways. He asks a woman, Ginger, to marry him. She tells him, "I just don't have those kind of feelings for you. I'm sorry. I'm not in love with you." He responds, "What is love, anyway? . . . I'll take care of you better than you'd ever imagine."

He's in control even when he's not. His words are taken out of context by the press, his cocaine-snorting wife plots to kill him, and his gaming license is revoked, but he stays preternaturally calm and self-assured, fighting critics on television and placing carefully worded phone calls. His friends do his dirty work.

Stephen appeared to study DeNiro's gestures—the loose hands, the fingertips-on-fingertips, the head tics—and incorporate them into his persona. Years later, he'd stand at podiums and conjure the old mobster in himself. "All these conservative guys can't help themselves, it's such a horrible cliché but they love the mafia," recalls one classmate. "The mobster is the perfect encapsulation of the conservative worldview, where there's no real law and order apart from might makes right." [16]

Stephen loved Las Vegas. He spent time there with family and friends wearing outfits inspired by the movies. "I won't describe what he would wear," Walter says. "He wore clothes that it was impossible not to see him. It's beyond peacocking . . . If you google Ace Rothstein casino outfits or suits, and you look at the pictures— you're directionally there." Stephen was skilled at craps. They ate at high-end steak restaurants, rented a cabana at the pool club and spent time in the sauna. They went to magic shows. Stephen wasn't into clubbing or getting wasted. He liked a classier vacation. "If you're not getting these hints about why he works for Trump, maybe it makes a little sense?"

The national attitude toward immigrants was less hostile than California's. "Immigration is not a problem to be solved," President George W. Bush said at a speech he gave in the summer of 2001 at Ellis Island. "It is a sign of a confident and successful nation."

He and Mexico's president Vicente Fox were in talks about a guest worker program to meet industry labor needs in a structured way.

It all came to a grinding halt on September 11, 2001, when the United States was attacked by terrorists. Miller watched the nightmare unfold on television: The Twin Towers were hit by two planes. The towers crumbled. People were burned alive, crushed to death or leaped from windows to their deaths. Another airplane crashed into the Pentagon. A fourth, believed to be headed for the Capitol, plummeted into an empty field after passengers overtook the hijackers. Nearly three thousand people were killed. It was the deadliest terrorist attack in history.

A multimillionaire Saudi extremist, Osama Bin Laden, had declared war on the US, citing its military presence in the Arabian peninsula, the war in Iraq and support for Israel. Bin Laden called those actions "a clear declaration of war on Allah, his messenger, and Muslims." It was, in his view, a war between Islam and the West. Historian Bernard Lewis wrote in *Foreign Affairs*, "To most Americans, the declaration is a travesty, a gross distortion of the nature and purpose of the American presence in Arabia. They should also know that for many—perhaps most—Muslims, the declaration is an equally grotesque travesty of the nature of Islam and even of its doctrine of jihad . . . At no point do the basic texts of Islam enjoin terrorism and murder."[17]

Walter sat next to Stephen in homeroom that morning. Geographically, they were nearly as far from the attacks as they could be in the US, but the images on TV had left them stunned and confused. What was going on? The boys waited for their teacher, an older gentleman, to help them process the attack. "He went on as though it never happened," Walter says. One student asked why he was ignoring it. "The teacher tried to be as calm and professional as possible with regard to describing this event," Walter recalls. "He was probably unprepared to say something."

Sarton Weinraub, a clinical psychologist who has done research on the trauma of Americans who witnessed the 9/11 attacks, says many people who were not in New York City had difficulty processing the attacks as well.[18] "It's almost as if the farther you go, the more that the ideas of what might have happened—the fantasy, the fear—was more intense," he says.

Walter says the school's response to 9/11 sparked Miller's political awakening. One teacher suggested that the terrorist attack was America's own fault for its actions abroad.

Miller wanted to stand in solidarity with the victims. Across California, as in other parts of the country, homes became decorated with American flags. He listened to "God Bless the USA" by Lee Greenwood. Meanwhile, President Bush's conversations with Mexico's president about a guest worker plan screeched to a halt. The US government created the Department of Homeland Security (DHS), which replaced the Immigration and Naturalization Service (INS), with Customs and Border Protection (CBP) and Immigration and Customs Enforcement (ICE).

Stephen wondered why his school didn't recite the Pledge of Allegiance. California's Education Code requires a daily patriotic exercise. He called into *The Larry Elder Show* and complained about his school's alleged reaction to the terrorist attacks. Stephen said a teacher had dragged the American flag across the floor and trampled it.

Other students recall it differently. The Canadian teacher pulled the flag from its stand and placed it on the floor. He asked students to discuss why a symbol, the American flag, mattered to them so much. Classmate Ben Tarzynski says he thought the lesson was valuable, but poorly executed.[19] "He just kept the flag there even after his point had been made, [with] a smirk on his face," He says it may have been "triggering" to some students still processing the attacks. "I don't think he was hoping to engender a backlash that would reverberate for twenty years."

Jenness Hartley confronted Miller about him twisting the details of the lesson about the American flag on *The Larry Elder Show*.[20] Stephen replied, "It doesn't matter what the truth is, but how it makes people feel," echoing a sentiment increasingly prevalent on the right—to value the gut over the brain. Hartley says, "He admitted he was just saying crazy shit in the worst way possible to get these conservative white people riled up."

Elder says, "[Stephen] came on my show and I thought he was amazingly articulate—full of energy and passion. And he seemed to understand concepts I didn't get until I was much, much older." He recalls that Miller told him how he prepped for his show. "He took it very seriously, almost like, like a game, like you prepare for a test or athletic contests. He said he thought about it all day, thought about what he was going to say . . . and I was just so impressed."[21]

Elder told him he could come on the show anytime. "Almost whenever he wanted to come on the air to talk about whatever was on his mind, I put him on. And he told me years later that he was on sixty-nine times. And I said, you counted them? He said yes." Elder was impressed with Miller's outfits. "He's been dressing well for years. And I asked him why, and he said he wants to make a good impression. He told me he always likes to have something that stands out on him, like some sort of affectation—it might be a ring, it might be a pocket square or something. And if you notice, it's always a little something . . . a little different."

Miller brought his friends to the studio to watch him on air, railing against the school's alleged liberal bias. "He made it seem like liberalism was the Antichrist," says classmate Adrian Karimi. "You could very clearly tell he had some sort of animus."[22] Alex Marlow, a future Breitbart editor, was listening to Stephen on the radio. It inspired him to ask Elder for an internship.[23] "I think I've given a lot of young people like Stephen and others a kind of confidence," Elder says. "It's not crazy to say that racism and sexism are no longer significant problems in America."

Elder appears to relish wrapping himself in the cloak of the villain. In a chapter on media bias in his book *The Ten Things You Cannot Say in America,* he wrote about his mother's hatred for a man named George who "was tall and muscular, with a beautiful face and sparkling white teeth."[24] She believed he was a bad person: a cheater and a fraud. Elder, then a child, argued that George was handsome. His mother so despised George that she couldn't see his handsomeness. He compared his mother's attitude to the media's attitude toward conservatives, saying journalists are so convinced conservatives are evil, they can't see anything else. "By the way," he writes at the end. "Mom was right about George."

CHAPTER FOUR

"PICK UP MY TRASH"

STEPHEN WAS MASTERING THE CONFIDENT and aggressive pose of his right-wing heroes. He wasn't the most popular boy in school, but he had the most attention. Trying his skills as a writer, he wrote an article in *The Samohi* titled "A Time to Kill." It read: "I am not going to lie. I relish the thought of watching Osama Bin Laden being riddled to death with bullets . . . Many people have rushed to point out that we are responsible for the incredible hatred that poor Islamic countries have for us. That is absolutely ridiculous. The reason that these countries are poor and failing is because they have refused to embrace the values that make our country great."

In 2003, Miller sat at the back of a bus in a white tennis shirt with classmates. He improvised into a handheld microphone. "As for Saddam Hussein and his henchmen, I think the ideal solution would be to cut off their fingers," he said, as his classmates cracked up.[1] "I don't think it's necessary to kill them entirely. We're not a barbaric people. We respect life." He fought back a grin. "Therefore torture is the way to go! Because torture people can live! Torture is a celebration of life and human dignity!" The others giggled. "We need to remember that as we enter these very dark and dangerous times."

Stephen enjoyed sparring with teachers in long-winded tangents. But while his monologues made some people laugh, they were exhausting and offensive to others. Adrian Karimi was in Stephen's AP government class senior year. He dropped out in part because Miller monopolized the discussions. "I'm just trying to learn about the intricacies of our government . . . but it became a [talk] show all the time between Miller and the teacher," he says.

Miller buttressed his arguments by firing off statistics, which left some people speechless. He deflected and derailed their criticism. He justified the Trail of Tears. "I've never heard of someone defending the way we treat Native Americans," classmate Nick Silverman says.[2] "Most people would admit we fucked that one up, we were awful—but Stephen was like, 'Oh the pioneer spirit, manifest destiny!' Romanticizing the mistakes we've made. And he was already so good at pivoting off the point you're trying to push him on. He'd pivot from us murdering Native Americans to, well, the Native Americans did *this*. Spinning the point around."

Miller would later publish his thoughts about his classes on a right-wing website, writing that his history teacher omitted "essential components of U.S. history," such as "the pioneers" and "the Second Amendment." They allegedly told students that capitalism had been "a sinister force" in the world and described the Mexican American War as the "North American invasion." He believed he had received poor grades for disputing those characterizations.[3]

Miller penned Silverman a note in chicken-scratch in one of his yearbooks: "Nick, what a year, huh? What a year. It's been great being in the two rows that control the class." Silverman says he was "traumatized" when he saw his old classmate at Trump rallies. He could hear Miller's voice in AP government when Trump talks about "America First" and "Make America Great Again." He says,

"Stephen's rhetoric has completely infected the tone and mantra of this administration. It's his." What Miller seemed to loath the most was multiculturalism. "He said we should be celebrating American culture and being Americans," Silverman says. "I mean, what is American culture? American culture is the different cultures."

An April Fools' Day issue of *The Samohi,* called "The Clamohi," ran a spoof article impersonating Stephen, rejoicing about the cancelation of "club day," in which student groups raise money by selling foreign food. "Samo is much better off without that gross display of multiculturalism encroaching on pure American values," the article read, capturing Stephen's voice. "The iron fist of ethnic culinary domination has held this school in its vice-like [*sic*] grip for too long . . . Finally we are free, free to eat the bland and over-cooked food that is our American birthright."

As much as Stephen stood out at Santa Monica High School, he was still a normal teenager in many ways. In keeping with his interest in retro-cool, Elvis Presley was his favorite musician. He enjoyed reality television shows like *American Idol* and *America's Got Talent.* He watched the movie *Ghostbusters.* Some classmates believe moving from North of Montana had an impact on him, contributing to feelings of inferiority that manifested as resentment. "I moved from North of Montana to half a block south of Montana and I felt it," says Jenness Hartley. She spent time with Miller because he was friends with Moritz, "a blue blood Republican, super rich North of Montana kid who has a wicked sense of humor and is pretty self-deprecating."

The group had a competitive culture. Hartley thinks Miller was going after kids who were less fortunate out of a vindictive feeling, because they were getting extra help. She says he was "obsessed" with the idea that Mexicans were not learning English. "That was very upsetting to him . . . he had intense hatred toward Mexicans in particular," she says.

Miller wrote a letter to the editor of a local publication in 2002, decrying the "rampant political correctness" at his school.[4] He claimed there were "very few, if any, Hispanic students in my honors classes," and that they "lacked basic English skills" because the school provided a "crutch" through bilingual education, which made "a mockery of the American ideal of personal accomplishment." Karimi says, "I was in three AP classes, and there were minorities in all my classes." Silverman adds, "We had a ton of Hispanic kids in all my honors classes."

In his letter, Miller criticized the school's policy of giving out free condoms. He criticized the club for gays and lesbians. He said the school did "nothing for American holidays but everything for Mexican holidays." He defended the genocide of the Native Americans. "I suppose then, that our country would have been better off if our soldiers never killed anyone, and we watched as our nation was obliterated by the evil in the world, as we sung songs of peace and love? Or, better yet, we could have lived with the Indians, learning how to finger paint and make teepees, excusing their scalping of frontiersmen as part of their culture."

That spring, Miller ran for student announcer. Like his father, he would give a speech that people would remember for years. He sauntered onstage before a large, noisy crowd of students in a half-circle Greek outdoor amphitheater. He wore a green snakeskin-print polo and grinned, feasting his eyes on the audience as they booed and cheered. He reached the podium and waved, still grinning. In Larry Elder's studio, he'd been practicing stoking the masses. Now, he stood face-to-face with the multicultural school he had so often criticized. The noise of them, the hysteria, contrasted with his calm. It seemed to fill him with a sense of superiority.

"Hi, I'm Stephen Miller," he said.[5] He gripped the microphone and squinted his face with practiced confidence. He was the only candidate, he said, "who really *stands out*. I will say and I will do things that no one else in their right mind would say or do." He continued, his face reddening with emotion, his voice rising to a shout, "Am I the only one who is *sick* and *tired* of being told to pick up my trash when we have plenty of *janitors* who are paid to *do it for us?*"

The school had thousands of students and about ten custodians, mostly people of color. Students erupted in a roar of disapproval. Miller's comments suggested the staff were the servants of the students. Student assembly president Coleen Armstrong-Yamamura was worried the students were about to riot.[6] "I just remember the crowd at that point going kind of nuts. We had very volatile racial relations," she says. She thought Miller's comments were classist and racist. "I can't remember if somebody threw things at him, but I felt it was on the brink of getting there," she says. She told him his time was up. "You need to get down," she said. He kept talking, relishing the moment. "So I took him physically, and I pushed him off the stage."

Miller's friend Walter says there were students who loved his performance. "Dozens of people came up to [Stephen] and said how awesome it was," he says. "We legitimately thought he had a chance of winning." Walter says the speech was pre-approved by the school, and that Miller was trying to showcase the entertainment he'd bring to announcements.

Not enough students were swayed, however. They chose a German immigrant instead of Miller. "So this guy with a thick German accent would read the announcements," Hartley says. She came up with an idea: to make a documentary about Miller. Rachel Greenberg and others joined her in interviewing classmates about him. "He's pretty right wing," said one. Another said he "adds flavor." A blond student hypothesized that Miller "enjoys the infamy, like some perverted power trip." His friend Moritz, sitting on a fancy chaise in a suit at his house, told the filmmakers that Stephen's comment about the custodians was a joke. "Most people are so uptight and they don't realize the humor in some of the things he says," he said.

It wasn't the first time Miller had made comments like that. One teacher recalls that a few times, while she told students to pick up their trash at pep rallies or on the quad at lunch, Miller came up to them and told his classmates to defy the teacher. "Throw your trash down. They need work, we pay them to do that," he said of the custodians. The teacher was always appalled and asked him to explain himself. Stephen replied, "What? That's their job."[7]

Greenberg and Hartley interviewed Miller for the film but ended up excluding the footage because he never signed a release. Greenberg, who edited the video, says Stephen's mother called the video center and told the teacher she "wanted the video destroyed. All copies destroyed."[8] Greenberg was disappointed because she was so proud of the cut and excited to show it to the world. "I never thought it was unflattering. If anything it was sort of flattering. I thought it was fun . . . It's someone who's unique and stands out, you know?" Lacking the signed release form, the girls created a cut without his interview. But they didn't submit it to film festivals as planned, for fear that they'd get in trouble with Stephen's parents.

DAVID HOROWITZ HEARD MILLER RAGING on *The Larry Elder Show.* He saw him as a kindred spirit, a potential recruit to his far-right movement. "He's very gutsy," Horowitz says.[9] "It's very hard to get people to stand up for what they believe in . . . it's very intimidating to be attacked in the way the left attacks. Very, very ugly." Horowitz ran the Center for the Study of Popular Culture, later renamed the David Horowitz Freedom Center——his School for Political Warfare. The foundation's website says it "sees its role as that of a battle tank, geared to fight a war that many still don't recognize . . . the political left has declared war on America and its constitutional system, and is willing to collaborate with America's enemies abroad and criminals at home to bring America down."

His School for Political Warfare taught white men to wear the armor of persecuted minorities in their fight to save the United States. Horowitz, who is Jewish, argues that Protestant Christian doctrines are fundamental to America and that they are under direct assault. He parrots the controversial political scientist Samuel Huntington, who envisions a "clash of civilizations" between Islam and the West, between Latin American culture and American culture. In the nineties, Horowitz coordinated with right-wing or libertarian lawyers to defend right-wing youths in trouble due to alleged racism, sexism or homophobia. When Cal State University Northridge's Zeta Beta Tau fraternity was suspended for passing out flyers for a party about Lupe—from the lyrics about the "Mexican whore"—Horowitz got involved. The hate song deeply disturbed Mexican American students; it was about an eight-year-old girl penetrated violently by a structure on which she was swinging, who became parasitically obsessed with sex, always wanting more to the point of sucking out people's guts. It was an especially vile expression of the statewide narrative of migrants as welfare-guzzling and subhuman.

But Horowitz thought the attack on the song was "overwrought." Spring of 1993, the fraternity was reinstated amid a lawsuit alleging free speech violations.[10] It was one of several cases Horowitz helped fight, pressuring universities to rewrite sexual harassment and hate speech rules, so that right-wing youths could more freely offend minorities.

Miller invited Horowitz to speak at Santa Monica High School. Days before his scheduled visit, administrators canceled. As a Horowitz acolyte, Miller would receive instructions for promoting "academic freedom." A seventy-page handbook gave tips for attracting media attention; documenting and protesting "classroom indoctrination and abuses"; organizing controversial events; obtaining funding; shaming administrators who refuse "to increase the scope of intellectual diversity"; investigating alleged partisan biases of faculty—with special attention to women's studies, African American studies, Chicano/Latino/Hispanic studies, Asian American studies, Lesbian/Gay/Bisexual/Transgender studies and more.

Miller and Moritz resubmitted the application for Horowitz to speak. They talked to local papers and went on *The Larry Elder Show* to complain, citing free speech violations. Horowitz was finally allowed to speak on November 1. When Horowitz arrived, the dean of students welcomed him and told him the school was glad to have him, according to an article Stephen wrote on Horowitz's website.[11] Horowitz said, "No you're not."

Horowitz stood in front of Miller's classmates and said, "You can't get a good education if they're only telling you half of the story." He said the idea of America as racist was a lie, and that the proof was that "there is no exodus of people fleeing America." He blamed liberals for "everything that is wrong with America's inner cities." Some of the students were offended, and "were rude, sometimes interrupting Horowitz's speech," Miller wrote.

After the event, Miller went on *The Larry Elder Show* to tell listeners about Horowitz's "less than courteous reception." The school superintendent allegedly called his house. "He wanted to speak with my parents because he was concerned with my appearances on the radio," he wrote. His parents defended him. Miller ended his article by listing several demands of the school, including that the Pledge of Allegiance be recited five days a week. He called for an "inclusive patriotism, rather than a multiculturalism that often seems directed at denigrating this country." The school instituted the Pledge of Allegiance. Jason Islas, Miller's middle school friend, wrote an article titled "Pledge Allegiance to Democracy and Free Thought," in the *Samohi*, arguing the Founding Fathers never meant to promote blind allegiance to authority. As Stephen stood in the mornings and recited it with gusto, many others remained seated in protest.

School administrators were worried about Stephen. He was brought into the office with a security escort.[12] When the school placed a tax increase initiative on the ballot to generate revenue after state budget cuts to education, "it failed, and right away I was blamed," he wrote. "I met with the superintendent and principal and carefully outlined the basic changes I felt needed to be implemented. I let them know this election was a wakeup call, demonstrating public disapproval, and that any positive steps the school should take would be dutifully reported on the radio." The principal distributed a memo to the teachers, ordering them to discuss the war in Iraq in a balanced way and to remain politically neutral, according to Miller's article.

Horowitz invited Miller over to his house. It was the start of a relationship that would last for years—like Miller's relationship with Elder.[13] Elder had given him a platform; Horowitz gave him the weapons. Squinty-eyed with a goatee, Horowitz had a raspy voice that dripped with a kind of fatherly exhaustion. Miller told him he'd grown up in a liberal household and realized those political views were wrong. Horowitz could relate. His own parents had been members of the Communist Party; he was steeped in left-wing views through most of the seventies and worked with the Black Panthers in California. But he became disillusioned after a white friend he had recommended to work on the Black Panthers' accounting was murdered. The murder was never solved, but David blamed the black activists. Horowitz wrote of his revelation, "By crowning the criminals with the halo of humanity's hope, the left shields them from judgment for their criminal deeds. Thus in the name of revolutionary justice, the left defends revolutionary injustice; in the name of human liberation, the left creates a world of oppression."[14]

Horowitz believes liberals have waged a wrongheaded war on whiteness. White European males, primarily English and Protestant Christian, created "America's unique political culture . . . [which] led the world in abolishing slavery and establishing the principles of ethnic and racial inclusion," he wrote in his book *Hating Whitey*.[15] "We are a nation besieged by peoples 'of color' trying to immigrate to our shores to take advantage of the unparalleled opportunities and rights our society offers them."

Stephen was awed by Horowitz's ideas. Receptive to his romanticization of immoral deeds by white men—such as slavery and genocide—while ignoring the central role of people of color in making once-false American ideals of equality and liberty true, he saw this country as a white-forged masterpiece, unfairly demonized by brown hordes.[16]

Horowitz studied the tools of the counterculture sixties New Left and gave them to white male conservatives. They adopted the principles of free speech and equality in order to attack them. People fighting racism and trying to lift up minority voices were "racists." Activists fighting inequality were "oppressors." It was, quite literally, gaslighting: psychological warfare to derail victims' sense of reality. Gaslighting is a form of emotional abuse recognized by psychologists. It involves deflection, projection, false or exaggerated accusations, misdirection, and doubling down when challenged—to keep victims on the defensive.[17] Harvard professors Eric Beerbohm and Ryan Davis wrote a paper about gaslighting, "The gaslighter doesn't just disagree with his interlocutor's assertions . . . The gaslighter deliberately refuses to treat the other agent's statements as inputs into a common deliberative process."[18]

The term has been overused and is often applied to explain President Trump's tactics on Americans. But Horowitz—who would shape Trump's campaign through Miller—was its architect as a central strategy of the new Republican Party.

MEANWHILE, SCHOOL COUNSELOR DE LA Torre launched the Pico Youth & Family Center to help disadvantaged students escape the cycle of violence. The Mara Salvatrucha gang had formed in Los Angeles as people fled a decades-long US-backed civil war in El Salvador, in which tens of thousands of civilians were massacred by right-wing death squads. They brought with them the trauma of the dead. Denied refugee status, they forged Mara Salvatrucha to survive. Deported, they spread across Central America, terrorizing people and triggering a new exodus.

"We destabilized those countries," de la Torre says. "[MS-13] was an American creation all the way, from creating the conditions in El Salvador, to creating the social conditions in Los Angeles which gives rise to the gang problem." Denied refugee status, Salvadorans were afraid of going to the police when robbed, assaulted or threatened in the US. But they had learned brutality for self-protection at home, thanks to US foreign policy.

America's involvement in Central America goes back to Sam Zemurray, the head of the United Fruit Company, who financed the liberal publication *The Nation* and was known as the Banana King. He was one of the world's richest men. In Central America, he ousted leaders unfriendly toward his Banana Empire, which controlled most of the region's natural resources. Subsequently, the United States intervened whenever a politician sought to redistribute Central American land. The mission of the US in the region was neither left- nor right-wing. It was capitalist. Its mission was to keep the veins of Central America open to American consumers.

Santa Monica was benefitting and had been for decades. The day Stephen was born, a pilotless US spy plane crashed in northeastern El Salvador.[19] It had been gathering intelligence for the Salvadoran government military. The R4E-40 Skyeye surveillance was made in Stephen's hometown.[20] The manufacturer, Lear Siegler, Inc., employed twenty-nine thousand people and had a revenue of close to $2.5 billion. It specialized in aerospace technology that fueled the wealth of the beach city and was seen by US officials as playing a key role in turning the tide of the war.[21]

The drone had fallen in Morazán, where US-trained right-wing troops had massacred hundreds of civilians four years prior. They raped women, beheaded fathers and shot at and hacked into children, rooting out the "cancer" of communism.[22] A woman named Rufina Amaya escaped the nightmare after hiding between the gnarled roots of a large crabapple tree. She heard the sounds of her children being dismembered—their small voices screaming her name—but she knew that if she crawled out to them, the American-backed soldiers would only kill her, too. "I promised God that if he helped me I would tell the world what happened here," she said later.[23]

The administration of Ronald Reagan, who had become president after his governorship in California, denied the reports as fake news. Still, a heated debate ensued in Congress about whether to continue supporting El Salvador's armed forces. Two decades later, the *New Yorker* published a comprehensive look at El Mozote. For a moment, when the genocide came to light, "the country's paramount Cold War national-security concerns were clashing—as loudly and unambiguously as they ever would for four decades—with its professed high-minded respect for human rights," wrote reporter Mark Danner.[24] Then it was forgotten. The US continued to back dictators in Central America with billions of dollars and M16 rifles, cannons, bullets and more. Fear of Communists outweighed their horror about the right-wing slaughters.

Danner wrote, "By early 1992, when a peace agreement between the government and the guerrillas was finally signed, Americans had spent more than four billion dollars funding a civil war

that had lasted twelve years and left seventy-five thousand Salvadorans dead . . . El Mozote may well have been the largest massacre in
modern Latin American history. That in the United States it came
to be known, that it was exposed to the light and then allowed to
fall back into the dark, makes the story of El Mozote—how it came
to happen and how it came to be denied—a central parable of the
Cold War."

Soon after, Mara Salvatrucha came of age in Los Angeles. The
Salvadoran gang was allegedly responsible for the drive-by shooting cited in the 1991 hate letter sent to hundreds of Santa Monica High School families, including the family of de la Torre. In
the mid-nineties, the gang started an alliance with the Mexican
mafia—La Eme, or "the M"—and became known as MS-13, Mara
Salvatrucha 13. The number "13" added for the thirteenth letter of
the alphabet—*M*—the Mexican mafia.

De la Torre told the young people he mentored that they didn't
have to get involved with gangs to feel at home; America was their
home. The MEChA idea that America belongs to brown people
struck fear in Miller. But the idea was not meant as a threat, de la
Torre says. It wasn't a zero-sum game. It was meant to help brown
students feel they, too, belong.

"When God said, where are we gonna put the Europeans,
there's Europe," he says. "When God said, where are we gonna put
the Africans, there's Africa. When God said where are we gonna
put the Asians, there's Asia. When God said where are we gonna
put the Mexicans, there's the Americas. See what I'm saying? When
God said where are we gonna put the salvadoreños or hondureños
or guatemaltecos: *the Americas*. These are *Americans*. These are people indigenous to this land. And to be called 'illegal' by the people
whose ancestors came here fleeing persecution, striving for a better
opportunity? It really runs contrary to human decency and the need
for all living beings to migrate, whether you're elephants, whether

you're butterflies . . . anybody whose ancestors come from some-where else need[s] to reflect on that. 'Cause they were given oppor-tunities here and they were blessed to be in a different place. *God did that.*" He compared the unfounded paranoia about a Hispanic takeover to fear felt by men who mistreat their wives. "They've been so abusive . . . They're sleeping with one eye open."

Both de la Torre and his wife sued the city over its at-large election system decades later, arguing that it systematically discrim-inates against Latin American voters. They won.[25]

IN MAY 2003, MILLER WAS featured in the *Los Angeles Times*. He was photographed cross-legged with books stacked on his knees—*Spartacus* by Howard Fast, two of Elder's books, LaPierre's book, *The Collected Tales and Poems of Edgar Allan Poe, Great American Speeches,* and Charles Dickens's *Great Expectations.*[26] His elbows rest on the tomes and his hands are folded loosely—thick golden ring visible, nails long and manicured. His serious face is in profile, his hair slicked back. "To be accepted into a university, you have to be a stellar student, athletic, musically inclined and involved in the community," he told a reporter.[27]

Miller graduated in 2003, having received more publicity than probably any other student in class. In his senior yearbook, he was voted "most outspoken," pictured in a long jacket with a pocket square and slicked-back hair, squinting, lips curling Elvis-like, pointing at the camera. His yearbook page is filled with pictures of him: on a spiraling staircase with a button-down shirt and his hand resting on the handrail, fingers outspread to showcase a fancy ring; in *Star Trek* uniforms with his brother Jacob; playing cards in a suit; leaning over a microphone in Elder's studio; resting his hand on the door of a white limousine; standing before the Twin Towers. He in-cluded three photos of himself in his black cowboy hat and a Theodore Roosevelt quote: "There can be no fifty-fifty Americanism in this country. There is room here for only 100 percent Americanism, only for those who are Americans and nothing else."

He published a self-promotional article on Horowitz's website: "How I Changed My Left-Wing High School." He recapped his wins, writing, "I just graduated from Santa Monica High School—an institution not of learning, but of indoctrination . . . In the 1970s, students started a political revolution on campus. Now is the time for a counter-revolution—one characterized by a devotion to this nation and its ideals. David Horowitz will soon launch 'Students for Academic Freedom,' an organization dedicated to just these principals [*sic*]. Acting together, we can succeed."

Horowitz was worried his mentee would not get the teacher recommendations he needed for a top-tier university, given how unpopular he allegedly was with his high school's authorities. He thought of Miller as a "second thoughts warrior" like himself, someone who had been brought up in one ideology and, upon second thought, decided the opposite was true. One day Miller came to him with some news: he'd been accepted at Duke University. He would study political science, with the hopes of eventually becoming a lawyer or a senator. Horowitz was relieved. His friend would go on rising. And he would take Horowitz's ideas with him.

CHAPTER FIVE

"THERE IS NO PALESTINE"

DUKE UNIVERSITY IS A PRIVATE university in Durham, North Carolina. It was created by the fortunes of tobacco barons, the Dukes that founded the American Tobacco Company. It had recently seen a meteoric rise in the national rankings thanks to an aggressive marketing campaign to attract high-profile professors, particularly in the humanities, and to improve its sports teams. By the late nineties, Duke was ranked third in all universities, behind only Harvard and Princeton, in *U.S. News & World Report*. The *Princeton Review* called Duke students "the happiest in the nation," with its temperate climate and beautiful campus.[1]

Freshman year, Stephen lived on the second floor of Pegram Dormitory. The dorm was on East Campus, with redbrick Jeffersonian architecture along a verdant quad. During orientation, a second-floor resident advisor asked his group of male residents to gather outside. Seated on the grass, the counselor asked them to introduce themselves: name, hometown, something about themselves. "Most people were playing the first-week-of-college game of keeping it short and sweet," recalls Michael Parker Ayers.[2] Most remained seated. But Miller sprang to his feet. "Steve stands up and puts his hands in that Mr. Burns pose, where the fingerprints all touch," says Ayers. Standing tall and straight, he began to speak: "Hi, I'm Stephen Miller," he said. "I'm from Santa Monica, California—*and I like guns*." His spectators chuckled, unsure if he was joking. He sat down. The introductions continued. But Miller had made an impression. He had a nickname now: *Guns*. His dorm mates called him Stephen "Guns" Miller.

There were signs early on that Stephen would pick up right where he left off in high school. The dorm residents gathered in the first-floor common room for pizza, salad and refreshments. They were getting to know one another during this first chapter away from home. When Miller threw his plate away, he missed the trash can and leftovers spilled on the floor. He walked away. A classmate asked, "Are you not gonna pick that up?" Stephen replied, "What hellhole are *you* from? We have people here for that."[3] Another recalls having lunch with him in the cafeteria. Every now and then, Stephen would leave his tray on the table, saying it wasn't his responsibility to clean up.[4] One classmate recalls that he tossed his tray on the ground, saying "there were people there paid to clean it up."[5]

A few weeks into freshman semester, a graduate assistant in charge of Pegram Dorm put a temporary lockdown on the first-floor common room because students were leaving it so messy. The dorm manager taped up a piece of paper letting students know that the custodial staff was not there to enable their filthy lifestyles. It encouraged them to pick up after themselves like grown-ups. Stephen taped up a typed two-page reply, protesting the punishment. Classmate Sean Hou says it described cleanliness as "a fine personal virtue, but ultimately it's the responsibility of the janitorial staff to ensure that it's clean, and it's too bad that forty thousand dollars a year doesn't make sure that people understand that." He says Stephen concluded by saying that regardless, the collective punishment was "fundamentally unjust."[6]

Miller was becoming disappointed with Duke. He didn't like the architecture of West Campus, known as a "Gothic Wonderland." He thought it looked superficial. He complained about it in the campus newspaper, *The Chronicle*. "West Campus is Gothic in the same way Disneyland's Main Street is New Orleans colonial," he wrote. Another building was the "ugliest" he'd ever seen. "It looks like a warehouse. It belongs at New York Harbor, not at the center of one of America's most elite universities." He didn't like the parking situation, either. He repeatedly got tickets for leaving his car where he wasn't supposed to. "Next time why doesn't Duke Parking just break my windshield," he griped.

Stephen enjoyed luxury-brand US-made Nat Sherman cigarettes. He was upset that the university lacked a smoking lounge where he could indulge in his habit "in rain, wet, cold and snow," without catching a cold. He imagined what the lounge would look like: "The room should have plenty of mahogany and leather, plasmas, darts, a grand piano and a professional full-service bar. This would be a great place to watch sports, recreate and relax."

Miller wandered around the dorm in a bathrobe and slippers: his signature outfit in his room and the common area. He drank whiskey or scotch from a rocks glass. He listened to Elvis Presley and kept leather-bound books. "He was a little bit strange, like an old man," says dorm mate Amy Terwilleger.[7] She recalls that his robe was "dark-colored terry cloth." For some dorm mates, he called to mind Hugh Hefner.

He was known as a mostly quiet and quirky dorm mate. Michael Parker Ayers says, "He was actually a relatively pleasant guy. A little weird, but pleasant." But he changed when he spoke about politics. "Like an alter ego or a different person. He was almost bordering on violent," he says. Some dorm mates recall he described himself as a "libertarian" at the time. Many tried to focus on apolitical topics with him. Alec Macaulay says when Miller wasn't talking politics, he "erred on the side of mild-mannered."[8] Alec, an extrovert, would say hello and slap people on the back. "Whereas he was much more quiet, hand half-way raised, a handshake in passing. This person you pass on the sidewalk is just about as completely different as you can imagine from the Stephen Miller standing on a stage of a Donald Trump rally."

Miller changed out of his bathrobe and into polo shirts, khakis and oxfords for class. From his desk, he launched into three- or four-minute monologues, smirking the whole time. "He would have people in fits," one classmate recalls.[9]

Some women found him charming, at least in private. He was romantically involved with a light-skinned Mexican American girl his freshman year. Her old friends at Pegram remember that she didn't want people to know she was intimate with Miller. "Yovana," a pseudonym, was conscious of her social image. "She didn't want to tell people about this 'cause he's weird and not necessarily attractive," says her then-roommate. "I think she felt a need to keep it a secret from the people she hung out with." Others in the dorm remember that Miller was more interested in Yovana than she was in him—like Ace's relationship with Ginger in *Casino*. Aaron Thomas Johnson says she was "almost like stringing him along," while he was "doting."[10]

Yovana came from a town just north of the US-Mexico border and, according to her old friends, expressed conservative viewpoints. On Twitter years later, she retweeted a pro-gun article and linked to an album by country singer Jason Boland. "They were always together," recalls Rebecca Suffness, one of Yovana's closest friends at the time.[11] Three dorm mates recall Miller bought alcohol for them because he looked older and could get away with it. He dressed up in a suit and launched into angry rants if anyone tried to card him. Since it was a dry campus, they snuck the alcohol into the dorm rooms from the windows with a makeshift pulley system.[12]

Stephen once placed recycling bins in front of Yovana's door to trap her inside, according to two dorm mates. It was creepy, but also playful. She left Duke at the end of freshman year. Her dorm mates lost touch with her, and her relationship with Stephen ended.

Freshman year had been low key for Stephen, wrapped up in his relationship with Yovana. He found his first issue worthy of a fight at the beginning of sophomore year, when Duke University scheduled a Palestine Solidarity Movement (PSM) conference from October 15 to 17. The PSM is a student organization that encourages divestment from Israel, seeing it as an occupation of Palestinian land. The movement has argued that "Zionism is racism," an extreme idea that took root in 1975, when the United Nations passed General Assembly Resolution 3379 condemning Zionism. In 1991, the resolution was retracted, deemed a product of the cold war.[13]

About three in four American Jews vote Democratic and favor a two-state solution to the Israeli-Palestinian conflict.[14] Most are Zionists. The Jewish intellectual Yehuda Kurtzer defines Zionism as the ideology of the project to build a Jewish nation-state, which includes Israelis and Palestinians recognizing each other and negotiating.[15] He says Zionism is sometimes wrongly construed as "loyalty to the existing version of the nation-state that is currently in place . . . whatever the state of Israel does." Kurtzer says, "Zionism is supposed to be a project of imagination as much as it is a project of loyalty. I'm committed to the Jewish nation-state. I'm committed to the project of building it and supporting it. But that also means I bring to bear moral critiques of what the nation-state does with its politics."

In recent years, a right-wing push in Israel has been mirrored in a minority of American Jews. Anxiety tied to low Jewish birth rates has led to intra-fighting about how to best ensure the community's survival, with the right-wing charge in the United States led by people like California-based talk-radio host Dennis Prager, the Zionist Organization of America's Morton Klein and Horowitz. The extreme right construes the Israeli-Palestinian conflict as a war between Islam and the West, just as terrorists in the region do. It denies Palestinians their right to a national identity. Horowitz tweeted, "There is no Palestine, there are no Palestinians." The far right demonizes Arabs, seeing them as a threat to Judeo-Christian values; it feeds the false view of Zionism as racist, as its own form of extremism. Kurtzer says both extremes express "a kind of chauvinistic or full-throated nationalism that sees the nation-state not just as a platform within which to build democratic societies, but as such, a profound goal in and of itself."

He emphasizes that nationalism is a useful tool for building societies. The problem, Kurtzer argues, is a narcissism that nationalism can engender, in which "nations start becoming obsessed with themselves, believing that the state is an end of itself that serves the purposes of this one nation as opposed to others—and then they oppress their minorities. Nationalism, in order to be moral, has to work in relationship to democracy. And one of the biggest category errors right now in Trump's nationalism, in right-wing nationalism, is that what makes a democracy is not the rule of the majority. You can have the rule of the majority—and that's called tyranny. What makes democracy is that you have the rule of the majority tempered by a major consideration for the rights of minorities."

In 2004, Miller was outraged that Duke was giving a platform to the Palestine Solidarity Movement. He launched a Duke chapter of Horowitz's Students for Academic Freedom and organized students against the conference. He handed out flyers linking the PSM to terrorist groups such as Hamas and Islamic Jihad and painting Israel as the "victim."[16] He made himself available for interviews with *The Chronicle,* local TV stations and papers. But they did not take him as seriously as Santa Monica news outlets had. "They either did not use my quotes or eviscerated them to the point where they were near meaningless," he later complained.

Despite protests, the university allowed the conference to take place, citing the importance of free speech. Just before, Duke held an antiterrorism concert, hosted a speech by a pro-Israel activist and displayed a bombed Israeli bus. Student M. Shadee Malaklou attended the display, which featured photographs of Palestinian children holding machine guns. She held up a sign asking, "What about state-sponsored terrorism?" Miller confronted one of her co-protesters. "He was like a set of audio files that kept running on repeat," Malaklou says. It was one of several encounters they had. "Whenever I tried to talk to him and engage with him about his ideas, he had no capacity to defend them. He was like a tape on repeat," she says, "like a narcissistic mother who gaslights you."

A few days before the conference, an inflammatory email impersonating two PSM student organizers went out to thousands of Duke community members. "The message included statements in support of terrorism and a slogan used by the extremist group Hamas," says John F. Burness, senior vice president for public affairs and government relations, in a letter to students and faculty.[17] "I am writing to inform you that the students did NOT send this message, which appears to be a deliberate act of disinformation and provocation on the part of people who do not want the conference to take place."

Burness says the university was never able to determine the source of the email. Computer security staff investigated.[18] They determined only that the message originated in California.

Miller met with Burness to tell him about alleged terrorist recruiting at the PSM conference. He planned to encourage people to stop applying to Duke and to stop donating money. Burness was struck by the vehemence of the young man's statements and his assuredness that his take was right. "That wasn't necessarily uncommon among students who would walk in my door who were passionate about an issue in one way or another," Burness says. "What was distinctive was that it didn't seem to matter what information you gave him."

The encounter was one of many Burness would have with Stephen. "He stood out more than any student I think I've ever encountered—and just so you know, I was vice president at Cornell before coming to Duke, and before that associate chancellor at the University of Illinois, and before that deputy to the president at Stony Brook. I had a very public role and dealt with students regularly who would come in and be passionate about an issue. But I never met anyone quite like him . . . the sort of cockiness, the arrogance." Burness says he knew him as a Horowitz acolyte, and always had the sense that Miller had been consulting with him just before. "The language he would use occasionally sounded exactly like Horowitz."

Burness told Miller that the student group that organized the conference had followed the proper channels and as such the views of the speakers didn't particularly matter. He thought it was ironic that the young man, relying on academic freedom arguments, took issue with them when applied to the opposite viewpoint. "He conveyed a sense that he had all the answers and that mine were made up," Burness says.

Miller went on *The Larry Elder Show* to complain. He wrote a piece for an online forum, saying Duke University had "invited evil onto its campus." He encouraged people to call or email Duke's president Richard Brodhead, express concerns about the "contemptible" actions and stop supporting Duke.[19] He wrote, "I was surprised there were not longer lines at the restrooms to use the sinks, considering how many people at the conference had blood on their hands." He said that Duke's president "prostituted the campus to terror."

He was shocked at the Jewish students supporting the PSM, writing that they had "fallen for the lies and propaganda, very similarly to how some Jews supported Stalin . . . [they were] disenfranchised college kids looking for a sense of belonging, of personal power, of importance."

THE SUMMER AFTER SOPHOMORE YEAR, Miller was still seething at Oscar de la Torre, the Santa Monica school district board member who told him that institutional racism did exist—the man who had been singled out by the 1991 hate letter promising to gas Mexicans "like Hitler gassed the Jews." Miller wrote a piece on Horowitz's website about him, having learned that de la Torre had recently been accused of bringing gang members to Santa Monica High School.[20] "When asked about his decision to bring gang leaders onto the high school's campus, de La Torre claimed that they were 'businessmen' . . . One has to wonder what kind of 'businessmen' wear gang clothes, have gang tattoos, and are suspected by the police department of being gang leaders," he wrote.

De la Torre had brought tattoo and graffiti artist Mark Machado, "Mr. Cartoon," and clothing apparel owner Steve Luciano, "Big Lucky," a former gang member, to talk peace at the high school after fights broke out between black and brown students. The idea was to inspire students to believe in their professional potential and to leave gang life behind. Police threatened to arrest de la Torre, writing in their report that his friends were covered with "mural-like" tattoos, "were holding their hands at their belt line, and their heads were tilted back in a gangster type of lean."[21] De la Torre says, "It was all bullshit . . . they tried to accuse me of starting a riot. When you and I know, all riots have been started by law enforcement fucking up people of color. We never riot just because. We riot because the police killed somebody."

Miller wrote that he had contacted the school superintendent John Deasy about de la Torre's alleged association with gang members. Deasy "refused to criticize De La Torres [*sic*] actions. This was another act of cowardice." His article was re-posted by the white supremacist website American Renaissance, which Miller grew so familiar with that he referred to it by its nickname, "AmRen."[22] He compared de la Torre to a doctor who is purposely making patients sick: "If the leeches aren't making the patient healthy, then more leeches need to be applied." He shared de la Torre's email address and encouraged people to "put him out of business."

De la Torre read the article. It scared him. He wondered why Stephen harbored so much resentment years later. But he also felt bad for him. "The thing with racism, it doesn't just hurt the darker-skinned person," he says. "It takes away from the white person the ability to interact authentically with other people that are not of his race or skin color . . . you keep yourself away from those interactions that make you whole." He blames us-versus-them rhetoric. "This separation between man and woman, between race, gender, class—all the way politicians divide people and cut them up into pieces for personal gain," de la Torre said. "That's really what's going on here. This shit is a game being played. Our job is to expose it. You know what I'm saying? 'Cause if we expose it, people get hip, people get smart—and we end that game."

MILLER STAYED IN TOUCH WITH Horowitz, visiting him back home in Los Angeles and attending his annual Restoration Weekends and West Coast Retreats. At luxury resorts in California and elsewhere, the events united right-wing lawmakers and media personalities with the aim of incubating conservative thought. Miller was on a student panel discussing alleged political abuse in schools and posed in a photo with former attorney general John Ashcroft.[23] Other guests were Wayne LaPierre, Andrew Breitbart and Congressman Tom Tancredo.

At Duke, Miller battled multiculturalism by redeploying its weapons, as Horowitz had taught him to do. Junior year, he secured a column in the campus newspaper, *The Chronicle*. He was seen as adding to the intellectual diversity of the university. On September 5, 2005, he published his first piece, "Welcome to Leftist University."[24] He said Duke's administration was "obsessed with multiculturalism." He criticized a freshman orientation speech by the legendary writer Maya Angelou, whom he described as having "racial paranoia." He ridiculed the idea that she had any wisdom to offer, arguing that she was recycling "multicultural clichés."

His column, "Miller Time," a beer reference, was printed with a brooding portrait of him against a stone wall. He criticized black classmates for calling out the right-wing pundit Bill Bennett's racist comments about how to reduce crime: "You could abort every black baby in this country . . . That would be an impossible, ridiculous and morally reprehensible thing to do, *but your crime rate would go down*." Miller called the critique of Bennett a "misguided and slanderous assault."[25]

The Chronicle newsroom was near the Gothic chapel on West Campus. With old clippings on the wall and rows of cluttered desks with computers, it resembled a real newsroom, with crushed beer cans lying around. Miller came in wearing a suit and battled vocally with editors who tried to tweak his work. In one column, he recounted an exchange with a woman who called him a racist.[26] "My skin, in addition to being somewhat pasty, is also very thick," he wrote. "I wasn't personally wounded by [her] remarks. On a moral level, I was disturbed by the private and public slander, by an accusation that was so grotesquely false and baseless; but sadly, it was far from the first time someone had created this paranoid illusion."

Rather than question his belief system after repeated accusations of racism from different people throughout his life, Miller doubled down. He chose to see the criticism as emotional. It reinforced his conviction that his opponents were at a loss for how to debate him.

"I am?" he asked the woman who called him a racist.

"Yes, you hate black people," she said.

"Really? I hate black people? What would ever give you that idea?" He wrote, recalling the exchange, "In similar encounters, I've found this simple question was often enough to render friendly slanderers incoherent."

The nameless woman said she'd read his columns. "You just think you're better than everyone else, don't you?" she asked.

Miller said, "I can certainly think of someone I've got beat." Then, "You have a mental disease. You're obsessed with race. You see everything in terms of race, and you see everyone who disagrees with your worldviews as racist. And guess what? Almost everybody you've been talking to thinks something is wrong with you. They've come up and told me. They're just afraid to tell you . . . they're worried you'll call them a racist."

Miller gained a reputation as a campus troll, melting the snowflakes and triggering the libs before those tactics became standard practice among the new Republicans, who drew from California's combative conservatism. "Today's archetypal college Republican is not a mini Mitt Romney with a copy of *National Review* tucked under his arm, but a red-capped rabble-rouser pranking the pious liberal students who fret that cafeteria is a form of cultural appropriation or demand free tampons in both men's and women's bathrooms in the name of 'menstrual equity,' " McKay Coppins wrote in *the Atlantic.* Conservative provocateur and Los Angeles native Ben Shapiro says, "To understand [Miller], you really have to understand the oppositional nature of conservative politics in Los Angeles. You're in the minority . . . You end up going to war enough times, you start to see everything as a war." [27]

Miller relished the thought of capital punishment. Wayne LaPierre had promoted the death penalty in his book *Guns, Crime, and Freedom*, Miller's childhood favorite. LaPierre distinguished between black and white crime. "Whites, too, kill, rape, and steal," wrote LaPierre, adding that "a larger percentage of white crime might be 'white-collar.' " LaPierre contributed to the insidious false stereotype that people of color have blood on their hands while whites stay clean in tailored suits. Miller called for the death penalty for rapists and child abusers without specifying any race. [28] "There must be no tolerance for this heinous, inhuman act," Miller wrote.

In his next column, "Sorry Feminists," he argued that women earn less than men because men take the hardest jobs. [29] "I simply wouldn't feel comfortable hiring a full-time male babysitter or driving down the street and seeing a group of women carrying heavy steel pillars . . . It's not chauvinism. It's chivalry." Like his "chivalrous" hero Limbaugh, he flirted with conspiracy theories. He peddled fantasies about a secularist war on Christmas. [30] He promoted pseudoscience, saying "unrelenting health fascists" were lying about the risks of smoking. [31] He wrote that Hollywood was a leftist "propaganda machine," citing films like 2005's *Brokeback Mountain*. [32] Twisting logic, he argued that dissent was unpatriotic unless it radiated patriotism. As an example of the "worst kind," he cited the case of the mourning mother Cindy Sheehan, whose son was killed in Iraq and who became an activist against the war. [33]

In column after column, he attacked multiculturalism, describing America as a female: "a living thing, with a beating heart. She is not simply some abstract ideal, but the very embodiment of the American people. Her greatness lies in us. Her perseverance, or her downfall, lies in us." [34] Like a self-dubbed knight battling to save a damsel in distress, he criticized Duke for celebrating Indian and Asian culture. He wrote, "As we obsess over, adulate and extol the non-American cultures we ignore the culture we all hold in common," he wrote in one column.[35] In another, "The nation of E Pluribus Unum threatens to be fractured across ethnic lines by racial animus and divisive multiculturalism."[36] He wrote that people should not "retreat back to the nationalities our ancestors eagerly shed in exchange for a greater, freer life."[37] He cited an all-male, all-white list (with one exception) of American heroes he thought were deserving of praise: "Jimmy Stewart, John Wayne, Frank Sinatra, Bing Crosby, Elvis Presley, Johnny Cash, Jackie Wilson, Theodore Roosevelt, Douglas MacArthur, Milton Friedman, Edgar Allan Poe, F. Scott Fitzgerald, Thomas Edison and again, for emphasis, Elvis Presley."

CHAPTER SIX

"CUT THEIR SKIN"

MILLER INVITED HOROWITZ TO SPEAK at Duke University in March 2006. Out of habit, he repeatedly flicked his tongue while introducing his mentor. Stephen pulled a piece of paper from his jacket pocket. "Making this event happen was not easy," he said. "We beseeched many departments, many institutions at Duke University, for funding. Many of them wanted nothing to do with us."

He began to read off the groups that had withheld support: the literature department, the philosophy department, the institute for US critical studies. The audience cheered with each one. Miller straightened his tie and said, "Try and save your emotion for the Q&A session, please." He frowned and licked his lips, then continued listing groups that rejected Horowitz. The audience erupted. "I see that many of you are happy that people on this campus don't want to support a debate of ideas." He continued, amusement on his face. When he reached women's studies, the cheering reached a climax. "Not surprising," he said.

Horowitz appeared on stage, much shorter than Miller. He shook his mentee's hand quickly, then took the podium. He complained about the lack of interest in his speech. "Things would be very different of course if I were a convicted terrorist," he told the students. Horowitz says women in the audience "were like Alvin and the chipmunks" purposefully giggling to mock him. Sounding tired and sad, he says, "When I was a radical at Berkeley, I always wanted to hear what the opposition had to say because I thought it would make me a better radical. These kids don't want to hear anything. It's really tragic."

Horowitz recruited Miller to lead a national Terrorism Awareness Project.[1] The project claimed to educate people about the threat of terrorism. But its website conflated Muslims and Arabs with terrorists. A video alternated photographs of terrorist attacks and piles of Jewish bodies in Nazi concentration camps. It made statements that vilify Arabs, "The goal of the Arabs is the destruction of the Jews" and "There were no Arabs in Palestine until the Muslim invasions."[2] A button labeled "Ammunition" led to a page advertising anti-Islam books, including three by a self-described Islamophobe named Robert Spencer, who wrote an article entitled "The Case for Islamophobia" that was published on Horowitz's website. Another section, "What You Should Know About Jihad," claimed the goal of Muslim "jihad" is "world domination." The meaning of "jihad," however, is complicated, as the Harvard Divinity School explains, "Muslims are sharply divided among themselves in their understandings of the term jihad, an Arabic term meaning 'struggle.'" Most interpret it as a struggle to be a good Muslim. Only extremists see it as a call to holy war. The Qur'an warns Muslims against instigating violence: "Fight in the cause of Allah those who fight and persecute you, but commit no aggression. Surely, Allah does not love the aggressors." Still, Horowitz and Miller used the term "jihad" to fuel hostility toward all Muslims. Horowitz says Islam is "a problematic religion" because of a passage in the Qur'an that calls for violence. (The Christian Bible also has passages that call for violence.) Miller distributed pamphlets such as "The Islamic Mein Kampf," published by Horowitz's organization.

Miller was invited onto *Fox & Friends* to discuss his efforts to run advertisements in campus newspapers with Horowitz's interpretation of jihad. A few colleges had rejected the ads. He spoke via remote satellite in front of shelves of leather books, somewhat plumper than he would become. "People on the far left, they claim to be about free speech and expression but as soon as you put something out there that offends them, all of a sudden, no, free speech out the window, it's about enforcing an orthodoxy. And I think it's terribly sad," Miller told viewers. Host Steve Doocy, evidently awed by Miller, asked, "Are you a college kid?" Stephen laughed. "Yeah, I'm a senior at Duke University." "Well you are *smart*!" Doocy said. Miller replied, "Well, I watch *Fox & Friends* every morning, so that probably has something to do with it."

In March 2007, Stephen organized an immigration debate with Richard Spencer, who became a well-known white nationalist. Spencer was a graduate student. A blue-eyed brunette with a slightly nasal voice, he developed the term "alternative right" with paleoconservative Jewish philosopher Paul Gottfried, who used it to label right-wing rebels. Spencer applied it to white nationalists radicalized on forums like 4Chan and Reddit: "the alt right."[3]

Spencer calls himself a "Zionist" for white people.[4] His appropriation of the Jewish term is ironic, given rampant anti-Semitism in the alt right. He has called for a "white ethno-state" through ethnic cleansing "done peacefully."[5] His followers have responded to him with Nazi salutes. At a 2016 conference, he said: "To be white is to be a striver, a crusader, an explorer and a conqueror. We build, we produce, we go upward. And we recognize a central lie of American race relations. We don't exploit other groups—we don't gain anything from their presence. They need us, not the other way around . . . America was, until this past generation, a white country, designed for ourselves and our posterity. It is our creation, it is our inheritance, and it belongs to us."[6] Spencer's argument, like Horowitz's, ignores the central role black people played in the building of this country and its economy, and that of all minorities in their struggle to make America's proclaimed ideals of equality, justice and freedom a reality here and across the world.

Spencer was a few years older than Miller. He says he mentored Miller, sharing articles with him.[7] "I don't think we were like the best of friends or something like that, but we were definitely friends. I respected him. He was very smart. He was definitely the smartest guy in [the Duke Conservative Union]. So I was kind of like, immediately attracted to him in that sense of someone who I could talk to." Miller said, "I have absolutely no relationship with Mr. Spencer. I completely repudiate his views, and his claims are 100% false."[8]

Spencer understands why Miller doesn't want to associate himself with him anymore, given his controversial profile. They didn't agree on everything, even at Duke. Miller was in favor of the Iraq War back then; Spencer was fiercely against it. Miller has never publicly said the things Spencer says about the white race. "He probably wouldn't say that explicitly—he might not even want to think about it explicitly," Spencer says. "Because we can't just assert ourselves and our [white] identity in this basic fashion, we instead want to focus on all these negative things and kind of dog whistle." He says Miller's demonization of the foreign-born results from this cognitive dissonance.

A full-page ad in *The Chronicle* for the Miller- and Spencer-organized immigration debate called it "the most controversial event this year."[9] It featured Peter Brimelow, the white nationalist author of *Alien Nation: Common Sense About America's Immigration Disaster*, and Peter Laufer, author of *Wetback Nation: The Case for Opening the Mexican-American Border*. Laufer, the pro-immigrant speaker, says Spencer and Miller worked hand in glove. They invited Laufer, Brimelow and their wives to dinner at a French restaurant prior to the debate.[10] Laufer says he ate a light meal of broiled fish and sparkling water; Brimelow ordered a very thick steak and lots of wine. "It was all very chummy . . . they couldn't have been more charming hosts, except for their repugnant points of view."

Laufer was quicker than Brimelow during the debate, perhaps because of what they'd consumed. He cited real-life examples of immigrants contributing to the United States, such as a Spanish-speaking young woman he'd met that day at McDonald's. Brimelow, on the other hand, made general statements about immigrants hurting the economy. After the debate, Miller and Spencer invited the speakers and wives to the Duke Conservative Union for drinks. The mood had darkened. "They were kind of sour," Laufer says. He and his wife left promptly. Miller and Spencer stayed in touch. When Laufer followed up a few times regarding his payment, Miller and Spencer exchanged emails. Laufer asked for a video copy of the debate for publicity. They never shared it. "They always had a reason why they couldn't locate it or hadn't made a copy," he says.

The experience had been life-changing for Miller. He began to think more about immigration. Brimelow's book *Alien Nation* contains some of the arguments Miller would later use to defend restrictions on legal immigration. The white nationalist cites the Cuban-born American economist George J. Borjas, who has found that immigration can have a temporary negative economic impact on high school dropouts. Brimelow criticizes the poem on the Statue of Liberty, pointing out that it was "added years after the dedication of the statue" and that the statue was meant "to symbolize not 'the Mother of Immigrants,' in Lazarus's phrase, but *Liberty Enlightening the World*." Miller later echoed Brimelow in a White House press briefing about a bill that would reduce the legal immigration of people who are not highly educated, saying, "The Statue of Liberty is a symbol of liberty enlightening the world . . . The poem that you're referring to was added later. It's not actually part of the original Statue of Liberty."

Brimelow says of Miller, "I certainly approve of his public statements."[11] But they are no longer in touch. "He's far too cautious to talk to un-PC figures," he says, referring to himself. In 2016, Brimelow was a featured speaker at a Spencer-led conference, where Spencer cried "Hail Trump," and the audience shouted, "Sieg heil!"[12]

Published in 1995, Brimelow's *Alien Nation* is dedicated to his young white son, blonde and blue eyed. He quotes Shakespeare, "This fair child of mine / Shall sum my count." His book contains bar charts and line graphs showing dark columns overtaking the white until they are nearly blotted out. Brimelow is the founder of VDARE.com, after Virginia Dare, said to be the first white baby born in the US. Brimelow says America's whiteness should be preserved, "The American nation has always had a specific ethnic core. And that core has been white."

Miller would later take articles from Brimelow's website and share them with Breitbart, encouraging bloggers to write stories based on their content.[13] Brimelow wrote that the latest immigration wave is different from the one of the early twentieth century because "then, immigrants came overwhelmingly from Europe . . . now, immigrants are overwhelmingly visible minorities from the Third World." He argues that America needs to pause immigration. His website promotes white genocide conspiracy theories,[14] which claim that people of color are systematically wiping out white people—a falsehood invoked by white terrorists to justify their massacres.

Brimelow describes an immigration naturalization office as an "underworld that is not just teeming but is also almost entirely colored." He fears people like him will be replaced by a darker shade.

He notes with anxiety that white birth rates have declined. "Now American Anglos are reproducing below replacement levels—generally defined as 2.1 children per woman."

It is the language of the dystopian novel *The Handmaid's Tale*, in which Gilead rose to power out of fear of declining birth rates. The men who launched a revolution enslaved women and repeatedly raped them to regain power. "Be fruitful, and multiply, and replenish the earth," wrote Margaret Atwood, quoting the Bible.

MILLER HAD CONVINCED THE DUKE Conservative Union to give him the executive director position so he could use the group for fundraising. David Bitner, who was in the group, says Miller was "like a guerrilla cell . . . very dedicated to what he believed. He was willing to sacrifice for it." He was openly disliked by many students. "Most of us can go through life and at least you can expect cordiality from people. He sacrificed that," Bitner says.[15]

At the beginning of senior year, Miller became so consumed in organizing and executing a 9/11 memorial—with a sea of 2,997 flags representing each victim and more—that he failed to take his LSAT exam to get into law school.[16] He memorialized 9/11 in *The Chronicle* with morbid descriptions of "severed limbs," "piles of flesh" and "charred corpses." He detailed meticulous preparations for his 9/11 event in a lengthy post on the forum Freerepublic.com, including coordinating with law enforcement and numerous school departments.[17] He described the product with relish: "When students woke up that morning they were greeted by a stirring image the likes of which they've never seen." Miller worried about how many people would come. "Right before an event starts there's always a huge knot in my stomach as the great question looms large: Will anyone show up? This experience is not helped by the fact that students usually don't arrive for an event before it starts. However, slowly but surely the audience started to build . . . I would say there was [*sic*] as many as 1,000 people."

During his senior year, Miller spent late nights working obsessively in the company of a junior, student body president Elliott Wolf. They had met through *The Chronicle,* where both wrote columns. "I tried to dig up dirt on the [school] administration," Wolf says. "I like to think I was being helpful on policies affecting under-grads. Stephen's angle, I felt, was to start a tire fire and just keep pumping oxygen into it."[18] Wolf didn't agree with Miller's politics, but he was curious about the world. He felt his opinions were "better served by hearing people who think differently than by having them affirmed."

The men plugged their laptops into electric outlets outside on the Plaza and bantered while they worked. But they were well known on campus, and it was distracting to have classmates come up to them. They started hiding away at a trucker's diner, Honey's, which has since closed. It was open twenty-four hours and had free Wi-Fi, bottomless coffee and a cigarette vending machine. They smoked cigarettes and crammed. "We would escape campus and tip the waitress at Honey's a dollar an hour and just hang there the entire night doing our work in relative isolation until the waitress shift change at six or seven in the morning," Wolf says. "We were nocturnal."

Wolf teased Miller by saying mathematics—Wolf's field of study—was a "real" subject, while political science was all opinion. Miller tried to argue the veracity of his claims and Wolf asked playfully, "What's wrong, Stephen, you don't have any *real* work to do?" Wolf says, "Most people came at it from an ideological angle, and I came at it from an intellectual angle of, 'Piss off, take a math class and see how biased it is, Stephen. Come on.' I think he was a little bit intrigued."

Miller wore a suit, while Wolf dressed casually. They were different but cordial. Wolf says, "His boundaries are defined by some antiquated notion of decorum. I don't remember him swearing for instance. He would get into aggressive, forward conversations but he would never name-call and he would never swear." Wolf studied Miller while they spent time together and tried to figure him out. He was a mystery, but one thing was clear: "He exemplified, better than anyone else I've ever known, a different life objective," Wolf says. "Some people want money, some people want power, some people want influence, some people want women, some people want scientific discovery and a lot of people run around not knowing what they want. Stephen very clearly wanted the tears of his enemies—and then went out and got them."

MILLER WAS CATAPULTED TO NATIONAL notoriety when a black woman accused white Duke lacrosse players of raping her. He defended the accused men on Fox News and *Nancy Grace*. In the end, the accusations were deemed false. The incident affirmed for Miller everything he had ever believed and filled him with still more confidence and certainty.

The Duke lacrosse team had thrown a party on March 14, 2006. All but one of the forty-one players at the house were white. They thought they'd ordered two strippers: one white, one Hispanic. But the women who showed up were Kim Roberts, half black and half Korean, and Crystal Gail Mangum, who was black. "There was some initial concern about whether the dancing should proceed, given the boys' preference for white dancers," wrote William Cohan in *The Price of Silence*, a comprehensive book about the ensuing scandal.[19] The girls began to dance as the raucous athletes cheered. One asked Roberts if she put "objects" up her vagina.

According to the team co-captain, she responded, " 'I would put your dick in me but you're not big enough.' " One guy grabbed a broomstick and asked if it would do. Roberts, feeling threatened, decided it was time to leave. She went to her car to change. She thought about leaving but didn't want to abandon Mangum. She was passed out on the back stoop of the house. A couple of the players helped walk her to Roberts's car. As the women pulled away, some in the team hurled racist epithets at them. Roberts called 911 and reported their slurs.

Ryan McFadyen sent an email to his teammates, allegedly a riff on Bret Easton Ellis's *American Psycho*.[20] "To whom it may concern," he wrote. "tomorrow night . ive decided to have some strippers over to edens2c . . . I plan on killing the bitches as soon as the[y] walk in and proceding to cut their skin off while cumming in my duke issue spandex."

That night, Mangum told Durham police that she had been raped by about five white men.[21] A Duke officer filed a report saying she had claimed she was raped by about twenty white men. Later, she reported she'd been raped by three men in a bathroom orally, vaginally and rectally. The players denied the allegations, but the police handed out flyers stating that the team had paid the "victim" to strip, then "sodomized, raped, assaulted and robbed" her. Many in the community presumed the players guilty. Complaints of underage drinking and late-night mayhem were common. Students puked in neighbors' yards and blocked driveways.

The Duke students were called in for DNA samples and photographed. District Attorney Mike Nifong took control of prosecution. The case grabbed nationwide attention. "It was too delicious a story," Daniel Okrent, a former *New York Times* editor, told the *American Journalism Review*.[22] "It conformed too well to too many preconceived notions of too many in the press: white over black, rich over poor, athletes over nonathletes, men over women, educated over noneducated. Wow. That's a package of sins that really fits the preconceptions of a lot of us."

Duke students and community members organized protests and a candlelit vigil outside of the lacrosse house. They pounded pots and pans and called for the expulsion of the players. Miller was watching this unfold. He saw it as a rush to condemn by radical leftists. "Being a white, male lacrosse player was all it took," he wrote in *The Chronicle*. "When our peers are accused of heinous acts, we should be the first to demand they be given the presumption of innocence." He was not alone in defending them. Across the US, people wore Duke lacrosse shirts in solidarity. Limbaugh called the strippers "hoes."[23]

Miller was invited to speak on *Nancy Grace* and lamented the fact that "two innocent people may have possibly just had their lives ruined." Grace said, "Oh good Lord!" They went back and forth. Grace closed her eyes and shook her head. *"Do you have a sister?"* she asked.

"Uh, yes I do, but I would appreciate it—"

"I assume you have a mother," Grace said. "I mean if your first concern is somebody's falsely accused—"

He lifted his hand. "Don't tell me what my first concern is, please."

"Those were the first words out of your mouth," Grace said. "Maybe I'm crazy? I don't wear hearing aids?"

Three players were indicted based on Mangum's testimony and review of a photo lineup that problematically lacked non-lacrosse players.[24] Prosecutor Mike Nifong would be accused of using the case to win reelection in the May Democratic primary race. His former campaign manager quoted him saying the case was worth "a million dollars of free advertisements." The press continued its coverage, invoking white privilege, elitism, racism, misogyny. The *New York Times* reported on Duke's strained town-gown relations with Durham.[25]

Miller was annoyed. He wrote a piece called "Welcome to the

Durham Petting Zoo." He opened with a reference to a drive-by shooting near the school. He said the university was the town's "lifeblood," and that Durham should be grateful to Duke. "I think it's about time the town started reaching out to the gown," Stephen wrote. "I have nothing against the town, but I wouldn't exactly describe it as a rich treasure-trove of life and culture." He was ignoring the city's rich African American history, its identity as a Black Wall Street. But Miller didn't feel like venturing into the city. It wasn't because he was afraid; he was a seasoned dweller of dangerous places, he wrote, from the "violent city" of Los Angeles.

"I personally don't feel unsafe . . . Mostly, I just feel bored." And then, the racially incendiary line: "Durham isn't a petting zoo."

His smoking buddy, Elliott Wolf, was advocating for student interests. He asked Miller about the column. "It was the least helpful thing you could've done for anybody involved," Wolf recalls. Miller just chuckled. Despite his irritation, Wolf says he, too, was struck by the university's bumbled response. "You're a student at an elite institution—you're supposed to have respect for the president of the university and the administrators . . . And then everyone just goes bananas . . . It taught all of us that the world is pretty unstable, and that these institutions don't necessarily have all the answers. I was coming at it sympathetic to the institution, he was coming at it hostile to the institution. But from both perspectives, the institution was not unassailable."

Coach Mike Pressler was forced to resign. The team suspended the 2006 season. Miller was outraged. He said the prosecution would never have proceeded had the players been black. Author William Cohan wrote, "My conclusion was exactly the opposite of Miller's: in my estimation, there is no way, had the indicted boys been black and their accuser white, that they ever would have been exonerated without a trial. There is no way a secret investigation by the state attorney general would have declared them innocent and no way that Duke would have paid them $20 million each—which is what the three accused white players received—as part of a legal settlement."[26]

Eventually, it came to light that Nifong had kept negative DNA results a secret. Defense attorneys analyzed the rape kit and found evidence of sexual activity with four males around the date of the alleged rape—and none was a Duke lacrosse player. Miller called for Duke president Richard Brodhead to be fired. He said Nifong should be disbarred and jailed. He defended McFadyen, who wrote the allegedly satiric email about cutting up and killing strippers. "Slightly altered, the content of his letter could easily find its way into a joke on *Family Guy*," Miller wrote, lamenting that the "sanctimonious hordes" had trampled him in a "merciless stampede."[27]

Miller's preconceptions were further affirmed when professors decided to go public together with their narrative of minority oppression. On April 6, 2006, the *Chronicle* published an advertisement signed by eighty-eight professors. The Group of 88 ad read, "Regardless of the results of the police investigation, what is apparent every day now is the anger and fear of the many students who know themselves to be objects of racism and sexism: who see illuminated in this moment's extraordinary spotlight what they live with every day."

Miller appeared on the *O'Reilly Factor* to condemn the ad, which he saw as an expression of the radical leftist agenda he believed had motivated the prosecution of the players in the first place. A Fox News cameraman confronted professors at their homes about their decision to sign it. One recalled Miller was with the crew. "He tried to force himself and his Fox News interview team into my home to ask questions," said Alex Rosenberg, a philosophy professor.[28] "I slammed the door on him." Miller told national viewers, "They were confronted about their radicalism and now they're all running for cover. Because if you take a professor that signed that *ridiculous* ad, and sat them down, and gave them even the most *mild* interrogation, they would fall apart."

O'Reilly asked why more people weren't speaking up. Miller said, "If you look at [Duke] President Brodhead, from day one, the man has been totally *consumed* by fear over his own radical faculty." O'Reilly said, "Yeah, Brodhead is a coward, we know that. He's been hiding in his office and he even allowed Professor Kim Curtis to give one of the accused boys an F in a course." Miller said, "I have reviewed the text of the complaint and I can say that it's an extremely valid complaint. The kid's mathematical grade was not an F."

White supremacist Richard Spencer published an article in *The American Conservative*, critiquing the professors who signed the ad: "Far from coming as a shock, the accusations that white students gang-raped a black stripper reached the Group as a kind of fulfillment of a dream." On the same day, Miller wrote a similar article in *The Chronicle:* "Is it any surprise radical students, activists and faculty latched onto these charges with such euphoria?"

Now Miller was the euphoric one. Ethics charges were brought against Nifong in late 2006. He asked the office of Attorney General Roy Cooper to take over the case. The next spring, Cooper held a press conference announcing he was dropping the charges, and that the players were innocent. He said, "The result of our review and investigation shows clearly that there is insufficient evidence to proceed on any of the charges . . . we believe these three individuals are innocent." Nifong was disbarred and served a one-day jail sentence. A few years later, Mangum was found guilty of murdering her boyfriend Reginald Daye.[29] Duke's Brodhead told students the media had fueled hysteria.[30] "Hysteria breeds extraordinary mental simplifications," he said. "People just reach for any old stereotype."

M. Shadee Malaklou, the student Miller confronted ahead of the PSM conference, believes the alleged rush to condemn the players was overstated. A first-generation Iranian American with sleek dark hair and bright brown eyes, she was also a columnist in *The Chronicle*. She says Mangum was "proscribed from access to even human recognition." More than a decade later, she wrote, "In claim after hysterical claim Stephen made to bolster the reputations of the indicted men, this Stephen, like Trump's Stephen, lamented the fate of white men who in an ostensibly 'post-racial' age feel themselves dislodged from atop their perch."[31]

More than three thousand Duke alumni signed an open letter denouncing Miller's actions in the White House.[32] Malaklou refused to sign it. She says the letter failed to reflect on the complicity of Duke, which gave him one of his first platforms. "His is not, to invoke Ta-Nehisi Coates's formulation, a 'uniquely villainous and morally deformed . . . ideology of trolls, gorgons and orcs,' but the banality of our liberal evil, which accommodated his racism and sexism," she wrote. "I am haunted by the knowledge that we could have shut Stephen down at the moment of his becoming, had we been more interested in the psychic and material health of the marginalized peoples with whom we shared our campus than in the doctrine of liberalism; that is, if we had momentarily stepped outside of our own privilege to hold space for those others."

Malaklou, a race and gender studies scholar, says Miller derives his power from liberalism, specifically the doctrine of free speech. "The assumption that you should have every idea available to you and you can pick and choose . . . that's the problem. It goads us to accommodate the far right, just as it legitimizes the far left," she says.

Liberalism sanitizes intolerance, absorbing it into its all-encompassing embrace. It encourages migrants to transcend their ethnic otherness. "The child of color looks in the mirror and says, *that's not me*," Malaklou says. "They literally identify with whiteness and see themselves as embodying all the things whiteness is said to embody: virtue, redemption, professionalism, civility . . . We are constantly performing or embodying what we think it means to be white—because our psyche is saturated in a discourse in which identification with whiteness prevails."

But in Miller's eyes, people like Malaklou were just obsessed with race. The lacrosse scandal had confirmed in his mind that he was right, as he had always known he was. During one of his appearances on *Nancy Grace*, Grace tried to rattle him again, as she had when she asked if he had a sister. "What are you majoring in?"

Miller replied without skipping a beat. "I actually want to become an attorney and I also even would like to go into prosecution," he said. "Although my ultimate career aspirations are political, I've always been interested in being a prosecutor."

Biting her pen and smiling cheekily, Grace asked, "For political reasons?"

"No," he said. "Because I want to get criminals and I wanna put them away so they never see the light of day again."

CHAPTER SEVEN

"OUR WHOLE COUNTRY IS ROTTING"

WHEN MILLER GRADUATED, ALABAMA SENATOR Jefferson Beauregard Sessions III, an elfin nativist with white hair, was attacking an immigration reform bill by a bipartisan team of legislators, the Gang of Twelve. President George W. Bush said, "I'm deeply concerned about America losing its soul. Immigration has been the lifeblood of a lot of our country's history . . . I am worried that a backlash to newcomers would cause our country to lose its great capacity to assimilate newcomers." By late June, the bill had died. "When talk radio got a frenzy going—Capitol phones crashed as the crucial vote loomed—nothing good could withstand the hot wind blowing across the Hill," wrote the *New York Times* editors in an op-ed titled "The Grand Collapse."

Miller traveled to Israel on a birthright trip that summer.[1] The ten-day trips, paid for by the Israeli government and philanthropists for young Jewish adults, are meant to foster Jewish identity. They come in many forms, from those that focus on religion, to those that focus on the outdoors and social activities. Miller chose a secular trip. He rode a camel and floated in the Dead Sea. He was encouraged to marry within the Jewish faith.

He didn't have a job. He drifted awhile, traveling in Europe. In the fall of 2007, Horowitz asked him to help coordinate an Islamo-Fascism Awareness Week about the alleged threat of Islam, featuring terror memorials and teach-ins in more than a hundred colleges. The Council on American-Islamic Relations said the events sparked "hostility" toward Muslims. Others called it an "Islamophobia tour." Miller said, "We're not going to back down an inch."[2]

Horowitz wanted to help Miller find employment. He had an idea. He had met first-term Minnesota congresswoman Michele Bachmann at one of his conservative forums, and he was under the impression she was one of the few Republicans with an outspoken perspective about jihad that aligned with his own.[3] Horowitz was concerned by the Bush administration's "denial" of an Islamic "holy war or jihad against the West." Horowitz thought she and Miller would be a perfect match, given Miller's work on the Terrorism Awareness Project.

Bachmann believed climate change was "voodoo, nonsense, hokum, a hoax."[4] (Horowitz also denies climate change science.) She criticized gays and lesbians. (Horowitz says he wasn't aware of her stance toward gay people and that he disagrees with her.)

Horowitz connected the two; Bachmann hired Miller as her press secretary. He moved to DC, where his family helped him buy a $450,000 condominium in the Metropole, a Logan Circle building that calls itself "a sleek, urban condo development."[5] Earning less than $60,000 a year, he bought a new collection of bespoke suits and got to work raising his boss's profile.

Immigration had proved successful at raising the profiles of California politicians during his childhood—as well as that of Colorado congressman Tom Tancredo, an associate of Horowitz's who ran for the Republican presidential nomination in 2007 by railing against a "Tower of Babel." On February 19, 2008, a Guatemalan woman ran a stop sign in Minnesota and hit a school bus, killing four students and injuring seventeen. Miller leaped on the tragedy. Olga Franco del Cid was in the country illegally. In 2006, she had been charged for driving without a valid driver's license. Miller declared that police hadn't done enough. "Officers can ask directly, 'Are you an actual citizen of this country?' " Miller said. Worthington Public Safety director Mike Cumiskey disagreed: "I can't ask someone if they are here legally."[6]

Miller knew that by elevating the crimes of people like Olga Franco del Cid, he could rally support for any leader who bashed them. The trick ignored reality: most studies show that immigrants—regardless of status—are statistically less likely than the native-born to commit crimes.[7] But it scored points with the base. Bachmann pushed for more collaboration between law enforcement officers and federal immigration officials in response to Miller's efforts. When Bachmann's opponent for the congressional district called it "untoward to exploit a tragic situation to advance a narrow ideological agenda," Bachmann responded that his remark was "highly offensive" to the victims of migrant criminals. She said migrants were "bringing in diseases, bringing in drugs, bringing in violence."[8] Her language reflected Miller's views.

Illinois senator Barack Obama won the 2008 election, defeating his Republican opponent John McCain. It was a historic moment, celebrated across the world. He had become the first black president of the United States, appealing to hope for change by adopting the slogan "Yes we can," one borrowed from United Farm Workers leader Dolores Huerta, who visited Miller's high school: *"Sí se puede."*

Miller perfected the art of the hyperbolic press release. He learned the ropes of Capitol Hill and the names of reporters covering Congress. But soon, he tired of working for Bachmann. He asked Horowitz for another recommendation.[9] (Horowitz developed a negative opinion of Bachmann as a "flake" and says he suspects Miller did, too.) By the time Miller left Bachmann, she was a darling of the Tea Party, earning "unprecedented media coverage," according to a press release from her office. She called Miller "an incredible asset." Horowitz helped him land a job with far-right Arizona congressman John Shadegg in early 2009.

He worked briefly with Shadegg as he participated in anti-Obama Tea Party protests alongside neo-Nazis. But after a few months, Horowitz learned his old friend, Alabama senator Jefferson Beauregard Sessions III, was looking for a press secretary. He knew Miller aspired to become a senator. Horowitz recommended Miller to Sessions, the leading nativist on the Hill, whom he knew from his Restoration Weekends at luxury resorts, uniting right-wing tribes. "As you can imagine, I couldn't have given [Miller] a higher recommendation, both because of his intelligence and his courage under fire, and because of how responsible he was," Horowitz says.

Miller jumped over to the other side of the Capitol. Sessions had been denied a federal judgeship as a US attorney in the eighties amid allegations that he had improperly prosecuted black voting rights activists and used racially insensitive language. He joked that he thought the Ku Klux Klan "was OK until I found out they smoked pot," according to Thomas Figures, a black assistant US attorney.[10] Another attorney testified that Sessions called the National Association for the Advancement of Colored People (NAACP) and the American Civil Liberties Union (ACLU) "un-American" and "Communist-inspired."[11] But Sessions won a Senate seat a decade later. With his southern charm, white hair and baby face, Sessions had the air of a sweet grandfather just pretending to be grumpy. The *Washington Post* ran the headline: "Jeff Sessions should have been a tough sell in the Senate, but he's too nice." Paul Kane wrote: "He is one of the more well-liked members of the Senate, a place that still retains elements of one of the world's most exclusive clubs. He is genial . . . [giving] fellow Republicans and even some Democrats reason not to scrutinize the more unsavory allegations of his political history."

Sessions's stance on immigration was vastly influenced by an experience he had in the eighties during a conference of US attorneys in San Diego. Former US attorney Pete Nuñez led a border tour in an effort to raise awareness in other parts of the country about the threat he believed illegal Southwest border entries posed to the country's national security.[12]

Nuñez would soon become one of the drafters of the 1994 California proposition denying social services to people without legal immigration status, including public schools—Prop 187, which was found unconstitutional. He stood with Sessions and the others on a rugged mesa overlooking Mexico. The sun was setting. Migrants gathered in Tijuana, preparing for the nightly charge. Once the sun dipped below the horizon, they scrambled into the US. Border Patrol tried to catch them, but there were too many. Nuñez says Sessions and the others were astonished and appalled. "It was just shocking to these people from everywhere else in the country—they'd never seen anything like it," Nuñez says. "And Sessions remembered."

At the time, border barriers were scarce and flimsy—some barbed wire here, some chain link there. Border Patrol officers likened their nightly activities to a game of cat and mouse. Nuñez continued corresponding with Sessions over the years. He knew immigration was not a major issue in Alabama, but Sessions had taken a personal interest in it, aghast at the sight of the migrants near the sloping canyons of San Diego. "What he had seen in the eighties had had an effect on his philosophy," he says.

Miller joined Sessions's office as press secretary amid confirmation hearings for Supreme Court nominee Sonia Sotomayor. She was Obama's first nominee to the court, and the first of Latin American heritage. Miller went to work trying to derail her nomination. Years earlier, Sotomayor said, "I would hope that a wise Latina with the richness of her experiences would more often than not reach a better conclusion than a white male who hasn't lived that life."

Sessions grilled her about the comment. "Aren't you saying you expect your heritage and background to influence your decision making?" he asked. "You have evidenced a philosophy of the law that suggests that a judge's background and experiences can and should . . . impact their decision, which I think goes against the American ideal and oath that a judge takes to be fair to every party."

Reporter John Stanton was covering Capitol Hill for *Roll Call*. He recalls getting calls from Miller, pitching him stories about why he thought Sotomayor was not qualified, calling her a "lesbian" or claiming "her position as a Latina woman created conflicts of interest because she would rule with a racial bias."[13] Stanton thought it was crazy. He says Miller's comments about Sotomayor were nastier than those he made about men he disparaged. "He always had an axe to grind, particularly against Latina women but Latinos in general," Stanton says.

Miller was having a hard time manipulating public perception through serious news outlets. Many journalists saw him as a gadfly and ignored him. But that year, Miller met someone who would change his life forever. Steve Bannon was working on a documentary, *Fire from the Heartland*, featuring Miller's former boss Bachmann. Bannon spoke with Miller and realized he knew him. He was familiar with his voice. He was the Los Angeles teenager who had appeared on the *Larry Elder Show* several years ago, sounding decades older than he was. Then he had become the person who had egged on Bachmann, his firebrand protagonist.

In his flip-flops and wrinkled cargo jackets, Bannon had the air of a cool but laid-back professor. He had unkempt silver hair. He was from a working-class family. He couldn't have seemed more different from the stiff, supercilious Miller. But Bannon loved the kid. He was a legend to him. He introduced Miller to Breitbart .com, a fiery far-right media blog that Bannon had joined. The blog's founder Andrew Breitbart was a conservative blogger and provocateur who envisioned a pitbull-like infotainment empire for the right. He had worked at the Drudge Report and the Huffington Post. He was told Miller was the California teenager who took his high school to task in the nineties. "That was you?" Breitbart asked, remembering him.[14]

A onetime Navy officer and former investment banker, Bannon was a bare-knuckle populist who later bragged: "I'm a Leninist. Lenin wanted to destroy the state, and that's my goal too. I want to bring everything crashing down."[15] When Breitbart died of a heart attack in 2012, Bannon took the helm of his blog. Miller became an informal part of the team, connecting with bloggers who'd help disseminate his ideas. He pitched stories that attacked bills and people he didn't like. They typed them up. One former Breitbart reporter said: "When I first joined the staff, the first email I got was from him. It said something like, 'Congratulations from everyone at Sessions' office, we look forward to working with you.'"[16] Miller participated in a Friday happy hour with Breitbart staffers.

Miller sent Breitbart links to overtly racist websites such as Peter Brimelow's VDARE.com, whose ideas about the dangers of non-white immigration had influenced him at Duke University. He encouraged the bloggers to pull from the white supremacist website American Renaissance, which he referred to familiarly as "AmRen," and which highlights the crimes of black and brown people.[17] Horowitz believes he helped Miller find that website when his mentee was a teenager. In 2002, Horowitz wrote about its founder

Jared Taylor. Horowitz calls him "a very smart man" with "a perverse point of view." [18]

Horowitz appreciates Taylor's articles about interracial crime, but he claims he rejects Taylor's emphasis on the need for whites to organize under white identity. Horowitz calls that perspective "racial," adding, "You can call it racist but it is no more racist than the general attitude in the Democratic Party." In 2002, Horowitz wrote, "Taylor has accepted the idea that the multiculturalists have won. We are all prisoners of identity politics now." [19]

He says he rejects Taylor's "racial schemata" and that Miller does, too. Horowitz advocates for a nation in which race is not a factor at all: a colorblind framework that rejects the unique cultures of people of color and their history. He thinks Miller used Taylor's website to pull content about interracial crimes to "emphasize that cultural differences are important and that unvetted illegal immigration is problematic."

But Miller's view *was* racial, just as Horowitz's views were. In conversations with his allies, Miller invoked "the heritage established by Calvin Coolidge." Coolidge had passed a law in 1924 that restricted immigration from non-white countries—a response to the eugenics movement of the time spreading the lie of white racial superiority.

Drawing from pseudo-intellectual white supremacist research sent to them by Miller, Breitbart editors created what Bannon later called the "platform for the alt-right." The blog used a "black crime" tag. It ran stories depicting non-white, non-male people as uniquely violent or inferior, with headlines such as "How Muslim Migrants Devastate a Community," "Anchor Baby Delivered Every 93 Seconds" and "Does Feminism Make Women Ugly?"

The melodramatic language of Breitbart was not part of reputable political discourse on the Hill prior to Miller's arrival. "You just didn't hear that kind of thing," recalled a former Senate aide.[20] But

Miller had immersed himself in the world of media provocateurs, and he began to transform the narrative in Congress.

Through lengthy press releases and emails, Miller focused on attacking legislation that sought to assist the marginalized, such as federal spending on food stamps for the poor in 2012. Perhaps he remembered the words in his favorite *The Way Things Ought to Be*. "The poor in this country are the biggest piglets at the mother pig and her nipples," Rush Limbaugh wrote. "The poor feed off of the largesse of this government and they give nothing back. Nothing. They're the ones who get all the benefits in this country. They're the ones that are always pandered to."

Battling programs for the poor, Miller cast Sessions as a champion of the poor. *Washington Post* reporter Glenn Kessler wrote a piece fact-checking a Sessions chart on welfare spending in 2013.[21] The chart claimed the government spends the equivalent of $168 in cash every day for each household in poverty. Despite "long discussions" with Miller about the figure, Kessler concluded that it was "misleading." He gave Sessions three Pinocchios. Miller contacted Kessler and insisted that he publish a four-paragraph response: "Who watches the *Post*'s watchman? Your piece is disappointingly anti-intellectual . . . unlike your post, our analysis is honest, accurate and, most importantly, a constructive step towards helping those in need."

Miller had been focused on the myth of migrants as criminals, and now promoted the idea that migrants were bad for the economy—an idea Sessions had used to derail immigration reform, and which Miller turbocharged with the California fantasy of welfare-guzzling migrants. The National Academy of Sciences has said that the effect of immigration on wages is "very small."[22] Long term, migrants generate more revenue than they cost the government.

Miller knew how to twist arms and wear people down, pressing buttons when they wouldn't budge. Miller told Stanton, "You *have* to write a story that favors me because you did a story that helps out those guys." And he was willing to play dirty. "If you wrote a story he didn't like or that didn't fit the narrative he wanted, he would come at you very hard," Stanton says.

In 2010, Stanton decided to do a story about a Sessions effort to protect a state sleeping bag manufacturer by adding a tariff to a routine tax measure. Miller asked him why he was even paying attention to it. "It's an earmark and your boss has come out against earmarks," Stanton told him. "It's not an earmark," Miller said, arguing that the tariff benefitting the state company aimed to reverse an "earmark" for Bangladesh and China. They went back and forth, disagreeing about the definition of an earmark. Suddenly, Miller said, "Okay, so we agree it's not an earmark okay bye," and hung up. When Stanton wrote about the earmark, Sessions called Stanton's boss. He told him Stanton had agreed not to call it an earmark and had gone back on his word. "No, man, I told him we were calling it an earmark," Stanton said. "[Miller] has this idea that through the force of his own will, he can just change reality. I hate to say it, but sometimes he has."

MILLER WORE A GOLD PINKIE ring with a gemstone and skinny ties. "That was very memorable, because the Hill was usually pretty buttoned up," says a former staffer.[23] "Skinny ties weren't really in yet." Another recalled that he wore Italian-looking pointed-toe shoes. He smelled of smoke, speedily clinking down the hallways. He was imperious, striding into the offices of older aides, plopping his feet up on their desks and launching into pedantic diatribes. He was a fringe figure, ideological and a bit scary, bombarding people with emails late at night with "FYIs." He had a staff of three and occasionally yelled.[24]

Former Senate aides spoke on condition of anonymity, fearing retaliation.[25] Two describe him as "vindictive." One says he was like "an aggressive, nasty street fighter." "He wants to project that he will do whatever he needs to do—and that anyone who crosses him will regret it." Miller showed little interest in working with Democrats or moderate Republicans. "He was a lone wolf." He told another aide: "You're not a real Republican."

Miller gave his peers headaches as he pushed negative stories about their hard-earned initiatives. One former aide says Miller pitched negative stories to Breitbart about her boss, a senior Republican senator who sought a compromise on immigration. Breitbart accidentally forwarded to her a memo critical of her boss that Miller had leaked. "It was pretty dirty," she says. "I recall saying this to him once, 'If illegal immigration is such a big problem, why don't we do something to solve it?' " She wondered if he wanted the problem to persist to have it as a wedge issue. While she gave presentations at conference meetings, "he'd sit there in the back lurking—and I just knew he was gonna take whatever I said and go send it to Breitbart."

In 2012, Obama announced Deferred Action for Childhood Arrivals, DACA, an executive action to protect young migrants brought to the US as children. About 1.7 million people were eligible. "It makes no sense to expel talented young people, who, for all intents and purposes, are Americans," Obama said. He emphasized that DACA was not amnesty but rather a temporary shielding mechanism while Congress worked on legislation. Miller helped Sessions bash DACA as "mass backdoor amnesty." Sessions criticized Obama for relying on executive action, "circumventing the will of the people and authority of its representatives."[26]

With the hope of justifying DACA in the eyes of Republicans, Obama ramped up deportations. During his first four years, Obama deported a record 1.6 million people. He became known as "Deporter in Chief." Sessions, however, was not satisfied. He complained: "The federal government has reached a point now where virtually no one is being deported, except those convicted of serious crimes." Many were parents with US-citizen children. Hundreds formed a homeless encampment in a river canal by the border in Tijuana. Many succumbed to mental health problems and substance abuse.[27]

Obama would later scale back deportations after images of sobbing children in the media provoked an outcry. He promised to focus on "felons, not families." In total, he deported nearly three million people—more than the population of Chicago. The Marshall Project later found that sixty percent of a sample of them were migrants with no criminal conviction.[28] In Miller's eyes, Obama had not deported enough of them.

MILLER CULTIVATED CONNECTIONS AT THE Center for Immigration Studies (CIS), the Federation for American Immigration Reform (FAIR) and NumbersUSA. He knew their statistics and research would help serious journalists take his attacks on migrants more seriously and give his beliefs a wider audience. All three think tanks had been bankrolled by Cordelia Scaife May, a bird-loving Pennsylvania heiress to the Mellon banking and industrial riches who believed the US was "being invaded" by foreigners who "breed like hamsters,"[29] and whose family also helped fund the David Horowitz Freedom Center.[30] The think tanks were founded with the help of John Tanton, a Michigan ophthalmologist who encouraged May to funnel her fortune into the groups and wrote, "As Whites see their power and control over their lives declining, will they simply go quietly into the night? Or will there be an explosion?"[31]

Both May and Tanton were environmentalists who believed in

population control for non-whites, fearing that population growth depletes America's natural resources. Tanton worked with the Sierra Club and Zero Population Growth (now called Population Connection). He supported the eugenics movement, which sought to breed a better human race using discredited race-based science. He wrote "The Case for Passive Eugenics." Like Horowitz, he believed the US needed a "European-American majority" for its survival. He fought for English to be the official language of the United States.

Tanton and May were animated in part by the French author Jean Raspail's racial-dystopian 1973 novel, *The Camp of the Saints,* whose title comes from the biblical scene of the apocalypse, in which the Devil and his beasts approach God's beloved city, "the camp of the saints," with their armies numbered "like the sand on the seashore."[32] The novel depicted the end of the white world after the arrival of a horde of savage refugees, led by an Indian "turd eater." They republished an English translation of the book and distributed it in the US. Many years later, Miller discovered it. He found it useful. The book is filled with frightening, dehumanizing, overtly racist descriptions of migrants: "[The old professor] pressed his eye to the glass, and the first things he saw were arms . . . Then he started to count. Calm and unhurried. But it was like trying to count all the trees in the forest, those arms raised high in the air, waving and shaking together, all outstretched toward the nearby shore. Scraggy branches, brown and black, quickened by a breath of hope. All bare, those fleshless Gandhi-arms . . . All the kinky-haired, swarthy-skinned, long-despised phantoms; all the teeming ants toiling for the white man's comfort; all the swill men and sweepers, the troglodytes, the stinking drudges, the swivel-hipped menials, the womanless wretches, the lung-spewing hackers; all the numberless, nameless, tortured, tormented, indispensable mass."

The idea of migrants as a nameless, repulsive horde en route to destroy a white society helped birth the May-Tanton think tanks—CIS, FAIR and NumbersUSA—which gave the anti-immigrant and white nationalist movements in America a veneer of intellectualism. Miller read their studies and stored them to use as ammunition. In July 2012, he helped organize an immigration-related event on Capitol Hill with Sessions, Louisiana senator David Vitter and Iowa senator Chuck Grassley. A FAIR representative handed out a report about Obama's "amnesty." It included a request for donations.[33] (Federal law prohibits solicitations for contributions on Capitol grounds, punishable by a fine or up to six months in prison.)

That year, Sessions released a statement celebrating the fifteenth anniversary of NumbersUSA. Miller had been promoted to communications director for Sessions. He credited NumbersUSA for derailing immigration reform in 2007. "The big lobbies pulled out all the stops, spent millions of dollars, and bore down hard in their push for mass amnesty. But Goliath fell to the grassroots David . . . The overwhelming grassroots response actuated by the NumbersUSA coalition was most evidenced when citizens called Capitol Hill in such volume that it shut down the Senate's telephone system . . . I commend NumbersUSA."

A few years later, Miller gave a keynote speech at a ceremony held by CIS. "I'd like to thank everyone here today, and especially at the Center for Immigration Studies, for everything they do to illuminate a debate that far too often operates, like illegal immigrants, in the shadows," Miller said, to laughter. He wore a mustard-colored jacket and a midnight blue tie, his forehead catching the light, his hair having receded notably since college. Twitchy but confident, he thanked CIS leaders on a first-name basis, revealing his intimacy with them. He criticized the idea that the term "illegal alien" is dehumanizing—again, to laughter.

Miller effusively praised the work of CIS, principally Steven Camarota, who directs the nonprofit's research with a focus on US

Census Bureau data. He's one of the more tempered voices at the group. Miller described him as a person "who knows more about immigration numbers, history, demography, the economy than anyone I've ever worked with. And one of the great pleasures of my professional life is just being able to get on the phone with Steve."

According to Camarota, Miller never asked racial or ethnic composition questions.[34] He focused his inquiries on economic impacts, such as the welfare use rates of migrants and the labor force participation rate of native-born people who are likely to compete with migrants. "He was always interested in getting it right," Camarota said. "He always seemed to be trying to do something . . . motivated by sincere concerns about what are, in my view, sometimes important costs that are unacknowledged . . . The media is always interested in the compelling anecdote about the immigrant . . . there has to be a consideration about the interests of the United States."

FAIR, CIS and NumbersUSA are designated as "hate groups" by the Southern Poverty Law Center (SPLC), a civil rights organization that helped bankrupt the KKK. The groups dispute the label. CIS executive director Mark Krikorian wrote an op-ed: "The SPLC long ago made a hate figure of John Tanton, a controversial Michigan eye doctor it breathlessly describes as the 'puppeteer' of various groups . . . whatever his vices and virtues, they are irrelevant to CIS; as he himself has written, 'I also helped raise a grant in 1985 for the Center for Immigration Studies, but I have played no role in the Center's growth or development.' "[35]

AFTER THE DEFEAT OF MITT Romney in 2012, Republicans concluded that the party needed change. In its election-autopsy report, the Republican National Committee wrote that it needed to become more inclusive: "We need to go to communities where Republicans do not normally go to listen and make our case. We need to campaign among Hispanic, black, Asian, and gay Americans."[36] A *Washington Post* headline called it "bold."[37] *The Atlantic* ran a story saying it was "astonishingly frank."[38]

Bannon invited Sessions and Miller for a dinner at the "Breitbart Embassy." The meeting would last five hours and proved fateful. Over split steaks and bourbon, Miller talked them through findings of RealClearPolitics senior elections analyst Sean Trende.[39] Miller sat at the table and explained that Trende's conclusion was the opposite of the RNC's. Trende's analysis showed Republicans had lost because of their failure to appeal to enough *white* voters, not Latinos. In his analysis, the three men saw an opportunity for a populist nationalist movement. Bannon tried to convince Sessions to run for president in 2016. He figured he wouldn't win, but they could make trade the number two issue and immigration number one. Sessions, sipping bourbon, wasn't convinced that he could be the star of the show. But at the end of the dinner, as Sessions left, a bit buzzed, he turned to Bannon. I'm not gonna do it, he said, but we'll find your guy. Sessions was into the idea, and Miller was already plotting.

Miller and Horowitz stayed in touch. They exchanged emails and got together in Los Angeles. In December 2012, Horowitz emailed him a strategy paper for Sessions and encouraged him to circulate it in the Senate. Miller expressed eagerness to share it and asked for precise instructions. "Leave the Confidential note on it. It gives it an aura that will make people pay more attention to it," Horowitz wrote.[40] The paper, "Playing to the Head Instead of the Heart: Why Republicans Lost and How They Can Win," did not blame Romney's loss on any demographic. Horowitz said the problem was failure to vilify the left.

"Behind the failures of Republican campaigns lies an attitude that is administrative rather than combative. It focuses on policies rather than politics. It is more comfortable with budgets and pie charts than with the flesh and blood victims of their opponents' policies," he wrote, adding that Democrats have the moral high ground. "They are secular missionaries who want to 'change society.' Their goal is a new order of society—'social justice.'" He argued that the only way to beat them is with "an equally emotional campaign that puts the aggressors on the defensive; that attacks them in the same moral language, identifying them as the bad guys . . . that takes away from them the moral high ground which they now occupy." He urged Republicans to "put *their* victims—women, minorities, the poor and working Americans—in front of every argument."

Horowitz wrote that hope and fear are the two strongest weapons in politics. Obama had used hope to become president. "Hope works, but fear is a much stronger and more compelling emotion." He argued that Republicans should appeal to Americans' base instincts. Rather than talk about Republicans' success at job creation, Republicans should attack Democrats as elitist job *"destroyers,"* he wrote. Republicans had to play dirty, he argued, "by framing [Democrats] as the enemies of working Americans."

Horowitz referenced the political utility of "hate" and other hostile feelings. He wrote that Democrats know how to "hate their opponents," how to "incite envy and resentment, distrust and fear, and to direct those volatile emotions." He urged Republicans to "return their fire." He urged Republicans to blame the problems of the "inner cities" on Democrats who "have their boot heels on the necks of millions of poor African American and Hispanic children and are crushing the life out of them every year."

Sessions participated in another of Horowitz's West Coast retreats with conservative lawmakers and other public figures. He had become one of the most frequent guests from Capitol Hill at Horowitz's events. At the Terranea Resort in Palos Verdes, Sessions gave a keynote speech praising Horowitz for his "profound contribution." He described a revelatory experience in bed while reading one of his books, *Radicals,* which suggests that Obama is a totalitarian extremist trying to destroy America. He praised the papers Horowitz had written for his office. He declared that the man was making "a difference in the way we approach things." Then Sessions invoked "the left's core slander: that the GOP policies are morally wrong. This is a direct attack on the integrity, character of Republicans and conservatives. It's a direct attack on who we are as people. Our decency as people. And I'm not sure Republicans are a lot better, but I think they're a pretty bit better," he said mischievously, to applause. "To paraphrase Larry Elder, you know, I think he said, 'you wanna bring a gun to a knife fight,' well Republicans tend to bring pie charts to a gun fight. We gotta do better. I'm learning, David, I'm doing the best I can do. Therefore we must and will make the moral case for conservative reform."

Republicans in Congress sought their own type of conservative reform. They decided to sit down with Democrats to work on an immigration compromise. A bipartisan coalition of lawmakers, the Gang of Eight, fought to create a comprehensive bill. The coalition included Republican senators Marco Rubio, John McCain, Jeff Flake and Lindsey Graham, as well as Democratic senators Michael Bennet, Dick Durbin, Robert Menendez and Chuck Schumer.

Miller launched a smear campaign assault against the bill, with Breitbart as his battle tank. He twisted the details to make it sound like a death sentence to America, a mass amnesty that would "decimate" the country and cost trillions in welfare.[41] Miller spread the myth that people who support legalization for migrants belonged to "the donor class."[42] The Gang of Eight were depicted as corporate agents looking for cheap labor. The narrative ignored and obscured a fundamental fact about legalization: that it legitimizes the workforce, which would require a fairer wage. In June, Sessions said of the bill: "The longer it lays in the sun, the more it smells, as they say about the mackerel." Horowitz wrote a tribute on his website to Sessions's "heroic stand."

Miller and Sessions knew the bill was going to pass in the Democrat-controlled Senate; they were focused on squashing it in the House of Representatives, where Republicans had the majority. "The whole point was to taint the bill in the eyes of Republicans in the House," says CIS president Mark Krikorian.[43] "Sessions, with Miller's help, really did succeed in preventing that bill from passing." Krikorian called it a "Christmas tree of a bill" for farm lobbyists, immigrant rights groups, immigration attorneys, border officers and more. "It was simply a rerun of earlier amnesty bills all the way back to 1986, which is that the amnesty happens first and promises of enforcement . . . would be broken," he says.

The bill sought to create a path to citizenship for the estimated eleven million people who live in the US without legal authorization, requiring that they pay a fine of up to a thousand dollars, back taxes, learn English, remain employed and pass a criminal background check. Only those who arrived before 2012 would be eligible. It gave DHS billions of dollars for border security, including fencing, surveillance drones and additional customs agents. The bill required US companies to implement E-Verify, a computer tracking system ensuring work authorization. It sought to bring migrants out of the shadows while fortifying the border for good. John McCain, one of the lead proponents of the bill, said it tackled the situation pragmatically. "A little straight talk. Republicans have got to compete. And I say compete for the Hispanic voter," he said.

The bill passed in the Senate in June 2013 with a strong majority, 68 to 32, picking up all Democrats and fourteen Republicans. Reince Priebus, at the time the RNC chairman, wrote an op-ed in the *National Review,* urging Republicans to engage with the Hispanic community. He noted that they were the fastest-growing voter segment. "If I can speak with Jorge Ramos and José Diaz-Balart about the future of the party, so can everyone else. Juntos podemos hacer más—together we can do more."

Miller led the charge in the opposite direction. He studied the Immigration and Nationality Act (INA) of 1965 and its amendments. He wished the law was more like the Coolidge-era law from earlier in the twentieth century—the one that set national-origin quotas, barring access to the Jews who were ultimately killed in the Holocaust.[44] Still, he gobbled up the INA, intent on identifying all of its loopholes and arming himself with knowledge of its text. People thought of him as a talking points guy, a mere PR professional. But he was going to show them. He had learned as a kid how to memorize facts he could use to derail his ideological opponents.

He distributed a thick binder with talking points and research in the House of Representatives, which was strange for a Senate employee to do. A staffer who saw it said it called for a double-wrapped wall and technical ways to reduce legal flows of people.[45] "It was like the beginning of the policy that we see coming out of the White House right now on immigration," they said.

In February 2014, Horowitz emailed Miller how proud he was.[46] Miller replied, "Many thanks. Priebus has made a huge mistake by playing defense on immigration. Every time Obama asks for a bill, Priebus replies: we must get 'something' done. Why not hold the President directly morally accountable for the harm his own policies have caused to low-income Americans?" Horowitz replied: "Republicans are attack-averse. Which is why they lose."

Miller expanded his network of extreme-right radio and TV media personalities, collaborating with them to broadcast anti-immigrant ideas. He courted Laura Ingraham and Tucker Carlson. He became chummy with Ann Coulter as she was working on the draft of her book *Adios America: The Left's Plan to Turn Our Country into a Third World Hellhole.* They bounced ideas off each other about immigration. She was stunned by his level of knowledge; he was like an encyclopedia. With Coulter's help and the help of an increasingly radical right-wing media machine, Miller fueled nationwide contempt for migrants and the political establishment that sought to reach a compromise on them.

An influx of unaccompanied minors from Central America began to arrive at the border, fleeing gang violence and extreme poverty after decades of US intervention. Border Patrol holding cells, built to house single adult men, became inundated with children and families. The cells were filthy; children slept on the ground. Breitbart published photos, which triggered criticism of the Obama administration on both sides of the political aisle. The left accused him of cruelty; the right said Obama had encouraged the surge. Tipped off by the Border Patrol union, a crowd of more than a hundred people gathered in Murrieta, in Southern California, on July 1. They stopped buses transferring migrant families from facilities in Texas. Waving American flags, they told the migrants to "Go Home," and chanted "USA!" Surrounding the buses, they forced the drivers to turn around. Forty-nine-year-old Roger Cotton said, "I wanted to say that I as an American citizen do not approve of this human disaster that the government has created . . . Who's going to pay for them? What kind of criminality will happen?" [47]

Miller's and Sessions's lobbying paid off. The Gang of Eight bill died in the House that summer as right-wing media again stoked hate. House Majority Leader Eric Cantor was defeated by the Tea Party–backed David Brat in the Republican primary, despite Bret being largely ignored by national media outlets. He had been propelled by Breitbart and other Miller allies, who characterized his opponent Cantor as pro-amnesty. The mogul Donald John Trump was paying attention. He gave an interview to Breitbart's Matthew Boyle. He said Cantor had lost because of "softness" on immigration, and that the defeat was a wake-up call: from now on, Republicans needed to start prioritizing Americans.

"Our country, our whole country is rotting, like a third world country," Trump said.

Miller emailed the interview to some friends.[48] "Trump gets it," he wrote. "I wish he'd run for president."

CHAPTER EIGHT

"I WANT TO HATE"

TRUMP HAD BEEN A STAR since the eighties, buoyed by real estate and casino wealth, his skill at crafting his public image by feeding stories to the press—sometimes fabricated, often exaggerated—and his ruthless silencing of critics.[1] He threatened them, insulted them, bullied them, sued them, got them fired. Born into wealth and power, Trump sought to outdo his father, Fred Trump, a callous developer. "We had a relationship that was almost businesslike," Trump told Tony Schwartz, who wrote Trump's best-selling book *The Art of the Deal*—a book that mythologized Trump in 1987. The opening lines of the book could have come straight from *Casino*, Miller's favorite movie: "I don't do it for the money. I've got enough, much more than I'll ever need. I do it to do it. Deals are my art form. Other people paint beautifully on canvas or write wonderful poetry. I like making deals, preferably big deals. That's how I get my kicks." He boasted about threatening frivolous lawsuits, "Sometimes it pays to be a little wild."

Publishers Weekly called Trump's book "boastful, boyishly disarming, thoroughly engaging." *Kirkus Reviews* described it as: "An engaging account of life as a major league hustler." The *Washington Times* celebrated it as "the most down-to-earth" guide to making a billion.

Schwartz felt guilty for writing it. "It's almost like I created a monster," he told PBS's *Frontline*. Schwartz spent hundreds of hours listening to Trump. He believes Trump has no values, that he is a sociopath with a binary worldview. He said, "You either dominated or you submitted. You either created and exploited fear or you succumbed to it."[2]

When Trump's career was taking off, the young magnate scored an interview with Rona Barrett on her NBC special looking at the "super rich" in 1980. Trump called Barrett multiple times to make sure he was going to appear on the network show. "We're a very highly motivated family," he told her. They spoke in the living room of his New York penthouse, overlooking the urban skyline. "I do understand it's all basically a game," the thirty-four-year-old Trump told her viewers, his longish hair glowing cherubic in the light. "We're all here to play the game and we're all hopefully gonna play it well, but some people obviously can't play it well . . . The world is made up of people with either killer instincts, or without killer instincts . . . And the people that seem to emerge are the people that are competitive and driven and with a certain instinct to win."

The next year, Trump's brother Fred Jr. died at age forty-two, after struggling with alcoholism and a tumultuous relationship with their father, who berated him for not being involved in the family real estate business.[3] In the Trumpian view, his brother had been bad at the game.[4] Trump had a dark side—overlooked, excused and glorified by Americans hooked on the anti-hero. He cajoled and coerced officials into more than $885 million in tax breaks, grants and other subsidies for his buildings.[5] In the 1970s, Trump had been sued by the Justice Department for allegedly refusing to rent apartments to black people. Trump settled with no admission of guilt. Former president of the Trump Plaza Casino John O'Donnell wrote that Trump told him: "Black guys counting my money! I hate it. The only kind of people I want counting my money are short guys that wear yarmulkes."[6]

In 1989, he paid tens of thousands of dollars to take out a full-page advertisement in four city newspapers calling for the death penalty during the developing case of the Central Park Five, in which five innocent black and Latino boys were falsely accused of raping and beating a white woman. (They were exonerated when the real attacker confessed in 2002.) In a rush to condemn, Trump wrote in his large advertisement: "Mayor Koch has stated that hate and rancor should be removed from our hearts. I do not think so. I want to hate these muggers and murderers. They should be forced to suffer and, when they kill, they should be executed."

The language echoed his future speechwriter, Miller, who expressed joy at the fantasy of murdering terrorists, and issued a public call for rapists to be put to death—changing his tone when the accused were white men.

As Trump's business floundered in the nineties, the media grew bored with him. But his image was resuscitated by a reality TV show, *The Apprentice*, with young professionals competing to work for him.[7] Trump became a household name. People loved Trump. People wanted to be Trump. In 2007, he started an ocean resort in Baja California, Mexico. He touted a cross-border lifestyle; Americans were increasingly going into Mexico to enjoy the beaches, food and culture. Trump appeared in a promotional video for the Trump Ocean Resort Baja Mexico, praising the location. "One of the things I love most about this project is the fact that it's in Baja, Mexico, and Baja is one of the really hot places," he said. Some were reluctant to buy in a foreign country. But with Trump's name all over the project, about 250 mostly American investors bought condos. They received a letter identifying Trump as a co-developer. When the housing bubble collapsed, the vision of a Trump resort in Tijuana vanished—as did the investors' money. Trump claimed he was not a developer on the project, and that he had merely licensed the rights to his brand. They sued Trump for fraud, and he settled under confidential terms.[8]

The sales office at the proposed Trump site was still standing years later, featuring posters of Trump and models of the towers that never materialized. While I was visiting the site during Trump's campaign, a security guard asked me to leave. "You can't be here," he said in Spanish. Then, revealing the power of Trump's myth-making, he made a false statement he believed to be true: "This is Donald Trump's."

DAVID CAY JOHNSTON, AUTHOR OF *The Making of Donald Trump,* who knew Trump for nearly three decades, called him "the greatest con artist in the history of the world."

Several years after the failure of the Baja resort, Trump left *The Apprentice* and once more faded. He made a final comeback: peddling a conspiracy theory about Obama not being born in the United States. Trading on racist anxieties about the nation's first black president, Trump sought to convince people that Obama was an African born in Kenya—an illegitimate president. "I have some real doubts," he told the *Today* show in 2011. He said he had sent investigators to Hawaii, Obama's birth state. "They cannot believe what they're finding." On *O'Reilly Factor,* he said Obama was hiding his birth certificate because "maybe it says he's a Muslim." Obama is Christian.

His comments thrilled racists convening on social media, where conspiracy theories about a Jewish/Muslim/Communist takeover gained a newfound virality, fueled by the far-right radio show *Info-*

wars and other pundits profiting on paranoia, and by algorithms that prize incendiary content on YouTube and other platforms. It was a perfect storm: a man and a digital revolution, colliding into a cataclysmic shift in the national zeitgeist.

Obama called a news conference to release his long-form Hawaii birth certificate, so the "sideshows and carnival barkers" could move on. Trump bragged about getting Obama to release it. "I'm very proud of myself," he said. But then Obama skewered him at the White House correspondents' dinner: "No one is happier, no one is prouder to put this birth certificate matter to rest than The Donald," Obama said, with signature charisma. "And that's because he can finally get back to focusing on the issues that matter—like, did we fake the moon landing? What really happened in Roswell? And where are Biggie and Tupac?"

Trump sat in the audience, stone-cold serious. Two days later, Obama was the hero, having taken out Osama Bin Laden—the man behind the 9/11 attacks. Trump seemed like the punch line. But people underestimated the power of his weapons. He doubled down. "An 'extremely credible source' has called my office and told me that @BarackObama's birth certificate is a fraud," Trump tweeted in 2012. "How amazing, the State Health Director who verified copies of Obama's 'birth certificate' died in a plane crash today. All others lived," he tweeted in 2013. In an interview with *ABC News*, he said he thought the issue had made him "very popular."

Meanwhile, things were looking up for Miller. In 2014, he was earning about $129,000 a year. He moved to one of Washington's poshest buildings, CityCenter, where his family helped him buy a nearly $1 million two-bedroom condominium with floor-to-ceiling windows. The complex features high-end global retailers such as Hermès and Gucci, which his future boss featured in his Trump Tower. Public records show "Stephen Miller Cordary, Inc."

as the buyer for the property. The company's address is the same as Cordary, Inc., his father's real estate company.[9]

Miller participated in a meeting with Robert Carey, the director of the Office of Refugee Resettlement (ORR)—the agency in charge of taking care of the child refugees. Carey briefed Senate staffers about ORR. Carey said something about the educational achievement of refugee youth, citing the fact that many had been accepted into prominent universities with scholarships. Miller interrupted. "He started yelling something to the effect of that not being true," Carey says.[10] "I was just kind of taken aback." He didn't feel that he'd said anything controversial; he had voiced well-known outcomes of ORR programs. "I found it kind of bizarre," he says.

In November 2014, Republicans won control of both houses of Congress for the first time in eight years. Sessions was in line to chair the Senate Budget Committee. But his chairmanship was in question. "Sessions has undercut party leaders with his strident opposition to President Obama's immigration action," wrote Paul Kane in the *Washington Post*. Moreover, Senator Mike Enzi held seniority due to a "totally random feature of party rules: They drew names out of a hat." Enzi won the chairmanship, allowing Sessions to focus on other matters.

Sessions attended another of Horowitz's Restoration Weekends, this one in Palm Beach, Florida, and criticized Obama. "This is the way they explain it. 'Well Congress won't act, so I have to act.' When Congress votes and rejects a bill, it is acting. It has made a decision. This idea that just because you won't pass the bill I want, I'm now able to do it through my executive powers is so far from the heritage of America, the constitutional order that we've been so proud of and served us so well, [it] is just beyond my comprehension," he said.

Horowitz emailed Miller to tell him he enjoyed spending time with him in Florida. He shared a note for Sessions, thanking him for his own "kind and thoughtful note," adding: "It's knowing that there are people like you, people with integrity and spine in Congress (albeit far to [sic] few at the moment) that makes it possible for me to keep my faith in our democracy. Thank you."

OBAMA ACTIVATED THE FEDERAL EMERGENCY Management Agency (FEMA) to create temporary facilities for migrant children and families while HHS ramped up bed capacity. Cecilia Muñoz, head of the Domestic Policy Council, co-organized a committee with the National Security Agency, convening heads of the Department of Justice, the State Department, DHS, HHS and more. "The intelligence community is giving us briefings on what's happening in Central America that's driving the spike in numbers. HHS is managing the shelter system. DOJ has a role because they're managing the immigration courts," Muñoz says.[11] "And we're working with the Congress to get the $2 billion we requested for the Northern Triangle countries [Guatemala, Honduras and El Salvador]. So, it's a robust process with multiple layers."

They started a program to process some minors' asylum applications in Central America, and convinced Costa Rica to offer temporary shelter to people in immediate danger. They did interviews with Spanish-language press, urging people not to believe smugglers' lies about US *permisos*, permission slips. They considered tackling the surge by prosecuting anyone who entered illegally. "But then it became clear that if we treated everybody like a criminal, we would have to take their children away. It was just clear to everybody in the room that that's a terrible idea on many levels," Muñoz says.

Nevertheless, the Obama administration was visibly—and loudly—going after migrants deemed "illegal," as Democrats had done for decades. The approach unwittingly bolstered the far right cause by perpetuating the narrative of migrants as criminals.

In early 2015, Sessions's office published an immigration handbook written by Miller titled "Immigration Handbook for the New Republican Majority." It read, "For years, Americans have been scorned and mocked by the elite denizens of Washington and Wall Street for having legitimate concerns about how uncontrolled immigration impacts their jobs, wages, schools, hospitals, police departments, and communities. But those who do the mocking are often ensconced behind gated compounds, guarded private schools, chauffeured SUVs, and fenced-off estates." Miller called for an end to welfare for undocumented migrants, closing asylum "loopholes," punishing sanctuary cities and more. "Please feel free to reach out to my office if you are interested in seeing legislative language for these reforms," he wrote.

In 2015, Sessions hired an attorney named Gene Hamilton to help with immigration legislation on the Senate Judiciary Committee. With thick hair and heart-shaped lips, Hamilton was two years older than Miller. He was from "all over the place," living in Arizona until he was sixteen, then Georgia, Florida and Virginia.[12] He worked at a commercial landscaping company and enrolled in Washington and Lee School of Law, where he was on the cover of the school's magazine. He got an internship at an ICE detention center in Miami, then went to work as a trial attorney for the Office of the Chief Counsel for ICE in Atlanta. While Hamilton worked there, the court became the toughest in the nation. More than ninety-eight percent of petitioners are deported.

Miller and Hamilton were in sync. They got to work honing the technical aspects of the immigration fight with Hamilton's legal background. The office waged an assault on H-1B visas, employment-based temporary status. Miller accused a bipartisan political group, FWD.us, cofounded by Facebook's Mark Zuckerberg, of hurting Americans by supporting "the importation of more foreign guest workers."[13]

Miller kept feeding the fear-based narrative. He reached out to the family of Kate Steinle, a thirty-two-year-old fatally shot by José Inez García Zárate on a pier in San Francisco.[14] The shooter, allegedly drugged on sleeping pills, said the gun went off by accident. He had been deported five times. Miller brought Steinle's father, Jim, to testify in the Senate. Mr. Steinle urged lawmakers to pass legislation that would protect people like his daughter, a golden-haired woman in medical device sales who died senselessly after the stray bullet ricocheted off the pier. Texas senator Ted Cruz drafted a bill creating a mandatory minimum five-year prison sentence for anyone who returns to the country after a deportation. He called it "Kate's Law." It has yet to pass the Senate.

ON JUNE 16, TRUMP RODE down the golden escalator at Trump Tower, his yellow eyebrows and hair glimmering in his gilded atrium. He pursed his lips at the podium. "Whoa," he said, glancing at the crowd. "That is some group of people—thousands!" He was running for the Republican presidential nomination. Like Miller, Trump was an outsider to the Republican establishment. He said politically incorrect things. "When do we beat Mexico at the border? They're laughing at us, at our stupidity, and now they're beating us economically. They are not our friend." Then: "When Mexico sends its people, they're not sending their best. They're not sending *you*. They're not sending *you*. They're sending people that have lots of problems, and they're bringing those problems with [them]. They're bringing drugs. They're bringing crime. They're rapists. And some, I assume, are good people." He evoked the image of a soiled America, "a dumping ground."

People had belittled Miller all his life for his views, deriding him as he stood on stage demanding that custodians of color pick up his trash. They called him racist. They called him classist. They questioned him. Here was a powerful magnate beaming Miller's own thoughts into American homes across the nation. Miller felt a jolt of electricity. He told the *Washington Post* it was "as though everything that I felt at the deepest levels of my heart were now being expressed by a candidate for our nation's highest office before a watching world." [15]

Trump's comments were widely perceived as racist. But he refused to apologize, telling CNN's Don Lemon: "Someone's doing the raping!"

Bannon was cringing a little. Trump's campaign had potential, but he needed help. Trump was focused mostly on his wealth. He had singled out the issues Bannon, Sessions and Miller had talked about during their lengthy dinner the previous year as they plotted a populist nationalist insurgency: trade and immigration. But Trump didn't present solid policy solutions. He promised a border wall and that Mexico would pay for it. But the wall had been conceived by consultants Sam Nunberg and Roger Stone to get Trump to remember to talk about immigration. It was a mnemonic device, not a policy proposal. Experts knew transnational cartels were digging tunnels ninety feet underground in San Diego, the most fortified border area with layered steel fencing, and that nearly half of all people in the country illegally were visa overstays who entered through airports and ports of entry.

Bannon reached out to the campaign and said he knew of a guy who could help. He could pull double duty: speechwriter and policy writer for Trump—two for one. Sessions gave Miller a glowing recommendation, comparing him to Karl Rove. But the campaign wasn't convinced.

Miller started contributing to the campaign anyway, in an informal capacity. He was enamored with Trump's refusal to apologize. "The fact that he, as I say, doubled down, breaking that apology-retreat cycle, gave enormous confidence to a lot of people," Miller said. [16]

Breitbart's Matthew Boyle put Miller in touch with Trump's campaign consultant Nunberg. "He was consumed with beating Marco Rubio," Nunberg says.[17] Rubio, a descendant of Cuban immigrants, was with the Gang of Eight. Miller sent Nunberg a strategy paper with talking points, advising Trump to attack Rubio as pro-amnesty. "A vote for Rubio is a vote for open borders," he wrote. Miller believed this would "drive his numbers down with blue-collar—and a segment of white-collar—primary voters." Nunberg sent it to Trump. He didn't think Rubio was as big a threat as Jeb Bush or Ted Cruz. Nunberg recalls thinking Miller was "not a bad guy," but "snooty" and "definitely not somebody you want to hang out with."

Campaign manager Corey Lewandowski dragged his feet on hiring Miller. Miller started reaching out to Lewandowski directly, bombarding him with emails at two o'clock in the morning.[18] "We have to talk immigration, we have to talk immigration," Miller told him. "Let me come to the campaign," he said. "Let me help draft your immigration policy."

Miller put together an immigration plan for Trump. With references to murders, rapes and beatings by people who lived in the United States without legal permission, the plan highlighted Miller's passion for the macabre. "An illegal immigrant from Mexico, with a long arrest record, is charged with breaking into a 64-year-old woman's home, crushing her skull and eye sockets with a hammer, raping her, and murdering her," the immigration plan read. It drew a contrast between Trump and "wealthy globetrotting donors." In Miller's view, the rich—excluding Trump—had a nefarious plot to pollute the US, as did Mexico. He took the seed Trump introduced and adorned it: "Mexico's leaders have been taking advantage of the United States by using illegal immigration to export the crime and poverty in their own country . . . US taxpayers have been asked to pick up hundreds of billions in healthcare costs, housing costs, education costs, welfare costs, etc."

The plan laid out steps to "Make America Great Again," in addition to the wall: tripling ICE officers, implementing nation-wide E-Verify, mass deportations, an end to "catch and release," defunding "sanctuary cities" (those that limit cooperation with federal immigration officials with the goal of encouraging the migrant community to report crimes and cooperate with police), enhanced penalties for visa overstays, an end to birthright citizenship, a requirement to hire American workers and ending "welfare abuse."

In January, the campaign announced it had hired Miller as a senior policy advisor. Ann Coulter, who compared migrants to cockroaches in an article published by Horowitz, tweeted: "I'M IN HEAVEN! Trump hires Sen. Sessions' brain trust . . . He's not backing down on immigration."

Miller finally got to work for his idol. Surely, neither man knew just how momentous it was. Trump introduced Miller to his daughter Ivanka, her husband Jared Kushner and others. They traveled together. They brainstormed together. They shared laughs and meals. Miller drafted tweets for Trump.

Meanwhile, Breitbart was turning into what some felt was a toxic cult—with Miller's help. Blogger Katie McHugh was in her early twenties, a Pennsylvania girl with large blue eyes. Breitbart editor Matthew Boyle had introduced Miller to her as someone who would influence the direction of her reporting. Miller called her and talked her ear off about immigration.[19] He bombarded her with links. As she read about the horrible crimes committed by people of color, she cried.[20] She wanted to help stop the madness. She began publishing overtly racist tweets such as "Funny how Europeans assimilated, unlike Third Worlders demanding welfare while raping, killing Americans" and "Indian tribes never bothered to build any kind of civilization. They killed each other and chased bison. Yawn~" and

"Mexicans wrecked Mexico & think invading the USA will magi-cally cure them of their retarded dysfunction. LOL."

Not everyone at Breitbart was comfortable with the overt rac-ism. Among the minority of those who protested was Texas editor Brandon Darby. Once a radical progressive who helped with Hurri-cane Katrina rescue and recovery, Darby became an FBI informant and found himself ostracized from liberal circles. Darby befriended Andrew Breitbart, who gave him a job. Darby had stayed on the platform after his friend had died.

Darby emailed McHugh, copying Bannon.[21] Darby wrote, "Ka-tie, You just retweeted 9 times in row retweets from Adolf Joe Biden, an open member of the American Nazi Party. They were tweets defending you. I am very concerned for your racially-tinged tweets, the fact that most of the American Nazi Party members follow you and commune with you, and the fact that most of the Ku Klux Klan accounts follow you and do the same. What is going on here?"

"WTF," Bannon replied. "Katie call me ASAP."

Darby went on. "I think you are a white supremacist," he wrote. "Am I correct? He is not a parody account at all and you know it."

"Brandon stop," Bannon wrote back.[22]

Breitbart did not punish McHugh. Instead, he basically pro-moted her. He chose her as a producer for his cherished radio show. Alex Marlow, the Breitbart editor who interned at the *Larry El-der Show* after hearing Miller on the radio, said at the time, "After reviewing these tweets, we're considering giving Katie a weekly column."[23] Miller and another Breitbart editor, Julia Hahn, became close. With rosy cheeks and fair skin, Hahn had grown up in Bev-erly Hills, another wealthy hub of Los Angeles County. During a social gathering at Hahn's apartment, Miller didn't want to talk about anything except immigration. "That was all he was fixated on," McHugh says, "even in a social gathering."

He recommended that Breitbart do a story about the racist-dystopian book *The Camp of the Saints*.[24] It was the book that helped inspire Tanton and May to create anti-immigration think tanks, the one filled with degrading descriptions of refugees, such as "kinky-haired, swarthy-skinned, long-despised phantoms," and "teeming ants toiling for the white man's comfort."

Miller suggested that Breitbart "point out the parallels" between the novel and real life. Days later, Julia Hahn wrote a four-thousand-word ode to the book. She compared Pope Francis to Raspail's fictional pope who preaches universal love, suggesting the book was prophetic. "Pope Francis is urging America to throw open her borders," she wrote.[25] (In fact, he had urged the United States to treat migrants "in a way which is always humane.") Hahn compared Hollywood celebrities to the book's "celebrity elites" who "throw bacchanalian bashes to celebrate and raise funds" for refugees. She likened Rubio to "one of the most dangerous characters . . . 'full of the milk of human kindness,' " Albert Durfort, who fights for an immigration policy that will "seal their doom." She wrote: "Importing millions of migrants from failed countries with different values and customs will not raise standards of living but will instead merely remake the West in the image of those failed countries."

After that, Bannon repeatedly cited the book to describe the situation at the border.[26] "It's not a migration. It's really an invasion. I call it the Camp of the Saints," he said.

MILLER BEGAN TO WRITE SPEECHES for Trump. He leveraged access to immigration experts on the Hill to improve the technical aspects and focus of his message. But the gut-punching emotion was a uniquely Miller-Trump mind meld, spiraling up from the underbelly of conservative media and a shared obsession with violent fantasies. They whipped up prejudicial white patriotism and transformed the myth of Trump from magnate to cult-like Mad Max hero-villain.

Miller repeatedly wrote the alleged threat of "radical Islam" into Trump's speeches, going so far as to have Trump say, "We're in a war against radical Islam," during a foreign policy speech in DC. He also highlighted the alleged danger of migrants. A couple of weeks before the Iowa caucus, Trump gave a speech in Cedar Falls, Iowa. He described the fatal shooting in 2008 of Jamiel Shaw, a seventeen-year-old football player, "shot right in the face purposefully. Stood there. Boom, boom, boom!" Another woman was "raped, sodomized and, killed by an illegal immigrant." Kate Steinle was "shot in the back."

Trump put on reading glasses and held up a piece of paper. "So I read this the other day, and I said, 'Wow, that's really amazing, that's really incredible,' " Trump told the crowd. "And it's the snake lyric." He began reading lyrics derived from an obscure sixties song by soul singer and social activist Oscar Brown Jr. "On her way to work one morning, down the path along the lake, a tender hearted woman saw a poor half frozen snake!" Trump paused and said, as if reflecting, "Interesting." He continued, "His pretty colored skin had been all frosted with the dew. 'Oh well,' she cried, 'I'll take you in and I'll take care of you.' 'Take me in tender woman. Take me in, for heaven's sake! Take me in, tender woman,' sighed the snake." She took the snake home and it bit her. She cried as she died, asking the snake why it had bit her. Trump said, " 'Oh shut up, silly woman' said the reptile with a grin. 'You knew damn well I was a snake before you took me in!' "

Trump looked up and spread his arms. "Does that make sense to anybody? Does that make *any* sense?" He looked consternated, shook his head and put his glasses back in his coat. "Hopefully that's not gonna be the case . . . We have no idea what we're doing! We have no idea who we're taking in and we better be careful."

It was the first of many performances of "the snake lyric." Trump was not a literary man, but Miller said it was Trump's idea.

"He spent several minutes describing to me—in meticulous, loving detail—" wrote McKay Coppins of the *Atlantic*, "how Trump conceived of this oratorical device himself . . . how Trump would go through each line and expertly 'hand edit' the page, making tweaks so that it works better as spoken word . . . how, on the days when he does [it], the opening lines are greeted as if they are 'the first three cords of 'Free Bird.' "[27]

Some of Brown Jr.'s relatives have asked Trump to stop using the song to excite his xenophobic base. His daughter Africa Brown told CNN, "Trump is the living embodiment of the snake that my father wrote about in that song."

In February, Miller helped convince his former boss to become the first senator to publicly endorse Trump. New Jersey governor Chris Christie, an establishment GOP leader, had already thrown his support behind him. *Politico* predicted that Sessions, a Tea Party idol, had tipped the scales away from Cruz and Rubio, validating "the New York City billionaire with the conservative grassroots."[28]

Miller touted Trump's promised wall in the media, falsely saying the barriers helped "cut down on rapes, human trafficking, drug trafficking, desert deaths." In fact, they had empowered violent cartels and ended a decades-long zig-zagging pattern of immigration in which people came to the US to work and returned south to live. They had trapped people north of the border. He claimed the wall was necessary to protect the United States from Mexico, "an extremely poor country."[29] But Miller knew the wall was not enough to convince everyone Trump was serious about border security. Mexico's president had declared that his country would never pay for it, and some media turned the idea of the wall into a joke. Miller needed another symbol for Trump, something to grab the attention of the masses, like the wall but different. Something that would give him real border security credentials.

CHAPTER NINE

"NEW DAY IN AMERICA"

TRUMP NEEDED ANOTHER ENDORSEMENT. WHILE working to kill the 2014 immigration reform bill led by the Gang of Eight, Miller had met the leaders of the unions for the Border Patrol (BP) and Immigration and Customs Enforcement (ICE). Now, during the campaign, he started courting the BP union chief Brandon Judd and the ICE union chief Chris Crane. "During the campaign, I would speak with [Miller] once a month maybe," Judd says.[1]

Miller wanted to know if the unions would endorse Trump. "We don't endorse anybody without them requesting an endorsement from us," Judd says. The Border Patrol union had never endorsed a presidential candidate before. It focused on local and state politics. But the union leaders were open to new ideas. Morale was at an all-time low; the public had vilified agents during the 2014 unaccompanied minor crisis. "The anger was completely and totally misplaced," Judd says, explaining that agents were merely doing their jobs and making do with the resources they had. "We decided that we had to have a voice and that we had to have a bigger voice."

Breitbart Texas managing director Brandon Darby had an idea for how to help Miller and the union. He was the editor who had called out Katie McHugh as a "white supremacist" the year before. One of the few pro-migrant voices at Breitbart, Darby led the "Cartel Chronicles," giving Mexican journalists a platform on Breitbart to expose crime and corruption under pseudonyms in Spanish and English. He felt Border Patrol agents were unfairly scapegoated for efforts to protect people. He wanted to help them secure a voice in the White House.

On March 23, 2016, Darby interviewed Miller on Sirius XM's *Breitbart News Daily* radio show.[2] In a perfectly orchestrated conversation, the two proceeded to paint an irresistible picture of Trump for the Border Patrol union. "We are here to be voices for Border Patrol agents and to bring their voices to the American public," Darby said. "They're out there risking their lives and they're often the most attacked group of law enforcement in the country. We found the National Border Patrol Council, which is the union—and yeah that's a bad word in conservative circles—but it isn't a bad word if you know about the union. They represent between sixteen and seventeen thousand of our nation's Border Patrol agents and they've been the *only* voice for those agents in the face of Obama appointees who do nothing but attack them and denigrate them. And so I would like to ask Mr. Miller, the senior policy advisor for the Trump campaign, what we can expect, what attitude can we expect, and what role can we expect the National Border Patrol Council to play in a Trump administration?"

"First of all, Brandon, I want to say to you in front of everybody listening today, what extraordinary work you have done in exposing the cartels, in exposing the gang violence and the criminal activity on our border . . . I am here today to say that we are going to work *closely, directly* and *intimately* with the National Border Patrol Council to develop a border policy for this nation. We're going to make *sure* they have the resources they need to get the job done. They're going to be sitting *with* us to craft the policy."

Darby said, "You're saying, in the Trump administration, as a senior policy advisor, that the *actual* agents, that the National Border Patrol Council is not gonna be sitting behind a door . . . they're gonna be playing an *active* role in determining border security policy? Am I reading that correct? Am I hearing that?"

Miller replied: "Absolutely. The day is over when people with political agendas are gonna write policies that work for the special interests and not the agents. The *agents* are gonna be the voice . . . they're gonna have a direct line into our policymaking on a routine basis. And we are gonna sit down with them and figure out how to secure this border and how to make life better for their agents and for the country. It will be a new day in America for the National Border Patrol Council."[3]

A few days later, the Border Patrol union endorsed Trump. The *New York Times* editorial board ran an article entitled "The Border Patrol's Bizarre Choice." It argued that the union had aligned itself "with vigilantes and nativists, birthers and borderline lunatics." They ridiculed the union's podcast, "The Green Line," which began "with a ludicrous bit of audio from *Game of Thrones*, a character reciting a watchman's oath: 'I am the shield that guards the realms of men.' " But the win was undeniable. Trump had secured the unprecedented support of the union of one of the nation's largest law enforcement agencies. It wasn't the same thing as the agency, but that didn't matter much from a public relations perspective.

Judd liked the message he had received from Miller about what Trump planned to do with respect to immigration. "If we can't get it done through Congress, then [look] within the laws and [look] at what can be done through regulation, through executive order."

Judd was into the idea of a president who would think outside the box rather than the "same Washington mindset."

Miller asked the union to put out a press release saying Hillary Clinton should be in handcuffs and that US cemeteries were filled with Americans killed by migrants. The union leaders pushed back; it was over the top.[4] The final press release, "Hillary Clinton's Immigration Plan," left out the handcuffs and cemeteries. But it did sound like Miller. The release said her proposals "victimized" cities and "destroyed" families, pandering to "liberal extremists" and hurting "minorities." The endorsement from the Border Patrol union helped distract from accusations of sexism being leveled at Trump. A few days earlier, Trump had tweeted a picture of his wife Melania next to Ted Cruz's wife under the words: "The images are worth a thousand words." Mrs. Trump is airbrushed, with a seductive expression and smoky eyes; Cruz's wife is in the middle of speaking. The infantile nature of the objectifying tweet grabbed headlines.

Miller appeared on CNN to defend his boss, trying to steer the conversation back to the border. It was one of his first national TV appearances on Trump's behalf, and it would show Trump just how loyal Miller was. He was part of a panel with other guests discussing politics. CNN's Jake Tapper asked Miller if Trump's attack on Cruz's wife was "presidential."

Miller said, calmly, "It would be nice if one-tenth of the outrage that has been spent and feigned indignation over this retweet had instead been spent this summer when Kate Steinle was murdered in cold blood by an illegal immigrant." Then, he cried, "We get wrong about what we're mad about in America! We don't get mad when Americans are murdered by illegal immigrants! We don't get mad when people have their jobs taken by cheaper foreign workers!"

Tapper interrupted, "I understand why you want to change

the subject." A fellow guest, former RNC communications director Doug Heye, told Miller he was refusing to condemn sexism.

Miller said, "You want to get into an argument?!"

They talked over each other as Tapper asked Miller to "hold on one second."

Miller said, "No!" Wagging his finger, he continued, "You. *Misquoted*. Me! That is a *lie*!"

Demonstrating his skills at misdirection, Miller said, "I just spent the other day in Johnstown, Pennsylvania—a once *great* American town—a *thriving* hub of industry! The steel industry shut down and the town is dying! You know why the steel industry is shut down? Because the political class in DC didn't care about product dumping."

Some of the guests laughed. "This is not a joke!" he said. "You wanna talk about women's issues? Here's something we should be talking about. This is a *fact*. As a result of uncontrolled migration into this country—you can look this up, it's a statistic from Equality Now—half a million U.S. girls in this country are at risk of female genital mutilation."

The study Miller was referring to, which drew from information from the Government Accountability Office, showed that about 500,000 girls born in or brought from countries where female cutting is a tradition were at risk of mutilation in the United States.[5] They would have been at risk regardless of whether they immigrated—and were at a lesser risk due to being in the US. But the image he had conjured in many minds was of migrants genitally mutilating "US" kids. In fact, many refugees were involved in activism against the practice, such as Maha Hussein, a Somali refugee who suffered mutilation and became an activist for women.[6] Neera Tanden, president of the Center for American Progress, called the claim "outrageous."

Walter, Miller's childhood friend, was watching.[7] He was concerned about Stephen. He called him. "Are you sure you're doing this right? I'm worried that after this you may not have much of a career." Miller said no, everything was fine. Later, Walter asked, "Aren't you worried someone's gonna come up and punch you, stab you, shoot you? That could easily happen." Miller said he was not worried about those things. "He's a very confident person," Walter said.

In a text message from one of Walter's friends was a picture of a person in a Grim Reaper costume and a Stephen Miller mask, manipulating a Trump puppet. High school classmates of his exchange photos like this, marveling at the weirdness of having a connection to someone so vilified. Walter recalls their trips to Vegas wistfully. "I don't think that'll ever happen again," he says.

Still, he says the idea that Miller has been enacting some kind of revenge on humanity is ridiculous. "Stephen is pursuing things he believes are for the benefit of the country," he says. But he does think Miller is changing. "I think Stephen has just been so consumed by his mission that he's almost turned into a different person, like Skywalker and Darth Vader," he says, emphasizing: "Except for the evil part."

BANNON REPEATEDLY PUT MILLER ON the radio. The duo was shaping the idea of Trump as a warrior for the working class, fighting the evil globalists. In February, Bannon asked Miller if Trump was like King Canute, "the mythical king that sat on the shore and tried to stop the rising of the tide . . . is Donald Trump sitting on the beach trying to tell the tide not to rise?"[8] He served him up question after question, which Miller slammed like teeballs. Miller intoned, "The one consistent through-line that stands out the most about the career of Donald Trump is his love of this country . . . when crime was rising in New York City, he stood up for the victims and stood up for the police. When our jobs were going overseas, he stood up for American workers. When illegal immigrants were pouring across our borders, he stood up for the border wall."

Miller had learned how to preclude enemies' arguments by inverting them. His own classist background obscured in the wake of his earnest-sounding arguments for lower classes, he turned Trump's riches into evidence of humility.

Bannon joked tongue-in-cheek about their listeners being "low information voters . . . hobbits and nativists and know nothings."[9] He asked Miller, "Isn't the beating heart of this problem right now, the real, beating heart of it . . . not illegal immigration, as horrific as that is, and it's horrific . . . [but] *legal* immigration?"[10]

Miller replied, "Yes, it's mind-boggling."

"It's scary. It's scary," Bannon said.

"There's no precedent for that kind of growth whatsoever," Miller agreed.

Miller told listeners how to win an argument with those who argue America should honor its history as a nation of immigrants. Echoing the white nationalist Peter Brimelow, he said, "The reply to that is: 'You're absolutely right, we should follow America's history, and the history of America is that an immigration "on" period is followed by an immigration "off" period.' "[11]

They discussed a "ban on immigration from Islamic countries."[12] When Miller complained about Cruz's success at picking up delegates, Bannon teased, "Stephen, I've known you for a long time and I hold you in the highest regard . . . you're one of the smartest guys in DC . . . a no-BS guy. And one thing you're not, is a whiner. Am I getting some whining here? Are you whining?"[13]

Miller praised Chris Crane, the ICE union president.[14] Bannon asked, "You're saying Chris Crane's not just a union hack?" Miller took a deep breath and said, "Chris Crane is one of the most virtuous people I've ever met . . . He could've gone to Rubio and said, I'll support your bill if you give me some particular benefit. Instead, he asked Rubio to protect the national security of the United States. He asked Rubio, don't give amnesty to sex offenders. Don't give amnesty to child molesters."

Miller's strategy worked. The ICE union endorsed Trump. The candidate now had the support of two major unions within the Department of Homeland Security.

Miller started to appear at Trump's campaign rallies. He warmed up the crowd before his boss took the stage, appearing to have the time of his life. He bopped up and down. He moved his arms like a conductor as people shouted their praise. He had come a long way from his days at Santa Monica High School. But old habits were hard to shake. He still licked his lips as he spoke. "Hillary Clinton loves special interests. Hillary Clinton loves Wall Street cash. Hillary Clinton loves open borders!" Then, his voice rising to a crescendo, face reddening, "Donald Trump loves American workers! Donald Trump loves secure borders! Donald Trump loves safe communities!"

In Dallas, Miller praised his boss for never apologizing and ended the speech in what became his signature style, whipping people into a frenzy with repetition. "I want you to shout so loud that they can hear you in Washington, DC! I want you to shout so loud! I want you to shout so loud that it shakes the boots of all the special interests!" Then, grasping the podium, he rode the crescendo of the crowd. "Are you ready to send to Washington a man who will put Americans first, last and always! Are you ready to elect Donald J. Trump!"

His staccato speeches were grandiose and played on the emotions of the crowd. His face was expressionless, though he occasionally grinned like a Cheshire cat. He flashed "V" for victory signs. He invoked Kate Steinle. Miller said, "The elites' day is over, their moment in the sun has passed, and a new era in American history will dawn where the people are the rulers again!"

And then, in the seeming culmination of Miller's dreams, he traveled to Vegas with Trump. "How are we doing today, Las Vegas?" Miller asked calmly, to cheers. With a somber expression, he said, "Very rarely in history do people get the opportunity to vote for true, real, profound change. I would venture to say that this is an opportunity that's not even just a once-in-a-lifetime opportunity. This is an opportunity that only comes once in many hundreds of years. And it's important—it's *crucially* important that every morning we wake up, that we're cognizant of just how historic and how rare this opportunity is. 'Cause folks, it's not gonna come again."

His energy rising, he swung from exaggerated claim to exaggerated claim about Mrs. Clinton, displaying his mesmerizing skill at complete earnestness in deception. He told the audience to read the book *Clinton Cash*. "Man, it'll turn your hair white, let me tell you somethin'—one corrupt deal after another," he said. "The corruption of Hillary Clinton would make many, many, many crime syndicates very envious. The sophistication—the scale—the scope—the dollars involved—we are talking about tens upon tens upon tens of millions of dollars!" The damage to Americans, he said, was "shocking and appalling and abhorrent."

Using the coded language of California conservatives, Trump dismantled the norms of political correctness. He repeatedly attacked federal judge Gonzalo Curiel, who presided over civil fraud lawsuits against Trump University. Drawing from Miller's playbook, Trump said Curiel could not be impartial because of his "Mexican heritage." He called him a "hater."

Miller wasn't coming up with all of the ideas. Throughout the campaign, he sought advice from his most trusted mentors. On May 9, 2016, Miller emailed Horowitz.[15] "What are some ways the government and the oligarchs who rely on the government have 'rigged' the system against poor young blacks and hispanics?" Horowitz shot back a list and multiple links, typing, "The inner cities are war zones . . . BLM [Black Lives Matter] makes criminals into martyrs."

Trump ramped up mentions of the inner cities and compared them to war zones following Horowitz's advice. "The victims of [Hillary Clinton's] policies will be poor African-American and Hispanic workers who need jobs," he said in New York City. "They are the ones she will hurt the most." Later, in Akron, Ohio, he said, "You can go to war zones in countries that we are fighting and it is safer than living in some of our inner cities that are run by the Democrats."

On June 30, 2016, Miller's other old mentor, Larry Elder, emailed him policy themes to share with Trump.[16] He told him to emphasize that "illegal immigration" is harmful to "unskilled, inner city mostly black and brown workers—and is a matter of national security. We lack the ability to vet Muslim immigrants coming in from [certain] countries."

"Second, tactics," Elder wrote. "Calling a judge, born in Indiana, 'a Mexican' was stupid. 65% of American [sic] considered it 'racist.' BUT, you can blast his critics for hypocrisy and selective outrage by pointing out, for example, the far worse bigotry of Sonia Sotomayor, who said 'a wise Latina' would make better decisions 'than a white male.' WTF!!!" Sotomayor was the Supreme Court nominee whom Miller disparaged with journalists while working for Sessions. Elder cited other examples of Democrats making what he called "bigoted" comments, such as when Al Gore's campaign manager said Republicans "have a white boy attitude." Elder wrote, "ARE YOU KIDDING ME!!!" He told Miller to have Trump slam Hillary Clinton by focusing on her private email server. ("Very likely people have been killed as a result of her negligence.")

Elder added that Bill Clinton's accusers, such as Juanita Broaddrick, a woman who claimed he sexually assaulted her in a hotel room, should be kept in their back pocket. "I'd sit on this until the debate. More on that later," Elder wrote. He also recommended two books about Mrs. Clinton's treatment of her husband's accusers. He urged Miller not to underestimate her. "She is a shrewd, good, talented debater. And she wants/needs this job WAY more than does Trump. He'd better be prepared. YOU SHOULD PREPARE HIM. When he holds his mock debates, you play the role of Hillary. In the first go around, you'll smoke him. And, hopefully, he'll raise his game." Elder advised the campaign to "lose that black woman who regularly appears on cable," he said, referring to Omarosa Manigault, a former contestant on *The Apprentice*. Elder said Miller should be "the face of the surrogates." "You are smart, calm, quick witted, dress well, look great . . . the Stephen Miller star is only just ascending. I hope to live to see the day when you become president. My thoughts. Mamba, out," Elder wrote.

Miller responded, "Can't thank you enough for this analysis. Also: your kind words are heartening beyond measure. And let us not forget: you were my first mentor, the one who gave me my 'break,' and the one true guide I've always had."

CHAPTER TEN

"WE LOVE DEFEATING THOSE PEOPLE"

OVERCOMING SKEPTICS AND GREAT ODDS, Trump became the Republican presidential nominee. At the Republican National Convention, he gave a speech written by Miller. He stressed that Obama "failed" the "inner cities." He talked about "the rollback of criminal enforcement," record-breaking homicides and "illegal immigrants with criminal records . . . roaming free to threaten peaceful citizens," such as Sarah Root, "killed the day after graduating from college."

"They said Trump doesn't have a chance of being here tonight, not a chance," he said. "The same people. Oh, we love defeating those people, don't we? Don't we love defeating those people. Love it, love it, love it . . . My opponent asks her supporters to recite a three-word loyalty pledge. It reads: 'I'm with her.' I choose to recite a different pledge. My pledge reads: 'I'm with you, the American people.' . . . I am your voice . . . To all Americans tonight in all our cities and in all our towns, I make this promise—we will make

America strong again. We will make America proud again. We will make America safe again. And we will make America great again."

Miller emailed Horowitz on August 14, 2016.[1] "The boss is doing a speech on Radical Islam. What would you say about Sharia Law?" Horowitz responded, "Islamic law is incompatible with the religious and individual freedoms guaranteed by our Constitution." He told Miller to instruct Trump to give examples from Iran—"Gays hung from cranes, jail for holding hands in public if you're not married"—and Saudi Arabia—"no Christian or Jewish bibles allowed." He added, "Referring to it as 'Radical Islam'— though inaccurate—is a good and necessary idea." He said Trump took it too far when he insisted that Obama "founded" ISIS. "He needs an iron discipline from here on in—no distractions from his anti-Hillary messages."

Miller spoke at a Fort Lauderdale rally for Trump. He called Hillary Clinton "guilty as sin" and blamed her for the creation of ISIS, saying she "nearly burned the entire Mideast to the ground." He laughed as the crowd chanted, "Lock her up! Lock her up!" When it was Trump's turn, he couldn't resist bringing up Obama. "He is the founder of ISIS . . . the cofounder would be crooked Hillary Clinton," Trump said, adding, "The media is almost as crooked as crooked Hillary Clinton." He criticized Clinton for not wanting to say "radical Islamic terrorism." "We have a real problem with *radical Islamic terror.* That's what it is. It's *terror.*"

Horowitz emailed Miller. "Great fucking ground-breaking speech," he wrote. "I spent the last twenty years waiting for this. Good work."

Miller replied, "Thanks! Keep sending ideas."

HOROWITZ SENT MILLER DETAILS FOR an education plan for Trump that included a promise of $100 billion in vouchers.[2] He wrote, "(1) it highlights the Democrats' lock in the inner cities and the destructive consequences of that lock; (2) it underscores that the Trump campaign will fight for inner city kids and is the only way out; (3) it dramatizes how inner city mothers and fathers are being scammed by the Democrats and their kids denied a shot at the American dream."

Later, Horowitz asked Miller for the text of the plan so he could share it with "the heavy hitters in the school choice movement." He wanted to secure funding for ads in battleground cities. On September 8, Trump gave a speech in Cleveland, Ohio, announcing his "school choice" plan. "I will be the nation's biggest cheerleader for school choice," Trump said. "I want every single inner-city child in America who is today trapped in a failing school to have the freedom, the civil right, to attend the school of their choice," he said. Trump unveiled his New Deal for Black America, including promises to protect "inner cities" from illegal border crossings and crime, as well as financial reforms to expand credit to the poor. The plan called the Dodd-Frank Wall Street Reform and Consumer Protection Act "a disaster." It had been passed in response to the 2008 financial crisis to rein in the banks, mortgage lenders and credit rating agencies. Trump said none of those entities were to blame for the recession. He said the Clintons were to blame.

His message reached some black voters. One Cleveland resident, Talessia Martin, had voted Democratic all her life.[3] By the time Trump came along, she was tired of politicians. "I grew up in a Democratic neighborhood, and they have not done anything. All they do is come around when it's time to vote to make all these promises," Martin says. Trump was calling those people out. And he was targeting migrants, who she felt were getting all this leniency from Democrats for breaking the law, when she and her friends had been jailed for minor crimes. She was hooked. She made T-shirts: "Conservative facts over liberal feelings."

Other black voters perceived the comments as degrading. Trump asked black voters, "What the hell do you have to lose?" He pointed to one black man in the audience. "Oh, look at my African American over here. Look at him. Aren't you the greatest?"

AS MILLER PREPARED TRUMP FOR his first debate with Clinton, the Aguilas del Desierto, a group of volunteers, searched for dead or dying migrants in the desert.[4] Construction workers, farmworkers and plumbers seek to give closure to families of the missing. They find bodies by following vultures, the scent of baking flesh, tips from relatives who received phone calls from the dying.

These routes are so full of death that it is difficult not to stumble on it. The routes hold human remains and tattered Bibles, backpacks, dusty teddy bears and black gallon jugs. A phone with several recent calls to 911. One of those who died near here was the brother of Aguilas del Desierto founder Ely Ortiz. The smuggler told him he had abandoned Rigoberto Ortiz because he was sick. But neither the consulate nor any US authority would help him find him. He went out to find him on his own—and discovered his brother's body sunbaked beneath a tree.

"I lost all illusions, all ambition for having things," Ortiz says.[5] "I stopped having desires to be somebody. I wanted to dedicate my life to helping people who suffer this." Ortiz, his friends and migrants face dangers besides the harsh environment. Beefed-up border security in the nineties meant mom-and-pop smugglers were displaced by cartel smugglers who could navigate the treacherous terrain. Migrants were pushed onto the same routes as criminal drug traffickers, and increasingly fell prey to murder, sex and organ trafficking.

The wall Trump was calling for would push these people onto

more dangerous routes. The lessons of history were lost in the desert with the anonymous bodies.

MILLER HELPED ORGANIZE A TELEVISED meeting between Trump and the National Border Patrol Council in Trump Tower.[6] The roundtable featured Trump, union president Brandon Judd and vice presidents Art Del Cueto and Shawn Moran. Del Cueto told viewers the government was fast-tracking citizenship applications so immigrants could vote against Trump. (Moran later clarified that they had no evidence of this.) Trump said, "To me, that's massive. They're letting people pour into the country so they can go and vote."

Within hours, a 2005 *Access Hollywood* video surfaced, revealing that Trump bragged about his power to sexually assault women. "When you're a star they let you do it. You can do anything. Grab them by the pussy," he said. Across America, people heard the disgusting comments. It seemed his chances were dead. But Miller was ready to drag his boss out of the grave.

Two days after the tapes were released, ninety minutes before the second debate, Miller acted on the advice Elder had given him earlier that year. Trump held a surprise press conference in the Four Seasons Hotel ballroom. It was streamed live. Steve Bannon, who had recently been brought on as chief executive of the campaign, stood in a corner, a smirk on his face. Trump referred to the Breitbart duo as "my two Steves." He sat next to four women, Juanita Broaddrick, Paula Jones, Kathleen Willey and Kathy Shelton, all of whom appeared somber.

A reporter broke the silence. "Mr. Trump, does your star power allow you to touch women without their consent?" Trump responded, "So thank you very much for coming—and these four very courageous women have asked to be here and it was our honor to help them." Jones, who had reached a settlement with Bill Clinton for alleged sexual harassment, said, "I'm here to support Mr. Trump because he's going to make America great again." Shelton was allegedly raped by two men in Arkansas when she was twelve. Clinton represented one of the men as the court-appointed lawyer. "Hillary put me through something that you'd never put a twelve-year-old through," she said. Broaddrick said, "Mr. Trump may have said some bad words. But Bill Clinton *raped* me and Hillary Clinton threatened me." When the women finished, the reporters tried to ask the nominee about the tapes. Jones screamed, "Why don't you ask Bill Clinton that! Why don't you ask Bill Clinton that! Go ahead and ask Hillary as well!"

Politico ran a story describing the "tawdriness" of the panel as "unprecedented in presidential politics."[7] Asked if he helped Miller organize the panel, Elder says, "Ha! No comment." Then, "People who know don't say. People [who] say don't know."[8]

MILLER'S CLOSEST FRIEND AT BREITBART, Julia Hahn, published a story calling out Paul Ryan for his outrage at Trump's "crass" words while remaining "quiet as criminal aliens have assaulted tens of thousands."[9] She described the same assault Miller had inserted in Trump's immigration plan: "Using a claw hammer, the illegal alien and his accomplice began savagely beating the elderly woman, according to police. Authorities say they shattered her eye sockets, strangled her, broke her neck bone, raped her, and left her for dead. [Marilyn] Pharis, described by her family as a 'gentle' woman, desperately tried to fight back as she was pinned down in her own bed under the heavy weight of her assailant as he was crushing the bones in her face."

Trump made a campaign stop in Johnstown, Pennsylvania. Miller's warm-up speech was personal this time. He talked about visiting as a child and riding the Johnstown Inclined Plane, "the fondest memories of my entire life," Miller said. "It broke my heart to see what happened to Johnstown when the steel mill shut down and the jobs left and the industry died and went to foreign countries." He looked out and asked, "How many of you know somebody or may *be* somebody whose personal dreams were shattered because our politicians let Johnstown down? Somewhere out in some other country, there's someone else who got that factory or got that job." He told the crowd that politicians were looking "down from their glass window condominiums at all of you. I have seen the elitism firsthand. And I can tell you, as bad as you think it is, it is so much worse."

Miller went back to his glass-window condominium. His uncle David S. Glosser decided to call him out. He posted on a Johnstown newspaper Facebook page. "Mr. Trump would have us believe that perhaps the mines and mills closed because the jobs were more or less stolen away to foreign countries," Glosser wrote. "The Appalachian soft coal industry around Johnstown died first because cheaper sources of coal and other energy were discovered elsewhere in the country." The industry also became mechanized—progress, he wrote, considering poisoned rivers and people. "Talk to the widows and children of black lung miners," he wrote. "Talk to the families of miners killed in cave-ins and explosions."

What bothered Glosser the most was the fearmongering. "My nephew and I must both reflect long and hard on one awful truth," Glosser wrote. "If in the early 20th century the USA had built a wall against poor desperate ignorant immigrants of a different religion, like the Glossers, all of us would have gone up the crematoria chimneys with the other six million kinsmen."

Buzzfeed ran the headline, "Stephen Miller's Liberal Family Is Publicly Wrestling with His Role in the Trump Administration." It included excerpts from the post, comments by other relatives and a screen shot of Glosser quoting Joseph Goebbels, the Nazi minister of propaganda who is thought to have gloated, "A lie repeated a thousand times becomes the truth." Miller's mother, Miriam, stopped speaking with her brother, except to correspond about their mother's health. She emailed him on May 23, 2017, under the subject line "deeply offended." [10] She attached images from his Facebook page and wrote, "I am extremely offended that you compare my son and by extension my entire family (and all of us deplorables who voted republican) to Nazis and reference Goebbels in particular. . . . The value of having done so, beyond your 15 seconds of fame, is beyond my understanding."

Glosser says, "Miriam and Michael appear to me to have been very much seduced by Stephen's success . . . So far as I can tell they have drunk the glitzy Kool-Aid of this administration down to the bitter dregs and have lost touch with their roots entirely."

He wrote back to his sister, urging her to read his actual post. "In the interest of preserving the peace, and repairing a very long ruptured family relationship, I have made it a point to not get into detailed political discussions with you or Michael for many years and have no interest in trying to convert you to a different way of thinking," Glosser wrote. "By the same token, you have little real idea of my adult life, my philosophical perspective, professional activities, business interests, circle of friends and colleagues, charitable activities, scientific research and scholarly publications, forensic work, or avocational intellectual pursuits. I have had a rewarding life with wonderful kids, colleagues and relationships; albeit not without tragedies. Your assumption that I am somehow motivated to seek 15 minutes of fame or to intentionally cause you pointless distress seems to assume that I am some sort of sophomoric ideologue with no life, no sustaining mission, or foundation of personal values . . . I don't know [your son] well enough to understand his motivations, personal morality, relationships, etc. and have never made any comment about it."

He affirmed his thoughts about Trump. "When listening to his campaign speeches about Muslims, I mentally inserted the word 'Jew' in place of 'Muslim' and was disgusted. When he character-ized Mexican and Central American illegal immigrants as murder-ers and rapists I found it odious and redolent of the kind of invective and hatred directed toward Jews by generations of our persecutors. So yes, I am 'uncomfortable' with Mr. Trump. I need not apologize for holding and expressing these opinions. They are supportable by the facts . . . I don't know what Stephen gets out of all of this in the end. I hope he approaches his job as one of public service and not just as a vehicle for his ambition . . . If you wish to talk to me about any or all of this I am more than happy to hear from you."

In Johnstown, behind still-abandoned storefronts with "No Trespassing" signs, forests of moss still grow on the floor. The side-walks are cracked. Billboards advertise opioid addiction clinics. Jack Roscetti, a local hairdresser who had the Glosser family as clients in the seventies and eighties, is a Trump-supporting former hippie. Roscetti's store is crowded with paraphernalia from the sixties and seventies: tie-dye T-shirts, a Woodstock record, a photo of a long-haired, younger version of himself getting arrested during a protest of the Vietnam War.

Over the years, Roscetti became disillusioned with both po-litical parties. Trump was exciting because he didn't seem like a regular politician. I asked what he thought about comparisons of Trump to Hitler, of Miller to Goebbels. "That's how Trump likes 'em," Roscetti says. "Because he fights like a Nazi. The extremists. Dedicated. Ferocious. He obviously is getting the job done, so he's there. If he wasn't, he'd be done. So he must be good at what he does. He might not be good for you or me . . . It's complicated. It's really complicated." [11]

I drive to West Virginia, to meet with a woman in the heart of Trump country. On the way was Pilgrim's Pride Poultry Plant with five "Now hiring" signs, offering "$12/hour." Most of the workers leaving the plant at the end of the day are Latin Americans. It reeks of blood. "If white people weren't so fuckin' lazy, maybe we wouldn't have to have [migrants] here," says Kassidi Heavner, who was working for the sanitation company contracted out of the plant. Smoking a cigarette after her shift, she added that migrants "work their butts off." [12]

In Pendleton County, Jamie Mitchell lives on her six-hundred-acre cattle and sheep farm, where her husband's family has lived for three hundred years, descendants of German Lutherans. We connected after I posted on a local Facebook group asking people for their views on Miller's immigration policies. So many spewed racist vitriol that Facebook took down the thread. But Mitchell was nuanced in her response.

Mitchell wore a gray, floral-printed shirt, fuchsia leggings and silver earrings. Her light brown hair was pulled back in a ponytail, showcasing her ice blue eyes. "You're surrounded by 150 cows," she says, smiling as she pulls out her lighter and flicks open the flame.[13] She watches me expectantly, mischief in her eyes, perhaps suspecting that I'm a globalist elite who will run in terror. I laugh, and she laughs, too, saying, "The methane from the cow farts!" We are in tears. She continues flicking open the flame. "Nobody blew up! There's 150 of them right around here. So I just want to let you know you're safe."

Mitchell and her husband have had to diversify: renting out four hundred acres, breeding emus, trying crop rotation. Many in the area work multiple jobs, such as driving school buses. Mitchell believes elites have been trying to destroy small farmers for decades. But small farmers are the ones who keep the land alive. They take care of it. They cut down trees suffering from mysterious plagues.

She shows me one of the dying trees, a skeleton of its old self. "Everything is dying and we don't know why," Mitchell says. I recall my conversations with campesinos across Latin America whose plantations rotted with new plagues, such as the fungus roya, amid rising temperatures. They, too, were driven out by forces outside of their control: trade deals, industrialization, climate change. "The campo is dying with us," an old campesino in Guerrero said.

Mitchell shows me her Suffolk sheep, with their dark faces and cream-colored wool. Her ancestors brought them. The early Mitchells thought black magic made them sick. Mitchell takes me to an old barn, where a counterspell written on a piece of paper is nailed up to the roof, repeating "Abracadabra" and declining numbers of the word's letters. Eventually, they learned about viruses and bacteria.

Mitchell believes immigrants are bringing infectious diseases because of stories she reads on Facebook. "You want to hug these children, but you see that they have rashes and whatnot and you see they have sicknesses and they're coughing and you don't know if it's TB . . . you want to help them all but you realize you can't. There is no way to help them all.

"What we're doing with these other countries—we're not saying no. We're letting anybody come. There's no desire to change their country. They just leave. The people who are left there are those who can't run away: the sick, the elderly, the people who have no money to leave. The single mothers with children. There's no one left to fight for them . . . we have to say no, go back and change it there."

She says her daughter was saddled with debt to pay for her college, while she saw immigrant girls with children get help from the government. "We can't afford to eat our own cows," Mitchell says. "So you see how they're playing us against each other?" She blames the political left. I ask why she thinks the left blames the political right. She says, with intensity, "It's like they've been *programmed*."

We wade through orchard grass and timothy on a hill near her home. The past of the place is preserved here: tombstones mark the graves of Mitchells as far back as the early 1800s. One house has the torn, dusty clothing of ancestors on the walls. She tells me about an elderly turtle her son found with her great-grandfather's name carved on its shell. A dilapidated farmhouse is full of antiques—a secret museum. The porch sinks into itself. A torn-up mattress adorns the grass. Inside is ripe with the past: an old organ with chipped keys. A record player. Cracked pottery. Frayed quilts. An antique wall phone. She picks it up. "Until we fix what's broken," Mitchell says, looking me in the eye, "we're not going to have cohesion."

AS ELECTION DAY APPROACHED, TRUMP prepared to lose. Most polls showed Clinton far ahead; the *New York Times* showed he didn't stand a chance, with a mere nine percent possibility of winning.[14] Trump complained that "dead people" and "illegal immigrants" were going to vote for his opponent in large numbers. Fact-checkers said his claims were unsubstantiated.[15] But Trump repeatedly made exaggerated claims about voter fraud. If he lost the election, he was going to blame the rigged system. Far-right militias prone to conspiracy theories about a New World Order prepared for battle. Their paranoia had been growing since the nineties. Bob Maupin, a San Diego County border resident and self-described vigilante, owns a bulletproof vest and AR-10 rifle, among other weapons. In an interview, he said that if Trump had not won, he and others would have started a revolution.[16] "I figured if I could do something for the good of the country, I would do it—and if I lost my life, so what?" He felt it was his duty to defend the country from invaders. "It was in place," he says of the revolt, "and it isn't going to go away."

The results started coming in. Miller watched the screens at Trump Tower as they began to tell him what he knew in his bones. Trump won Ohio. He won Pennsylvania, Miriam Miller's home state. He won other states he was supposed to lose. He kept winning. Trump was going to be president. And Miller was heading to the West Wing. They'd done it.

MILLIONS OF AMERICANS WERE SHOCKED. The America they had known—one in which a person like Trump could never win the presidency—was gone. People wept and comforted one another. Meanwhile, millions of others celebrated. They were going to Make America Great Again. Back in Los Angeles, Horowitz was thrilled. Speaking into a microphone in December in a room of supporters, he reached into his coat and pulled out a list of people with positions in the administration who were "friends" of his Freedom Center. He read: Sessions, Bannon, Vice President Mike Pence, Kellyanne Conway. "My personal favorite is Steve Miller, because Steve, who was today appointed the senior policy adviser . . . is a kind of protégé of mine," he said, adding, "The Center has a big stake in this administration." [17]

Horowitz's influence reveals the extent to which certain nonprofits can get involved in politics, making use of millions of dollars in taxpayer subsidies as federal laws that prohibit such activity are rarely enforced.[18] According to the Internal Revenue Code: "All section 501(c)(3) organizations are absolutely prohibited from directly or indirectly participating in, or intervening in, any political campaign on behalf of (or in opposition to) any candidate for elective public office. Contributions to political campaign funds or public statements of position (verbal or written) made on behalf of the organization in favor of or in opposition to any candidate for public office clearly violate the prohibition against political campaign activity. Violating this prohibition may result in denial or revocation of tax-exempt status and the imposition of certain excise taxes."

"This is a shadow political universe," Horowitz bragged.[19]

During his confirmation hearing for attorney general, Sessions was grilled about his relationship with Horowitz.[20] The Southern Poverty Law Center lists his Freedom Center as a "hate group," but Horowitz disputes the label. Sessions leaned into the microphone. "He's a most brilliant individual and has a remarkable story," he said. "I don't believe David Horowitz is a racist or a person that would treat anyone improperly, at least to my knowledge."

During the transition, Miller advocated for the ICE and BP union leaders' pick, Kansas's secretary of state Kris Kobach, to be nominated as the secretary of the Department of Homeland Security.[21] Kobach had given an air of legitimacy to voter fraud conspiracy theories, despite the fate of his law requiring people seeking voter registration to show citizenship documents. It was struck down as unconstitutional after the American Civil Liberties Union argued it was meant to stop the demographics of the electorate from changing.

Kobach put together a plan to lead Homeland Security, promising "extreme vetting questions for high-risk aliens," regarding their support for Sharia law, jihad and more. Miller introduced Kobach to Trump as "a rockstar on immigration," Kobach says.[22] "Stephen knows so much about the subject. His endorsement, his seal of approval, was certainly important." But the transition team had concerns. Leaked vetting documents cited "white supremacy" as a Kobach vulnerability.[23] "Past political opponents have accused Kobach of allying himself with groups that had connections to white supremacist groups," the document read. During his congressional run in 2004, a TV ad sponsored by his Democratic opponent Dennis Moore said, "People in groups tied to white supremacists gave Kobach thousands." Kobach lost. He had received money from a political-action committee affiliated with John Tanton, the ophthalmologist who helped create the anti-immigration think tanks classified as "hate groups" by the Southern Poverty Law Center. Later, Kobach said on KCMO 710, a Kansas City radio station, "What protects us in America from any kind of ethnic cleansing is the rule of law." [24]

Miller knew when to push and when to yield. He had a knack for political maneuvering. The unions wanted Kobach at the helm of DHS; they had been helpful in securing Trump's victory. Beyond that, by some accounts, Miller had little use for them. When he got pushback from the transition team on Kobach, Miller dropped it. But he had a plan.

Trump nominated John Kelly, a retired Marine general and former chief of the US Southern Command. Miller called the cabinet confirmation team in DC from the Trump team's New York headquarters to ask that Kelly recite talking points during his Senate confirmation hearing. Kelly and his team declined. [25] Miller requested that the Border Patrol and ICE union presidents, Judd and Crane, be nominated as secretaries of his department's agencies. Neither had been supervisors in their lives. Judd was based in Montana. The idea was absurd. But during Kelly's ceremonial swearing in at DHS headquarters in late January, Kelly found himself standing next to Trump, Pence and the union heads, Judd and Crane, on stage.

"It was just completely bizarre. I mean, if someone from the White House planning a cabinet swearing in had even proposed the idea in the Bush administration—hey, we're going to have the component agency heads of CBP, Coast Guard, the Secret Service, FEMA down in the audience, and the two union heads on stage—

the reaction would have been, 'are you crazy?' Nobody would do that. Not just a Republican administration. The Obama administration wouldn't do that," says a former high-ranking Bush DHS official who was in attendance.[26]

Miller knew how to put on a spectacle. Neither Judd nor Crane would be nominated to lead their agencies, but at least they got to stand on the stage. They stayed on good terms for now.

ON JANUARY 13, MILLER MET the person whose role he would take over as head of the Domestic Policy Council. In many ways, Cecilia Muñoz was Miller's opposite. Muñoz had served twenty years at the National Council of La Raza, an immigrant advocacy organization. But she had come under fire from former allies for Obama's deportations while she was in the White House. "There will be parents separated from their children," Muñoz told Maria Hinojosa on PBS's *Frontline*. "They don't have to like it, but it is a result of having a broken system of laws and the answer to that problem is reforming the law."

When the unaccompanied minor crisis occurred in 2014, Muñoz again drew criticism for keeping children in detention. "I'm an immigrant rights advocate who had to make decisions about immigration enforcement that some people in my community will never forgive me for," Muñoz says.[27] But, she adds, "Whatever anyone might have to say about the decisions that we made . . . I know for sure that everybody in that room was worried sick about those kids."

Obama told officials to facilitate a gracious handoff, regardless of how they felt. "We had very clear instructions from the President," Muñoz says. "The transition is sacred to the democracy." Lisa Monaco, Obama's homeland security advisor, organized a disaster exercise in room 350 at the Eisenhower Executive Office Building with outgoing and incoming cabinet members. Miller arrived late and sat next to Muñoz, whose office he would be taking over in the West Wing, where Muñoz previously spoke a lot of Spanish. ("It's still in the walls," she told *Politico*.)

Monaco detailed disaster scenarios: a pandemic, a devastating hurricane and a cyberattack—all of which the Obama administration had tackled. Miller fiddled with his phone the whole time.

During a break, Muñoz turned to Miller. "Is there anything I could do that would be helpful to you?" she asked. Miller immediately said yes. "What's the best way to really grab control of the immigration issue?" he asked, adding that he wanted to bypass the National Security Council. "How do you make sure you're the person running the show?"

Muñoz was taken aback. "Well, we work collaboratively . . . you don't want to elbow the National Security Council out of the way because you need their perspective at the table."

She told him that different agencies had different areas of focus; they all were critical to provide sound advice to the president. Miller chuckled. Muñoz says, "Knowing how many terrible things can happen, no matter how you feel about the people coming in, you really want them to be on their game. It was distressing."

CHAPTER ELEVEN

"AMERICAN CARNAGE"

TRUMP PRESENTED HIS INAUGURAL ADDRESS, which was classic Miller, with references to "American carnage" and "rusted-out factories scattered like tombstones." Trump promised, "From this moment on, it's going to be America First." *The Atlantic* called the speech "long on anger and dystopia."[1] *The Guardian* said it cast a "shadow."[2] But Miller had long learned that there is value in outrage. The more upset the media was at his boss—or pretended to be—the better. They'd fixate on him, elevate him. As opponents grew numb, supporters grew strong.

He helped secure positions in the White House and elsewhere in the bureaucracy for allies from Capitol Hill. Gene Hamilton, Sessions's attorney, was brought in as senior counselor to the homeland security secretary; Julia Hahn, Miller's Breitbart ally and *Camp of the Saints* acolyte from Los Angeles, was made special assistant to the president; Julie Kirchner, former executive director of the May-Tanton group FAIR, was ombudsman in US Citizenship and Immigration Services (USCIS); Lee Francis Cissna, who worked for right-wing senator Chuck Grassley on Capitol Hill and as a lawyer at DHS, was nominated to head USCIS; John Zadrozny, who worked as a legislative counsel for FAIR, was placed in the Domestic Policy Council; and more.

The Domestic Policy Council went to work brainstorming how to restrict legal and illegal border crossings from Mexico—anything the administration could do without Congress. FAIR had issued recommendations, such as an end to "catch and release," a term, borrowed from anglers, that describes the practice of releasing asylum seekers on parole while they await their day in court rather than keeping them detained. It suggested halting: all amnesties, "chain migration," welfare benefits for people unlawfully present in the United States, Obama's strategy of prioritizing "felons, not families" and birthright citizenship. It proposed a "merit-based" immigration system. Miller's team adopted the wish list almost verbatim in policies and goals.[3]

WITHIN DAYS, THE ADMINISTRATION ISSUED a flurry of executive orders. The first, "Enhancing Public Safety in the Interior of the United States," made it easier to round people up for deportation. It targeted "sanctuary jurisdictions," revoking funding to those cities. It mandated a new ICE office, eventually named Victims of Immigration Crime Engagement (VOICE), for victims of crimes perpetrated by migrants.

Miller asked for the weekly publication of a "comprehensive list" of migrant crimes through VOICE and the White House press office. Some warned that the list could inspire violence against people of color. "This strategy—one designed to single out a particular group of people, suggesting that there's something particularly sinister about how they behave—was employed to great effect by Adolf Hitler and his allies," wrote *Washington Post* editor Amanda Erickson. (The Nazi periodical *Neues Volk* published photos of Jews next to their alleged crimes.)

He also directed the communications team to showcase photos of the alleged criminals. He was especially interested in seeing their gang tattoos. "He wanted literally a daily demonization of immigrants," recalls one former DHS official.[4] It made some people uncomfortable. David Lapan, deputy assistant secretary for the DHS media team, says it wasn't just about shaping the public's perception but also his boss's. "He wanted to be able to put more stories like that in front of the president," he says.[5] Officials had not previously released such information about detainees who had not been convicted or charged; they worried it could constitute a breach of privacy. Miller pointed to the executive order. It instructed agencies to "exclude persons who are not United States citizens or lawful permanent residents from the protections of the Privacy Act."

Internal emails obtained by students at Vanderbilt University Law School and published by the Intercept show officials struggling to implement the order: "If a location has only one egregious case—then include an extra egregious case from another city," an ICE official wrote offices nationwide.[6] In July, ICE issued a press release about a twenty-year-old Idaho man, Jesus Nieto, sentenced to twenty-five years in prison for "enticing and coercing two underage girls . . . [he] used social media sites to communicate with the minor girls, ages 11 and 15, for the purpose of soliciting sexually explicit pictures. He also persuaded and coerced the girls into engaging in sexual intercourse."

Spanish-language news networks attempted to counter the demonization.[7] Univision ran a story about "undocumented heroes never mentioned by Donald Trump," including Mexico's Antonio Díaz Chacón, who saved a neighbor's six-year-old daughter from being kidnapped, and Costa Rica's Carlos Arredondo, who made a tourniquet for a man injured in the Boston Marathon bombing.

But the press—charged with informing the public—was still mostly white and male. They were late to identify the dangers of the demonization. According to the Pew Research Center, more than three in four newsroom workers were white in 2018; sixty-one percent were male.[8] The dominance of white male perspectives extends to all forms of storytelling, from literature to cinema. Seven of the ten highest-grossing authors were white men in 2018.[9] Of the more than one thousand highest-grossing films in the last decade, nearly three-quarters were produced by white men.[10] The people framing the public narratives rushed to sanitize the actions of the Trump administration. Until the spring of 2019, journalists were warned against using the word "racist."[11] The term was seen as polarizing and presumptuous. With white male perspectives the default and dominant, it was easier to give the president the benefit of the doubt than to consider the consequences for the demonized.

A second executive order authored by Miller called for Trump's promised wall—which had become a fixture of the Trump brand—and an end to catch and release.[12] It set the stage for taking migrant children from their parents with its directives, and laid the groundwork for a policy that would effectively end asylum at the US-Mexico border. But people were distracted by a third order also crafted largely by Miller.[13] It suspended travel from six Muslim-majority countries—Iran, Iraq, Libya, Somalia, Sudan and Yemen—for months, placed an indefinite ban on travel from Syria and paused refugee admissions. It called for publication of reports about foreign nationals committing acts of terror in the US.

During his campaign, Trump had called for "a total and complete shutdown of Muslims entering the United States." Miller and Bannon publicly discussed "a temporary ban on immigration from Islamic countries."[14] Protests erupted after the executive order, which appeared to be the manifestation of those plans. Attorneys, activists and others converged on the airports to try to protect people's rights. Chaos and confusion reigned. It was unclear if the ban applied to people with green cards and people whose flights were midair. Miller had failed to share the final order ahead of time with US Customs and Border Protection (CBP), the agency in charge of enforcing it. Joseph B. Maher, DHS acting general counsel, saw a draft an hour before it was signed. Emails show officials frantically trying to understand it. CBP commissioner Kevin McAleenan emailed Hamilton about green card holders. "We have 300 in the air inbound right now," he wrote. Hamilton told him that they could be exempted on a case-by-case basis.[15]

Hameed Darweesh, an Iraqi father whose life was in danger after working for the US military for years and who had been granted a visa, was detained at the airport and threatened with deportation. Tareq and Ammar Aziz, two brothers from Yemen with valid immigration documents en route to be reunited with their father in Michigan, were handcuffed after their long flights and sent back to east Africa. Ali Vayeghan, an Iranian who had waited a dozen years to be reunited with his son in Indiana, was also sent back after his plane touched down.

Miller appeared on TV to defend the order. On *CBS This Morning*, he stood in the snow outside of the White House, pursing his lips like Trump. "I think anytime you do something hugely successful, that challenges a failed orthodoxy, you're going to see protests," he said. "In fact, if nobody's disagreeing with what you're doing then you're probably not doing anything that really matters." The American Civil Liberties Union sued the administration, saying the order discriminated against people on the basis of their country of origin and thus violated their equal protection rights under the due process clause of the Fifth Amendment.[16] Some noted the ban excluded certain countries with Trump business ties, such as Saudi Arabia, where most of the 9/11 hijackers came from.[17] On February 3, a federal judge in Seattle ordered a halt to the enforcement of the travel ban across the country. (It would be revised twice before it was upheld, and later expanded to include nearly a quarter of the people in Africa.)

Officials said Miller's inexperience revealed itself in the failure of his actions to withstand court challenges, evident from Trump's first few days in office. A Bush-era DHS official says the administration could have paused immigration from certain countries without an executive order. "You could have done that just by changing protocols or targeting rules for how CBP does inspection based on threat information from these countries. We did that all the time," says the former DHS official. "[Miller was] just utterly incurious about learning from people . . . Is the goal actually to fix things, or to continue to have the political issue?"

Bannon bragged that the chaos of the roll-out had been intentional. They had done it "so the snowflakes would show up at the airports and riot." [18]

Miller appeared on *Face the Nation* and fulminated against the judicial branch for its decision to halt the travel ban. "We have a judiciary that has taken far too much power," he said. Then he uttered a line that would become infamous: "Our opponents, the media, and the whole world will soon see, as we begin to take further actions, that the powers of the president to protect our country are *very* substantial and will *not* be questioned."

Miller continued defending his boss, regurgitating his false statements about voter fraud, shouting on *ABC News*, "It is a fact, and you will not deny it, that we have massive numbers of non-citizens registered to vote in this country! . . . You have people who have *no right* to vote in this country registered to vote canceling out the franchise of lawful citizens!" He was ridiculed on the *Late Show with Stephen Colbert* and became a favorite punching bag on late-night television. Trevor Noah called him "Sméagol in a suit." Seth Meyers called him "Montgomery Burns."

Miller became more secretive. He rarely sent emails and often lurked in the background during conference calls. He sought power without accountability. He bypassed agency heads, placing strategic calls to civil servants he thought he could coerce or cajole into compliance. Some days, he called more than a dozen people, from cabinet secretaries down to supervisors at the border. "Miller knew how to intimidate people," recalled one former State Department official, citing an incident in which he called a civil servant from Air Force One and chewed him out about a draft discussion paper he didn't like because it cast refugees in a positive light. A former DHS senior official said, "Miller never hesitated to pick up the phone and call people at DHS and tell them what he wanted—and this infuriated John Kelly when [he] was the DHS secretary."

He did not tell the cabinet secretaries what to do, but rather regularly made suggestions to them about "what would make the president happier," according to a former government official. Miller heaped praise on Trump. He depicted himself as a mere vessel of his will, saying: "Every day of my life I thank God for having the privilege to come and work here for this president . . . my sole motivation is to serve this president and this country, and there is no other."[19] Miller slyly teased out Trump's prejudices, too. He slipped him reports that made him look bad, quelling his insecurities by telling him who was *really* to blame. During meetings about how to revise the travel ban, Miller pushed back against those who argued that certain African countries met national security standards. Miller referred to them as "shitty countries."[20]

In June, Miller prepared a document for Trump. The president stormed into the Oval Office, clutching it and seething.[21] He read aloud. Thousands of Haitians had received visas in 2017. They "all have AIDS!" Trump cried. He complained that forty thousand Nigerians had received visas; now they would never "go back to their huts," he said.

Miller kept a somber face in public. But it's not hard to imagine him and Trump letting loose together behind closed doors. Trump enjoyed listening to Miller shout down ideological opponents.[22] He was fond of his combative style and organized actual debates in the Oval Office to see it on display. Watching people beat each other up verbally was his favorite way to process information—and Miller could play both sides. He could verbally dominate men who outranked him, while remaining ever-obsequious to Trump.

Hamilton and two of Miller's allies in the Domestic Policy Council, John Zadrozny and Andrew Veprek, understood his special relationship with the president.[23] They invoked Miller in conversations with career officials who tried to push back against them, saying things like, "This isn't going to fly with Stephen."

It was unprecedented in the memories of experienced leaders. "I was a government bureaucrat for thirty-four years," says James Nealon, who served as assistant secretary for international affairs at DHS from July 2017 to February 2018, and from 2014 to 2017 was the US ambassador to Honduras.[24] "He is by far the most successful bureaucrat that I've ever experienced. Here's a now thirty-four-year-old guy who grabbed immigration policy by the throat and single-handedly changed it."

Miller was not acting alone. Among Miller's chief contacts at DHS were Hamilton; Dimple Shah, a deputy counsel who later became assistant secretary for international affairs; Tracy Short, ICE principal legal advisor who had worked with Hamilton in Atlanta; and Chad Wolf, the DHS secretary's chief of staff. Hamilton, the lanky attorney who was just a few years older than Miller and who came from Sessions's office, too, had his own gift with the bureaucracy. Both he and Miller outworked everybody else. "He was just tireless in trying to accomplish this thing with his little cabal of people, and that counts for a lot in a bureaucracy," recalls a former senior DHS official. "If you outwork other people, out-hustle them, out-write them, out-influence them—then you can actually get a lot done."

Miller and Hamilton pulled from the May-Tanton think tanks. They asked operators at ICE and CBP for thoughts. If Miller was cast as a lone puppeteer, it was because once he stumbled upon an idea he liked, he took it and ran with it aggressively, framing it in polarizing terms that resonated with Trump. He knew how to transform operational realities into campaign-style sound bites, the stuff of headlines—the language of Trump.

One of the obstacles Miller hoped to overcome was a consent decree called the Flores Settlement. During the Obama administration, Homeland Security secretary Jeh Johnson had opened family detention centers to try to deal with an influx of mothers and fathers arriving at the border with children in 2015 and 2016. The strategy aimed to deter fraudulent cases, pulled by the promise of release on parole while awaiting their court hearing (catch and release). More than half of asylum seekers show up for court.[25]

In 2015, a federal judge ruled that by detaining families together, the Obama administration was violating the Flores Settlement, which limits how long migrant children can be detained by border officials to twenty days. The agreement sprang from the detention of an unaccompanied fifteen-year-old girl from El Salvador, Jenny Flores, alongside adult strangers. In 2015, the judge said the Flores Settlement also applied to minors who arrived with parents. The Trump administration, like the Obama administration, asked the judge to reconsider, and allow them to keep children detained if they arrived with parents. But they, too, were denied. Judge Dolly Gee cited the "deplorable and unsanitary conditions in CBP facilities."

Miller told people at DHS that he wanted them to come up with a work-around to the Flores Settlement to end catch and release. On February 14, the administration held a meeting in a conference room in the headquarters of CBP. Alongside acting CBP commissioner Kevin McAleenan, officials from Immigration and Customs Enforcement (ICE), the Department of Justice's (DOJ) Executive Office for Immigration Review (EOIR), and the Health and Human Services (HHS) Office of Refugee Resettlement (ORR) participated. ICE officials spoke about plans to target migrant children. They said they were considering separating migrant children from their parents as a way of deterring family migration and ending catch and release.

Jonathan White, the deputy director of ORR's unaccompanied children program, was there, according to subsequent congressional testimony. Bespectacled, with expressive eyes and a bald head, White was a commander in the US Public Health Service Commissioned Corps, an elite team of uniformed public health professionals trained to respond to natural disasters, disease outbreaks and terrorist attacks. He had served in the corps since 2008 and had helped the Obama administration deal with surges in Central American families.

Commander White was alarmed. A licensed social worker with a long history of protecting kids, he raised concerns to his superiors at HHS, including Maggie Wynne, counselor for human services policy. His concerns were twofold. First, he warned that the plans could overwhelm the capacity of ORR, crashing the program. "There's no question that separation of children from parents entails significant potential for traumatic psychological injury to the child," he later said in Congress, when the policy came to light. "The consequences of separation for many of these children will be lifelong." Childcare experts argue that family separation contributes to post-traumatic stress disorder, attachment issues, anxiety and depression. Dr. Colleen Kraft, a former president of the American Academy of Pediatrics, called it "child abuse."

His concerns were ignored. On February 20, DHS secretary John Kelly sent a memo to acting CBP commissioner Kevin McAleenan, acting ICE director Thomas Homan and others: "The Department no longer will exempt classes or categories of removable aliens from potential enforcement."[26] The next day, ICE's Matthew Albence issued a similar memo: "Effective immediately, ERO officers will take enforcement action against all removable aliens."[27] The memos replaced Obama-era guidance ordering DHS to protect family unity and prioritize serious criminals.

Border Patrol agents and CBP officers at ports of entry began to increase family separations. Illegal entries dropped during the first few months of the administration. Trump's tough rhetoric, it seemed, had worked. Some called it the "Trump effect."[28]

MILLER GAINED A REPUTATION AS a stand-up comic on Air Force One. He stood in the middle of flights and riffed on themes, as people loosened up with glasses of wine. He told policy-related jokes with a straight face. Michael Anton, National Security Council spokesman at the time, said Miller was "extremely hilarious."[29] The routines revealed his superhuman energy. One time, people were exhausted after a grueling trip. "[Miller] comes back and he starts with his routine. Everybody just wanted to zonk out. And Sarah Sanders finally got fed up. She was like, 'Stephen, seriously, you have to get out of here. Just go away. Not now.' "

Anton was a senior fellow of the Claremont Institute, a California conservative think tank supported by Miller's parents that called for an end to birthright citizenship. In the days leading up to the election he had penned a controversial essay, "The Flight '93 Election," that was published in the *Claremont Review* under the pseudonym Publius Decius Mus. The piece said the need for voters to elect Trump was like the need for passengers to fight for control of the 9/11 flight that crashed in an empty field—killing everyone aboard—before the plane could reach what was believed to have been the terrorists' target: the Capitol. Electing Trump might prove disastrous, but it was better than the alternative: "The ceaseless importation of Third World foreigners with no tradition of, taste for, or experience in liberty . . . just like Angela Merkel after yet another rape, shooting, bombing, or machete attack. More, more, more! This is insane. This is the mark of a party, a society, a country, a people, a civilization that wants to die."

His essay captured the zeitgeist of Trumpism, disgusting both liberal and conservative media figures. Bill Kristol, the Republican editor of the *Weekly Standard,* compared Anton to Nazi theorist Carl Schmitt. Bret Stephens, an op-ed columnist for the *New York Times,* called Anton's writings "vile" and "hallucinatory." *Salon*'s Chauncey Devega placed him alongside Miller and Bannon in Trump's white nationalist "genius bar," injecting "polite" Nazi "poison."

The administration's first overseas trip came in May for a summit in Saudi Arabia. Trump met in Riyadh with the Saudi monarch, Gulf coalition leaders (Bahrain, Kuwait, Oman, Qatar and the United Arab Emirates) and representatives from more than fifty other Muslim countries. Trump planned to give a speech on May 21. "Stephen worked really hard on it," Anton says. "He had this wonderful draft." But someone leaked it to the Associated Press. The day before Trump was to deliver it, the headline read, "In draft of speech, Trump using softer language about Islam." Anton says everyone was upset because the important speech would no longer come as a surprise to the public. "We were all up in arms and angry and consoling to Stephen, and a bunch of us, including I, I said this to him, 'Stephen, just don't give them the satisfaction. Don't acknowledge that the draft is real, just deliver it and whatever. Who cares.' "

Stephen responded, "You're right. I won't give them the

satisfaction . . . I'm just gonna stay up all night on the plane and rewrite it."

Anton tried to talk him down. "You worked on this speech for a month." But Miller had made up his mind.

Anton and the other staff went back to the plane, watched a movie and fell asleep. "We were going to land at ten a.m. local time and then have whole full days' worth of events. And by God, true to his word, he stayed up all night and rewrote that speech with the same content, the same message, but entirely different verbiage just so that he could say screw you . . . I marveled at that. If I had been in his position, I would've just said, this is too bad, but it's a good speech. We worked hard on it. It's all interagency cleared, it has the right messages, we're just gonna go with it. He was stubborn. But in a kind of heroic way."

MILLER OBSERVED EARLY THAT TO survive in Trump's orbit, he would have to ally himself with Trump's beloved daughter Ivanka and her husband, Jared Kushner. It wasn't hard. Miller had been crucial for Trump's victory; the family appreciated him for it. Kushner and others joked that if they got "key man's insurance" on anyone, it would be Miller. Bannon was getting in trouble by railing against Ivanka and Jared as a sort of merged globalist monster, "Javanka."[30] Miller distanced himself from his friend. He worked with Kushner's Office of American Innovation, the White House's main point of contact for the tech industry, and helped Ivanka on women's issues.[31] In February, Bannon's face appeared on the cover of *Time*. He was christened "The Great Manipulator." The media had decided he was Trump's brains. Trump didn't like that. He said, "I'm my own strategist."[32]

Cliff Sims, a White House communications aide, was walking behind Miller and Trump when Miller "plunged in the knife."[33]

Sims heard Miller tell Trump, "Your polling numbers are actually very strong considering Steve won't stop leaking to the press and trying to undermine Jared." Sims was surprised by Miller's willingness to betray Bannon, who saw eye-to-eye with him on immigration. Miller had once told Sims, "I would be happy if not a single refugee foot ever again touched American soil." Trump replied, "So you think that's really hurting me, huh?" Miller said, "It's getting nonstop coverage. If Steve wasn't doing that, I bet you'd be ten points higher." [34] Miller would soon become Trump's favorite Steve.

ORR'S DIRECTOR WAS A POLITICAL appointee named Scott Lloyd. Despite broad shoulders and a strong chin, Lloyd seemed boyishly shy. His soft-spoken demeanor contrasted with his aggressive anti-abortion activism. He reached out to Miller in the summer of 2017.[35] Miller responded, and the two began to meet in the White House and talk on the phone. They got along. Lloyd felt a kinship with Miller. They were ideas people, "somebody who focuses on a good idea and pursues that good idea, even when people's feathers are getting ruffled," says Lloyd. Like Miller, Lloyd also made a name for himself with a single-minded focus on one issue.

After cofounding a pro-life law firm in Virginia, Lloyd helped craft a twenty-week abortion ban that became law in several states.[36] His advocacy, like Miller's, started early. As a first-year law student at Catholic University, he recounted the experience of driving a pregnant partner to the clinic and paying for half of her abortion after trying, in vain, to convince her to have the child. "The truth about abortion," he wrote, "is that my first child is dead, and no woman, man, Supreme Court, or government—NOBODY—has the right to tell me that she doesn't belong here."[37] Lloyd's essay likened abortions to the Holocaust. He continued penning op-ed articles against abortion. In 2011, he wrote an article for a Catholic publication, recommending state laws ordering that "women must notify the men of their decision to abort, and gain their consent."

Formerly with the Catholic organization Knights of Columbus, Lloyd had an obsession with abortion that paralleled Miller's with immigration. Lloyd felt Miller was misunderstood. He thought it was important to give people the benefit of the doubt. And Miller had gotten back to him right away. "I took that as a nice thing, given how busy he was," Lloyd says. "If he really was the type of person he is portrayed as in the media, then he wouldn't do those sorts of things."

Lloyd found it easy to imagine good intentions in lots of people, and believed it was important to let them make their own decisions. But there were others he expressed an interest in controlling. Under the Bush and Obama administrations, the ORR agency had routinely allowed migrant girls to get abortions if they had private funding. Shortly before Lloyd's arrival, the administration prohibited federally funded ORR shelters "from taking any action that facilitates an abortion without direction and approval from the Director of ORR."[38]

Lloyd began to hit the brakes on abortion requests, including in the case of one girl who was pregnant as a result of rape. He instructed shelters to send girls to religiously affiliated anti-abortion pregnancy crisis centers and undergo medically unnecessary ultrasounds. The American Civil Liberties Union sued to stop him. Lloyd thought he was acting in the interest of the children—consistent with ORR's mission—because he saw fetuses as children in his care. In the case of a girl who was suicidal, Lloyd wrote, "Clinician should work to identify any pressures that might be leading her to desire termination (does she feel pressure to get to work, is there emotional abuse, etc.) and what is leading to her sadness and anger . . . if she has not had her ultrasound yet, she should do so at the following place . . . once we know the gestational age, that will be material, as it may already be too late to legally obtain an abortion . . . she should not be meeting with an attorney regarding her termination."[39]

While Lloyd was absorbed in his quest to save the unborn, ORR began receiving an unusual number of migrant toddlers and infants classified as "unaccompanied." Infants who could not have traveled to the border alone from Central America. Children who said they came with their parents. Clearly, they had been separated. But ORR officials were confused. DHS secretary John Kelly had appeared on CNN in March saying he was considering separating children from their parents as a way of deterring migration. Shortly after that, he told Senate Democrats there was no such plan. Was DHS separating families, or not?

Lloyd wasn't worried. He trusted the White House. No policy had been announced. Perhaps the increase was the result of more fraudulent families arriving at the border, or Border Patrol chiefs exercising their wide autonomy. Still, ORR officials contacted DHS to ask what was going on. "We didn't get a response for a while," Lloyd says. "We followed up with them . . . they just said, 'You shouldn't see this anymore.' We got the impression that, okay, they weren't sure exactly what was going on, they drilled into it, and they took care of it."

Lloyd says he doesn't recall discussing family separations with Miller. But they did have one-on-one conversations about another policy targeting migrant children that they were both passionate about: a memorandum of agreement that was in the works between ORR and DHS. It would mandate increased information sharing between the agencies, including fingerprinting and biographical data for all adults in a household where migrant children are expected to be transferred.

Lloyd guessed that heightened collaboration between ORR, a childcare agency, and ICE, the deportation agency within DHS, could cause a backlog of cases and discourage sponsors from taking in children, since many sponsors were undocumented. But Lloyd didn't think that was the goal. He wanted to help the White House stop killers and rapists. Miller argued for swift action. "People are dying!" His words stuck with Lloyd, who felt the two were driven by the same urgent desire: to preserve life. "It really spoke to what was motivating him," Lloyd says.

He told Miller about concerns that career officials raised, such as the possibility that the plans would crash the ORR program. According to a former ORR official, Lloyd came back from a summer meeting and said, "We have our marching orders from Miller—if we can prevent a backup, we should do everything we can to do that. But it is better that there be a backup in the border stations than that we not enforce the immigration laws and that we not deter migration."[40] Lloyd isn't sure if those were his exact words, but he doesn't deny them either. The important thing, he says, is that it was never anyone's intention to crash the program. He thought to himself, "We could overcome the capacity concerns with proper management."

Lloyd was finishing a semi-autobiographical novel, *The Undergraduate*, about a college student who lacks direction as he drinks heavily at parties. He gets a friend pregnant and must come to terms with her decision to abort against his will. He finds purpose through prayer. The publisher compared Lloyd to Bret Easton Ellis, the author of *American Psycho*, saying the book was like his novel *Less Than Zero*, exposing "how privileged youth can be torn asunder by the sudden intrusion of adult responsibility and burning questions of moral culpability."

From November 2016 to March 2017, the percentage of children referred to ORR who were known to have been separated from their parents jumped from 0.3 percent to 2.6 percent. By August 2017, the percentage had increased to 3.6 percent—a more than tenfold increase.[41] Unbeknownst to ORR officials, El Paso's sector started a pilot program of separating families in July 2017. Children were being systematically pulled from mothers' and fathers' arms. ORR career officials were so alarmed, they began to keep a list of minors whom they learned were separated by DHS. When the list was leaked to the press, Lloyd told his staff to stop maintaining it, sources told *Politico*.[42] Lloyd disputes the allegations. He says he merely asked staff to communicate with DHS on a "case-by-case basis." He did not want another leak to "create a news cycle over a policy that did not exist, according to our understanding."

Miller had waged a rhetorical war on MS-13. Despite their relatively small numbers—less than one percent of the country's total gang members—the administration brought them up at every opportunity. In September 2017, Attorney General Sessions mentioned an "unaccompanied minors issue," saying MS-13 gang members arrived in the United States as "wolves in sheep's clothing."

Lloyd was horrified by the violence of MS-13. The Los Angeles–born Mara Salvatrucha had expanded to Long Island and other parts of the US, chopping up other youths with machetes in the woods, stuffing their bodies in drainage pipes. "How many rapes or murders are an acceptable number of rapes or murders among our unaccompanied minors population?" Lloyd asked. "The answer is zero." Lloyd expanded the reasons for which migrant minors must be sent to jail-like secure facilities—rather than shelters or homestays—to include any allegation of gang affiliation, past or present. He ordered that no migrant children could be released from secure facilities unless he personally approved. This created backlogs. In May 2017, ICE launched Operation Matador, arresting hundreds of suspected "gang associates" and placing them in ORR secure facilities. One boy was detained and deported for a drawing he made. Another, who had never spent a night apart from his mother, was removed from his home on gang allegations that were "soundly rejected" by a judge.[43] But he was kept in detention for more than seven months. Lloyd allegedly kept him locked up despite the boy's mother's pleas.[44] "It was hard to keep up with the pace of human rights violations that were getting rolled out through our office," says a former ORR official.[45] "It became quickly demoralizing because there were so many."

In August, the American Civil Liberties Union filed another class action lawsuit against the administration for its prolonged detention of migrant minors, alleging that officials were violating the due process rights of the children. "To become an MS-13 member, recruits have to commit a serious act of violence—like assaulting a rival gang member—and endure a group beating," wrote Hannah Dreier for ProPublica.[46] "But there is no process to become a 'gang associate'—a classification used only by law enforcement. ICE designates people as gang associates if they meet two out of eight criteria, which include frequenting a known gang hangout (which can be a bus stop or a park), wearing gang colors and displaying symbols." She noted that police officers who add "gang associates" into the database rarely speak Spanish.

Meanwhile, Miller expanded his control over the Department of Homeland Security. Trump brought in General Kelly to be chief of staff, and Kelly was replaced at DHS by acting secretary Elaine Duke. A descendant of Italian immigrants, Duke served under both Obama and Bush. She was not seen as a Trump ally and was kept in an acting capacity. Under Trump, cabinet members were often kept in an "acting" role, giving him more flexibility to get rid of them.[47]

Miller began to more aggressively push his agenda at DHS. Hamilton began writing immigration policies at Miller's behest. "He was basically telling senior bureaucrats within the department, including the acting secretary, 'this is what we're going to do,'" says James Nealon, who served as DHS assistant secretary for international affairs. "I've never seen anything like it."

Miller took a special interest in any policy that involved young migrants. He turned his attention to the Central American Minors Program, which allows parents lawfully in the United States to request a refugee resettlement interview for their children in Guatemala, El Salvador and Honduras. It was started under Obama to process people prior to their dangerous trek. But for Miller, it was another way for youths with possible gang affiliations to come. It was terminated.

He spoke with Hamilton about ending DACA, the Obama-era program that protected migrants brought to the US as children. Hamilton wrote a memo to terminate, which Trump signed despite his reservations.[48] Trump had sympathy for the so-called Dreamers, whose stories he knew struck a chord for many Americans. But he trusted Miller's feel for the hardliners who'd helped elect him. The pushback from the left was relentless and immediate. Attorneys general in California and other states sued, alleging that the decision violated the youths' due process and equal protection rights. About ninety-four percent of DACA recipients are from Mexico or Central America. The injunction was granted. Trump tweeted, revealing uncertainty about what he was doing: "Does anybody really want to throw out good, educated and accomplished young people who have jobs, some serving in the military?"

Apprehensions at the border had been surging since the summer. The Trump Effect wasn't real after all. Across Central America, hundreds of families formed a caravan organized by a pro-immigrant group called Pueblo Sin Fronteras. The cross-border organization sought to help poor and desperate families reach the US without smugglers, as gang violence tore their worlds apart. The idea was safety in numbers; migrants were a frequent target for kidnapping, rape and extortion.[49] Hundreds had been found in clandestine graves in Mexico. Together, they made the dangerous journey on the roof of a freight train known as La Bestia, the Beast. Human rights groups, priests and others donated food and provided shelter during their journey. Jose Fuentes, his partner Olivia Caceres and their two young sons, one-year-old Mateo and four-year-old Andree, left El Salvador. They were fleeing death threats.[50] On the journey north, when Mateo wept, Fuentes would rock him to sleep. Sometimes, he stayed up late into the night taking care of him. He and Olivia were worried about him because he was so young. As they approached the US, Mateo began to show signs of dehydration and exhaustion. Fuentes rushed to the San Diego–Tijuana port of entry with him while Olivia stayed behind with Andree and the caravan.

Fuentes asked for asylum, cradling Mateo. He always strove to be a good and present father because he never knew his own. He had been raised by a single mother, who died just before he graduated from El Salvador's Catholic University with a journalism degree—just before the gangs took notice of him and his family.

He and Mateo had the same cinnamon skin and almond eyes. Fuentes shared his boy's birth certificate and his national identification with CBP. They were found to have a credible fear. But then ICE officials told Fuentes they were going to take his boy. He clutched his child. An officer pried them apart. ICE sent Mateo to an ORR facility fifteen hundred miles away in Texas. Fuentes was placed in a for-profit detention center in east San Diego County. Fuentes wept in fear and confusion in a small, all-white room.[51] "I feel powerless," he said.

CHAPTER TWELVE

"COSMOPOLITAN BIAS"

DURING A MARCH 2017 MEETING in the Roosevelt Room, Miller brought up a soon-to-be-released report on the cost of refugees. "The president believes that it costs too much to resettle refugees," he said. "This report shall not embarrass the president."[1]

He sat in a leather chair at a long conference table with a handful of State Department officials. A portrait of Theodore Roosevelt hung over the mantel, a depiction of the politician in a cowboy hat on a rearing horse, part of the Rough Rider cavalry. Roosevelt was the president Miller had quoted in his high school yearbook: "There can be no fifty-fifty Americanism in this country. There is room here for only 100 percent Americanism, only for those who are Americans and nothing else." He had pushed the president's powers to their limits, writing ten times as many executive orders as his predecessor. Roosevelt wrote, "I did not usurp power, but I did greatly broaden the use of executive power."

As Miller spoke under his image about how expensive Trump

thought refugees were, and the importance of creating a report that aligned with the president's views, senior State Department official Lawrence Bartlett thought of all the research showing the opposite. He brought up one of those studies, showing refugees were net positive contributors to the economy over time. Miller changed the subject. When the meeting concluded, he asked aides if they knew the name of the older gentleman.[2] Soon after, Bartlett was reassigned out of his role as head of refugee admissions. He had served in the department since 1999. One former State Department official says, "In the early days, we hadn't fully gotten the message that any suggestion of countervailing facts and evidence would land you firmly in the suspect category—that you would be personally targeted for your views and be deemed disloyal and part of the Deep State."

Jennifer Arangio, a senior director in the National Security Council international organizations and alliances division, was ousted after heated exchanges with Miller about the importance of providing accurate information to the president. Other critics, such as advisor Sahar Nowrouzzadeh, were sent elsewhere. The State Department's inspector general began investigating the possibility of unlawful political retaliation. One investigation found that at least one career State Department employee had been forced out for inappropriate reasons, and that department leadership had subjected career employees to politically motivated harassment, calling them such names as "Obama holdovers," "traitors," "disloyal" and "Deep State."[3]

Meanwhile, a draft of the refugee report leaked to the *New York Times*.[4] It showed that refugees brought in $63 billion more in government revenue than they had cost over the past decade. Miller was upset about the leak. He requested a meeting with officials involved in refugee issues. In the meeting, Miller told officials that the final study had to consider only the costs of refugees, removing fiscal benefits from the math.

During a June 5 meeting on refugee admissions co-chaired by
Miller and Hamilton, the two banged on the same message, as recalled by a participant. "As we know, the president believes refugees
present a clear and imminent danger to the US," Miller said. "So
this year, we're going to turn to DHS to tell us what number we can
safely bring to the US."

"He was always speaking for the president," a former official
says. "I've never seen a president personally invoked so much, as in
like, 'he *believes* this, and irrespective of what the facts and evidence
suggest, we will all organize ourselves around this belief.' "

The president had to tell Congress by the start of the federal
fiscal year in the fall how many refugees he believed should be re-
settled in the country. Miller and Hamilton told National Security
Council staff that the Domestic Policy Council would be taking the
lead on the refugee cap—not the NSC, which historically coordi-
nates refugee admissions with the State Department, the Department of Defense and intelligence agencies. "They were pulling the
rug out from all of us who have worked on this program for years
to say your input is not needed here," says a former official. "What
Miller tried to do was turn refugee resettlement into an immigration issue [as opposed to a foreign policy issue], and therefore put
it under the purview of the DPC . . . it took them time to get their
head around the fact that there's this whole international component."

NSC staff raised concerns with National Security advisor H. R.
McMaster about Miller's plan to run a policy process on a national
security issue outside of the NSC. McMaster had already had issues
with Miller. He told him to stop writing "radical Islamic terrorism"
in Trump's speeches.[5] The phrase was known to provoke hostility toward Americans among terrorists who used it to paint us as
anti-Muslim, fueling myths of a war between Islam and the West.
Still, the phrase kept popping out of Trump's mouth.

McMaster made sure the NSC interagency process was put in motion. In discussion papers on refugee resettlement, NSC staff found creative ways to add information alongside the misleading paragraphs Miller and his allies had written, such as that refugees posed a terrorist risk and were a drain on the economy. Civil servants typed in evidence showing the opposite.

During preparations for an important meeting related to the cap, Miller's assistant sent out an Outlook calendar invite to "decide the ceiling this week," a former official says. The invite was sent to a small subset of stakeholders and flouted the process of alerting agencies seventy-two hours in advance through a formal system. Hamilton put forward a refugee cap of twenty-six thousand.[6] He asked NSC staff to cite the Department of Homeland Security for the figure in the report. "We thought that was very unusual because the alternative option said 'the Secretary of State recommends fifty thousand.' So we told him we had to say 'the Secretary of Homeland Security,'" recalled a former staffer. Hamilton said he would follow up. The DHS secretary number came back at forty thousand. "It exposed the extent to which they were going rogue. It was Gene's number that he cooked up with Stephen, and they were going to make acting secretary Elaine Duke be the face of it." Ultimately, the cap was set at forty-five thousand: a compromise with the secretary of state, but still the lowest since 1980.[7] The next year, Miller and his allies slashed the cap to thirty thousand, and to eighteen thousand for 2020. Miller wanted to get the cap down to zero.[8]

"I'll never really understand why there was such a disproportionate obsession with refugees," says a former State Department official, who adds that they're "the most intensively vetted" newcomers. Refugees wait for years in camps to get into the United States. On the other hand, asylum seekers ask for protection at the border without prior approval. The official hypothesized it was because of the increasingly Arab-Muslim demographics of refugees.

Mark Hetfield, president and CEO of HIAS, says lowering the cap has forced resettlement agencies to dismantle infrastructure that took years to build. "I can't overemphasize the harm that that's causing," he says. In 2018, resettlement agencies were asked by the administration to collectively close thirty-five sites in the country. Critics argued that by choking off the flow of refugees, Miller was ruining America's reputation as a global leader in refugee admissions and hurting allies who need our help, such as Jordan and Lebanon. Experts say the decision to slash admissions hurts homeland security as well. The Department of Defense brings in Iraqis and others who help the US Army as translators and informants. They're promised resettlement in exchange for endangering their lives and their family's lives on behalf of the United States.

Miller turned his attention to the Global Compact for Migration, an intergovernmental agreement the US had joined under Obama. It aimed to address the global migration crisis through increased cooperation. McMaster convened a meeting in the Situation Room to discuss it. Several cabinet secretaries, including acting Homeland Security secretary Elaine Duke and Attorney General Sessions, were present with their deputies. Miller was seated at the table. Ambassador to the United Nations Nikki Haley was present via video conference. McMaster asked if the US should participate in the Global Compact conference. Some thought it would best serve our interests to be present at the negotiating table, even if the US didn't sign the agreement.

Miller spoke up.[9] He read aloud from a document about the need to "protect human rights" and "strongly condemn xenophobia." When Secretary Duke asked what he was reading—it sounded a bit kumbaya to some of the people present—Miller explained that it was the universal declaration of the Global Compact. He launched into a speech, describing migration as "out of control" and saying the US couldn't possibly be a party to the compact.

"Isn't is a *fact*—does anybody deny that it was the *Obama administration* that signed onto this resolution?" Miller asked. One official asserted that it was the US that signed. Miller looked across the table and enunciated each word, "Is there seriously *anyone* sitting along this table who believes that the United States should participate in this process?" The cabinet secretaries were stone silent, shrinking in the face of his question. Miller was channeling Trump. He had learned to dominate meetings by personifying the president; few dared challenge him. One participant in the meeting recalls that Haley piped in, "Well, you know what, Stephen? This is the kind of thing we eat for breakfast every day at the United Nations. We participate in all kinds of things, and we're big boys and girls and I think we should participate. But if that's what you all think, then I've got things to do." Haley stood up and left. They voted to disengage.

Miller was expanding his control across the government. He dispatched ideological allies to key positions within the bureaucracy that would allow him to export his ideas overseas. John Zadrozny was sent to the State Department to oversee policy planning. In addition, his pal Andrew Veprek was moved from the Domestic Policy Council to the State Department, as deputy assistant secretary in the Bureau of Population, Refugees and Migration.

While editing a draft United Nations Human Rights Council resolution, "The Incompatibility between Democracy and Racism," Veprek wrote that world leaders should not have to condemn hate speech.[10] They should not use words like "populism and nationalism" as if they were "dirty words." He wrote, "There are millions of Americans who likely would describe themselves as adhering to these concepts. (Maybe even the President.) So are we looking here to condemn our fellow-citizens, those who pay our salaries?" Veprek argued against "xenophobia" as well. He wrote, "[W]hat real or perceived offense is next to be considered 'xenophobic'? How does that square with our historic respect for the right of free expression?"

A few days later, the United Nations High Commissioner for Human Rights condemned the US practice of separating migrant children from parents as "unconscionable." The US announced it was withdrawing from the Human Rights Council, which the US had joined under the Obama administration. Ambassador Haley called it a "cesspool of political bias." The decision was condemned by human rights leaders who said the council played an important role across the world and that America's participation was critical. But the Trump administration wasn't interested.

MILLER WAS LASER-FOCUSED ON IMMIGRATION, even amid distractions that lingered for months. Early on, FBI director James Comey had confirmed he was investigating whether members of Trump's campaign had colluded with Russia to influence the 2016 election. Russia had spent tens of millions of dollars to manipulate American opinion through the Web.[11] Russia's Internet Research Agency had leveraged algorithms that enabled far-reaching information warfare.

Trump was furious at the implication that Comey was investigating him, even more so when Sessions recused himself. He said he never would've appointed him as attorney general had he known that he would do that.[12] Trump called him "our beleaguered A.G." in a tweet.

On May 5, at a dinner in Trump's Bedminster, New Jersey, resort, Trump turned to Miller for comfort. He told him he had decided to fire Comey and asked him to help him write a letter. They were sitting at a table with Kushner and others. Miller took notes as his boss dictated.[13] "While I greatly appreciate you informing me that I am not under investigation concerning what I have often stated is a fabricated story on a Trump-Russia relationship—pertaining to the 2016 presidential election, please be informed that I, and I believe the American public—including Ds and Rs—have lost faith in you as Director of the FBI," Miller's notes read. The final version of the letter was more eloquent, with some added flourishes in Miller's style: "Dear Director Comey, While I greatly appreciate your informing me, on three separate occasions, that I am not under investigation concerning the fabricated and politically-motivated allegations of a Trump-Russia relationship with respect to the 2016 Presidential Election, please be informed that I, along with members of both political parties and, most importantly, the American Public, have lost faith in you as the Director of the FBI and you are hereby terminated."

Trump wanted to know if it was legal. Miller did some research and concluded that he "had the authority to terminate Comey without cause," according to a report by special counsel Robert Mueller, who initiated a probe shortly after Comey was fired. Trump never delivered the letter Miller wrote to Comey because White House counsel deemed it problematic. But the president still dismissed Comey, citing his handling of Clinton's email investigation.

The history-making letter Miller helped write would contribute to years of blowback. The Mueller investigation initially examined any links or coordination between the Russian government and people close to the Trump campaign. Then it widened to explore whether Trump had tried to obstruct justice. The probe dominated headlines as hundreds of witnesses were interviewed and subpoenas were filed. Trump called it a "witch hunt."

Miller didn't let it pull him away from his obsession. He continued to push hardcore immigration policies, bypassing cabinet heads in his quest to tighten up, micromanaging civil servants. He pressured DHS to transfer unlawfully present migrants to "sanctuary cities." But there was some concern over the legal liabilities.[14] He sought ways to make it easier to deport migrant youths and took an interest in individual cases. During Trump's first trip to France as president, Miller and other aides strolled along the banks of the Seine in Paris, enjoying a moment of leisure. Miller's phone rang, and he answered. For several minutes, he shouted at the caller to deport an individual in detention. It struck some officials as bizarre.[15]

In May, he supported deporting the son of a Montagnard hill tribesman veteran who fought alongside the Green Berets in the Vietnam War.[16] Officials had trouble removing him because the Vietnamese government was not providing the necessary travel documents. Chuh A feared he would be tortured at home, where Montagnards are viewed with hostility. Chuh was thirteen when his father brought him to the US. He was being held at an ICE detention facility in Irwin County, Georgia, where he had to speak by videoconference with an immigration judge in Atlanta. He'd been detained after completing a state prison term for a first-time felony conviction of "trafficking" MDMA, a synthetic party drug known as ecstasy. The conviction invalidated his green card. When Vietnam's prime minister came to Washington, Miller raised the issue of their struggle to deport people like Chuh. A few weeks later, the US received Chuh's documents. He was deported.

Miller and Kushner continued to work and travel together extensively. The two did not always agree on immigration. Miller wanted to pick fights with Democrats by targeting sanctuary cities and highlighting wedge issues.[17] Kushner was willing to compromise with Democrats. He could give them protection for the Dreamers in exchange for some restrictions. Miller thought amnesty for young people would encourage more people to come and ruin the US.[18] But he and Kushner worked courteously together even in their disagreements.

On August 2, Trump endorsed a bill that would cut legal immigration in half over the next decade, from about a million to roughly 500,000 green cards a year. Sarah Sanders greeted reporters in the press briefing room and said Miller would be answering their questions about the RAISE ACT, introduced by Republican senators Tom Cotton and David Perdue. "I know you guys will have lots of fun. Take it away, Stephen," she said. Miller grinned happily. He had been working with the senators on the bill, which favored high skills over family ties in determining who obtained green cards. It set up a points-based immigration system that would take into account whether an applicant speaks English, whether they are paid high wages and so on.

CNN's Jim Acosta recited a portion of "The New Colossus," the Emma Lazarus poem on the Statue of Liberty. "Give me your tired, your poor, your huddled masses yearning to breathe free," Acosta said. It was the poem criticized by the white nationalist Peter Brimelow, whose work Miller had encountered at Duke University. Acosta observed that her sonnet doesn't list credentials that migrants must have. "Aren't you trying to change what it means to be an immigrant coming into this country?" Acosta asked.

Miller recited the argument from Brimelow's writings. "I don't want to get off into a whole thing about history here," he intoned, "but the Statue of Liberty is a symbol of liberty and lighting the world. It's a symbol of American liberty lighting the world. The poem that you're referring to, that was added later, is not actually a part of the original Statue of Liberty."

White supremacist Hunter Wallace tweeted: "Stephen Miller just echoed us on the Statue of Liberty."[19] It was the argument of white supremacists who believe the poem is part of a Jewish conspiracy to destroy the United States. White supremacist David Duke, formerly with the Ku Klux Klan, wrote a book detailing an alleged Jewish conspiracy to pollute America with immigrants using the same arguments, "The beautiful jade-colored colossus had no original connection with immigration and predated the Ellis

Island immigration center. It was a gift from France to commemorate the American Revolution, not to honor the arrival of 'wretched refuse.' " Andrew Anglin, founder of the neo-Nazi website the Daily Stormer, wrote of Miller in 2018, "Everything that he does is intended to stop brown people coming in while getting as many as possible out. . . . There is nothing I have seen this Jew do that I disagree with. I don't know what that means."[20] His website has a "Jewish problem" tab and is fiercely anti-Semitic.

Acosta told Miller, "The Statue of Liberty has always been a beacon of hope to the world for people to send their people to this country. And they're not always going to speak English, Stephen. They're not always going to be highly skilled. They're not always going to be somebody who can go to work at Silicon Valley right away."

"Jim, let's talk about this," Miller said, then fired off the statistics he'd stored. "In 1970, when we let in 300,000 people a year, was that violating or not violating the Statue of Liberty law of the land? In the 1990s, when it was half-a-million a year, was it violating or not violating the Statue of Liberty law of the land?" He shouted over Acosta's replies. "Tell me what years meet Jim Acosta's definition of the Statue of Liberty poem law of the land! So you're saying a million a year is the Statue of Liberty number? 900,000 violates it? 800,000 violates it?"

He inhaled deeply and licked his lips, repeating "Jim" as Acosta pressed on. They went back and forth for a while. Miller tried to suggest that Acosta didn't understand how people obtained green cards. Acosta explained that his father was a Cuban immigrant who had obtained a green card and that he was aware of how people obtained green cards. "They do it through a lot of hard work," he said. "And yes, they may learn English as a second language later on in life. But this whole notion of 'well, they have to learn English before they get to the United States,' are we just going to bring in people from Great Britain and Australia?"

"Jim, it's actually—I have to honestly say I am *shocked*," Miller stopped to stare, then continued, "at your statement, that you think, that only people from Great Britain and Australia, would know English! It's actually—it reveals your cosmopolitan, uh, bias to a *shocking degree*."

"Sir, it's not cosmopolitan—"

"No! This is an amazing moment! This is an amazing moment. That you think only people from Great Britain or Australia would speak English is so insulting to millions of hardworking immigrants who do speak English from all over the world."

Miller's assertion that Acosta was elitist, while advocating for a premium on credentialed immigrants, was top-notch gaslighting. And the epithet "cosmopolitan bias" served as a dog whistle for white supremacists who often use the term. The neo-Nazi forum Stormfront.org has a page devoted to "cosmopolitanism," in which contributors share thoughts such as: "The enemy is the global-istic elite who view themselves as cosmopolitans. In their eye we are one world on a happy trip to a one world utopia. They are heavily a thorn in the side of those who would like to see eth-nic nationalism . . . nationalism is the ideal savior of white people." VDARE.com, the website by white nationalist Peter Brimelow, promotes similar ideas. One contributor wrote: "White Americans will have to fall back on their inherited racial and ethnic identities. Only then will the historic American people find the strength to turn the tables on cosmopolitan elites."

Acosta brought up the bill again, saying, "It just sounds like you're trying to engineer the racial and ethnic flow of people into this country through this policy."

"Jim," Miller said. "That is one of the most outrageous, insult-ing, ignorant, and foolish things you've ever said, and for you that's still a really—the notion that you think that this is a racist bill is so wrong and so insulting."

Miller's attacks on the press, like his gaslighting, mirrored Trump's. The duo continually worked to blame journalists for polarization, in the process of producing it. They echoed Hitler's characterization of Jews and journalists. "The struggle between the people and the hatred amongst them," Hitler said in a speech in 1933, "is being nurtured by very specific interested parties. It is a small, rootless international clique . . . It is a people who are at home both nowhere and everywhere. Who do not have a soil on which they have grown up, who live in Berlin today, Brussels tomorrow, Paris the day after, then Prague, Vienna or London. And who feel at home everywhere." A member of the audience cried: "Jews!"

But it was easy to shrug off charges of anti-Semitism. They had plenty of Jews in the administration, including Miller and Kushner. The white supremacists plotting to hurt people in that very moment could be written off as aberrations.

CHAPTER THIRTEEN

"WHITE LIVES MATTER"

MILLER'S FORMER COMPANION AT THE Duke Conservative Union, Richard Spencer, was organizing a Unite the Right rally in Charlottesville, Virginia, with white nationalists, white supremacists, neo-Nazis and militias. Some came to protest the possible removal of a Confederate statue. The first evening, on August 11, 2017, a large group of mostly white men marched with tiki torches. Their faces lit with orange flames, they chanted: "Jews will not replace us!" "You will not replace us!" "White lives matter!" and a Nazi slogan: "Blood and soil!"

The next day, James Alex Fields Jr. idled in his Dodge Challenger, eyeing a crowd of people who had gathered to protest the rally, carrying "Black Lives Matter" signs and chanting against hate. He reversed, eyes on them, then stepped on the gas and rammed into the protesters. Screams filled the air. People rushed to help one another amid the chaos. Heather Heyer, a thirty-two-year-old paralegal, was killed. Jeanne Peterson's leg was shattered. Wednesday Bowie almost bled to death after her pelvis was crushed in six places. Dozens were injured.

Trump was at his golf club in Bedminster, New Jersey, on a "working vacation." He addressed the events in Charlottesville. "We condemn in the strongest possible terms this egregious display of hatred, bigotry and violence on many sides, on many sides," he said. The neo-Nazi Daily Stormer celebrated his remarks. Some were stunned by his refusal to single out the white supremacists. Even a few Republicans admonished him. Colorado senator Cory Gardner tweeted, "Mr. President—we must call evil by its name. These were white supremacists and this was domestic terrorism." Facing criticism, the White House issued a brief statement, adding, "Of course that includes white supremacists, KKK, Neo-Nazis and all extremist groups."

Homeland security experts argue that the administration's rhetoric encourages white terrorism. "Stephen Miller promotes, through his language and through the policies and programs he has convinced the president to support, an anti-immigration agenda that is wholly consistent with the agenda of extremists, in particular white supremacist or white nationalist extremist thought leaders," says John Cohen, a homeland security intelligence and counterterrorism expert who worked under Bush and Obama and has since focused on helping the FBI and law enforcement agencies understand the threat of extremism. He says white supremacist thought leaders mainstream their beliefs by speaking in terms of culture rather than race and skin color. Depicting the foreign-born as criminals, terrorists and job stealers with a different culture serves to inspire hatred in a subset of the American population. The words are amplified by social media, which premiums the incendiary through algorithms. Mentally unwell, violence-prone individuals absorb the negative characterizations and see them as a call to action.

"The words and themes being promoted by the Trump administration and specifically by Stephen Miller are inspiring people to violence the same way the messaging of groups like Al Qaeda, ISIS, or even neo-Nazi groups are," Cohen says. "I'm not saying that's their intention—but as somebody who has spent thirty-four years working in law enforcement and homeland security for both Republicans and Democrats, what concerns me is that while it may not be their intention to inspire acts of violence, it is achieving that result all the same."

More than seventy percent of extremist-related fatalities in the United States between 2008 and 2017 were committed by members of the far-right or white-supremacist groups, according to the Anti-Defamation League's Center on Extremism.[1] And while Trump has singled out brown terrorists with an emphasis on "radical Islamic terror," white terrorism is proving more deadly. The number of white supremacist murders more than doubled in 2017 from the previous year in the US, "far surpassing murders committed by domestic Islamic terrorists."[2] Extremists with right-wing ideologies were tied to at least fifty domestic murders in 2018, more than in any year since 1995, when white terrorists bombed a federal building in Oklahoma City. Across the world, over the past five years, far-right extremist violence more than tripled.

BANNON HAD BEEN INSTRUMENTAL IN shaping Trump's populism and garnering support from the white voters. He left the White House on August 18, having received too much credit for Trump's successes, chattering with the press—helping paint a chaotic picture of the West Wing. Miller had shifted alliances early, showing Trump his loyalty was with him. Writer Olivia Nuzzi wrote of Miller: "[He] easily assumed the role of Cronus, who in Greek mythology is the power-hungry son who castrates his father, Uranus, and tosses his balls into the sea."[3]

Several months later, Miller made an appearance on CNN to attack his old friend. Bannon had told author Michael Wolff that a meeting between Donald Trump Jr. and Russians had been "treasonous."[4] Miller told viewers that Bannon was "out of touch with reality" and "vindictive." He praised Trump's skills as a speechwriter and political leader. Tapper reminded Miller that Bannon had gotten him his job. Miller chuckled softly. His voice cracking, he said, "Cory Lewandowski is the one who, um, offered me the job in the Trump campaign."

"Bannon didn't help you get that job on the campaign?"

Miller looked nervous. "I think the person who probably helped me most get the job on the campaign was probably—Cory," he said, folding his hands and regaining his composure. "But the most important thing to say about this is that the president's first speech that he gave, unfiltered, unscripted, that was Donald Trump . . . A phenomenon was happening that the rest of the political class didn't see. All these so-called political geniuses in Washington—"

Tapper interrupted him. "The only person who's called themselves a genius in the past week is the president," he said.

"Which happens to be a true statement. A self-made billionaire who revolutionized reality TV, and who has changed the course of our politics—"

Tapper was exasperated. They argued. "Stephen, settle down, settle down. Calm down," he said. "I have a question for you about issues . . . is it really the position of the Trump White House that Steve Bannon had nothing to do with the presidency?"

Miller mentioned people being "slaughtered" by migrants. Tapper gave up on the Bannon issue and asked about Trump's letter firing Comey. "The first line of the letter mentions the Russia investigation . . . is that true?"

Miller said, "The final draft of the letter has the same line about the fact that there is a Trump Russia investigation that this has nothing to do with . . . to point out about the f-fact," he swallowed, nervous, and breathed, "that notwithstanding, having been informed that there's no investigation that, the um, that the move that is happening is completely unrelated to that. So in other words it was a *disclaimer.*" Miller again tried to praise Trump as "a self-made billionaire."

"I get it," Tapper said. "There's one viewer that you care about right now and you're being obsequious, you're being a factotum in order to please him. And I think I've wasted enough of my viewers' time. Thank you, Stephen."

Tapper introduced a new story as Miller cried: "Jake! Jake! You know who I care about? You know who I care about?" But the camera was no longer on him.

FAMILIES CONTINUED TO ARRIVE AT the border by the thousands, spurred by rumors that this was their last chance. Miller was tracking their numbers. Apprehensions were a clear metric of how the administration was doing on policy priorities. In June 2017, they were at sixteen thousand. They creeped up to eighteen thousand the next month. In both August and September, more than twenty-two thousand people were apprehended. In October, they swelled to forty-six thousand.

Miller was in a panic. A former DHS senior official recalls an unpleasant period in the fall of 2017 when Miller put intense pressure on the department to "close every opening, shut every door, close every loophole and then some." Hamilton took control of meetings. Acting secretary Elaine Duke just listened. "This is what we're gonna do," Hamilton said. He demanded memos about how to deter the numbers. He mentioned family separations. "I want them very quickly."

The former DHS official says, "Needless to say, we didn't give them ten memos in two days, because bureaucracy can't function that way. We had to go back and say, okay, let's look at what the current law says, what we're trying to accomplish, what the legal mechanisms are, what the policy consequences and impacts will be . . . [Hamilton] got upset, obviously, because Miller was pushing him very hard. He started getting pressure from [Secretary Duke's] chief of staff [Chad Wolf] because the secretary's chief of staff was getting pressure from Miller."

A few weeks later, Wolf sent Hamilton an email.[5] "Hey, please keep this close hold as the components are still reviewing and editing," he wrote, explaining that he had worked on the memos with ICE principal legal advisor Tracy Short and DHS deputy general counsel Dimple Shah. He asked Hamilton not to forward the memos to Miller yet because he wanted more input. Hamilton told him he would be happy to review the memos that night, after posing for family photographs with his children.

The memos called for migrant children to be separated from their parents, either through a zero-tolerance policy—prosecuting anyone who enters the country illegally—or a simple family separation policy. They noted this "would be reported by the media and it would have a substantial deterrent effect." Family separations were skyrocketing for months, with hundreds of children torn from parents' arms, concerning ORR career officials who'd raised alarms. Under Obama, separations had occurred in limited instances— when the parent was deemed a danger to the child. Now the administration planned to formalize systematic separation of children from their parents just so that they could keep the adults detained.

MEANWHILE, MILLER DEMANDED THE TERMINATION of Temporary Protected Status (TPS) for a number of countries. "TPS is everything," he once wrote a Breitbart blogger in the midst of a deadly hurricane in Mexico that he evidently feared would bring Mexicans into the United States.[6] TPS is for foreign-born individuals who can't return home due to conflicts or disasters at home. When Miller's allies tried to remove language about an ongoing crisis of human rights violations in one of the countries' discussion papers, a civil servant pushed back. "It IS bad there," he wrote. Francis Cissna, Miller's ally from Senator Grassley's office who was nominated to lead USCIS, observed in an email, "The memo reads like one person who strongly supports extending TPS for Sudan wrote everything up to the recommendation section, and then someone who opposes extension snuck up behind the first guy, clubbed him over the head, pushed his senseless body out of the way, and finished the memo. Am I missing something?"

The administration canceled TPS for more than 200,000 Salvadorans, 50,000 Haitians, thousands of Nicaraguans and around a thousand Sudanese. The American Civil Liberties Union sued for alleged discrimination and rulemaking violations. The US Circuit Court for the Northern District of California issued an injunction. The ACLU argued the actions were "based on animus against non-white, non-European immigrants in violation of Equal Protection guaranteed by the Constitution." The judge wrote that the cancellation seemed to have been done "to implement and justify a pre-ordained result." The administration relented. It extended TPS.

With nearly every attempt, the courts were blocking Miller and Hamilton's efforts. If the goal was to terrorize migrants, the duo was effective. But they were not deterring migration or deporting nearly as many people as Obama. Michael Anton, the former senior national security official, says the problem was there weren't enough people like Miller in the White House. "If Stephen had more Stephens, more people who believed what he believed seated throughout the government and who had his skill at bureaucratic lever-moving, the president would have been more successful so far at implementing his agenda," Anton says.

Others say Miller's lack of regard for due process was the reason his actions were ineffective at deterring illegal entries or deporting as many criminals as Obama. "The policies and written guidance and executive orders have been excruciatingly poorly written," says Peter Vincent, ICE's principal legal advisor and senior counselor for international policy under Obama.[7] "When everything is a priority . . . nothing is a priority."

ICE deportations under the Obama administration totaled more than 385,000 a year during his first four fiscal years. Under Trump, total ICE deportations plummeted to 226,119 in fiscal year 2017 and about 250,000 in fiscal 2018. Obama's ICE had issued prioritization rules early on to rein in overzealous enforcement because of limited resources as far as officer time, attorney time, bed space and the ability to expeditiously and safely remove people, which involves complex negotiations with foreign countries. Vincent knew how easily a logjam could be created, interrupting meaningful action. "That rigorous, disciplined, legalistic approach toward these written prioritization standards did not make political appointees such as myself, and attorneys, very popular with the rank and file within ICE," says Vincent. "Because many of those individuals are predisposed, almost genetically wired to want to round up every noncitizen, willy-nilly, regardless of their threats to national security."

ICE, an agency of DHS, is made up of Enforcement and Removal Operations (ERO) officers, who focus on rounding up migrants, and Homeland Security Investigations (HSI) agents, who investigate serious criminal activity, such as human trafficking, terrorism, weapons smuggling. Special HIS agents in charge of human and drug trafficking investigations were sidelined for a crackdown on non-criminal migrants. Human-smuggling cases started by HSI dropped nearly sixty percent during the first fiscal year of Trump's presidency.[8]

ICE ERO officers saw Miller as a "demi-god" who "freed them from their shackles," Vincent says. Under Obama, ICE officials proposed moving ERO out of ICE and into DOJ's Bureau of Prisons. Under Trump, with Miller's influence, officers in the ERO division—once mocked by investigators as mere "jailers"—took the reins with Miller's ally Thomas Homan as acting director. "ICE's mission shifted from focusing on the most lethal threats to our homeland . . . to obsessively focusing on women and children who were in the United States without authorization or who had overstayed their legitimately obtained visas," Vincent says.

In the summer of 2018, special agents in charge at HSI wrote a letter asking the DHS secretary to spin their division off from the agency.[9] Their critical investigations were being compromised by their association with ERO. "Many jurisdictions continue to refuse to work with HSI because of a perceived linkage to the politics of civil immigration," they wrote.

Border Patrol, a division of US Customs and Border Protection (CBP), is one of the largest humanitarian aid groups at the border, rescuing migrants in extreme temperatures after they have been abandoned by criminal smugglers. But a secret Border Patrol Facebook group with nearly ten thousand members showed many agents joking about migrant deaths and exchanging racist memes.[10] Agents have been implicated in the killing of migrants, such as Anastasio Hernandez, a Mexican father who was repeatedly tased while he lay on the ground in San Diego, begging for help. In 2018, the ACLU published a report with an overview of CBP child abuse allegations from legal service providers and internal agency records from four years prior, including complaints of a child's head punched three times, a child kicked in the ribs, a boy run over with a patrol vehicle and more.[11] A quarter of the more than one hundred children involved in the allegations reported physical abuse. More than half reported verbal abuse.

The Border Patrol and ICE unions attract some of the most politically extreme individuals in the ranks, according to people familiar with those agencies. "To see the unions, through Stephen Miller, guide the policy decisions and the operational strategy and tactics is truly horrific and extraordinarily dangerous," Vincent says. "When attorneys with DHS and the DOJ are no longer serving as the guardrail or a restraint on the natural proclivities of undisciplined law enforcement officers, that is a very dangerous step."

TRUMP STILL DIDN'T HAVE MONEY for the central element of his campaign: the wall. It was little more than a symbol, buying Border Patrol agents time while cartels developed more creative ways to bypass the barriers—but Trump and Miller, both showmen, understood its importance.

The administration unveiled eight prototypes for his wall in South San Diego County. Silver, peach, beige, gray and blue colors were used on the barriers. Some were solid concrete; others were spaced steel barriers to allow Border Patrol to see through them. The $5 million prototypes generated buzz on Fox News, Business Insider and more. They quoted unnamed officials describing the barriers as "virtually impassable," and "nearly impossible to scale."

But the actual results of testing by tactical teams—obtained through a Freedom of Information Act request—showed that every mock-up was deemed vulnerable to at least one breaching technique.[12] "The [redacted] breaching technique was rescheduled to be [the] last breaching technique on each mock-up, since the technique had the potential to impact the structural integrity of the entire mock-up," the report states. It took testing teams by surprise. Most of the techniques were redacted, but the document reveals that one mock-up was thoroughly breached by a quick saw. The testing teams did not analyze for how well the barriers resisted tunneling; tunnel resistance was one of the requirements in the request for proposals, as tunnels have proliferated wherever walls are built, such as in San Diego, where they have been found with railways, lighting and ventilation dozens of feet under the infrastructure.

The administration was mocked for the ineffectiveness of the prototypes, and Trump continued to lack the wall funding he wanted.

JARED KUSHNER AND IVANKA TRUMP invited Miller for dinner with Democratic senator Dick Durbin and Republican senator Lindsey Graham.[13] They were working on an immigration compromise and hoped to get Miller and his allies on board. The lawmakers were offering $25 billion for a wall in exchange for protections for 1.8 million Dreamers.

Senator Durbin got the president on the phone. Trump sounded enthusiastic. When Durbin and Graham arrived to discuss it in person, however, the Oval Office was packed with anti-immigrant hawks invited by Miller, including Congressman Bob Goodlatte and Senators Tom Cotton and David Perdue. When Graham started talking about the bill, Trump was condescending. The money wasn't enough, he said. When Graham mentioned TPS for places like Haiti, Trump said, "Haitians. We don't need more Haitians . . . Why are we having all these people from shithole countries?"[14] Later, Graham told reporters at the Capitol: "As long as Stephen Miller is in charge of negotiating immigration, we're going nowhere."

Breitbart and other far-right media began attacking the bill. From the perspective of immigration hardliners, Trump's sympathy for the Dreamers was his Achilles' heel. Senator Susan Collins and others tried to cobble together a replacement. Katie Waldman, DHS deputy press secretary, banged out a press release. Waldman, a twenty-six-year-old from Florida, would soon start dating Miller. She was Jewish, and her father was an attorney, like Miller's. She, too, had stirred controversy in college. While studying agricultural economics at the University of Florida, Waldman accompanied a classmate as he threw away newspapers ahead of a student government election. The paper featured an endorsement for a candidate from their opposing party.[15] "I do not question her qualifications, passion or work ethic. I question her ethical and moral fiber," wrote classmate Max Stein in *The Alligator*. Waldman denied wrongdoing. She was elected to chair the student senate's allocations committee.

The press release she helped craft blasted the senators' compromise. "It would be the end of immigration enforcement in America and only serve to draw millions more illegal aliens with no way to remove them," the statement read. "It ignores the lessons of 9/11." Republican senator Lindsey Graham called the statement "poisonous" and "ridiculous."[16] It had done the job, helping to derail negotiations. Lawmakers had reached another impasse.

CHAPTER FOURTEEN

"THESE ARE *ANIMALS*"

ON FEBRUARY 26, THE AMERICAN Civil Liberties Union sued the Trump administration over its practice of separating migrant children from their parents. The separations had been going on for months, but the administration had yet to acknowledge what it was doing. Asked if DHS could confirm or deny its practice of separating families, Waldman responded, "As a matter of policy, we don't comment on pending litigation. Thanks."[1]

The lead plaintiff in the ACLU lawsuit, referred to as Ms. L, was a Congolese mother whose seven-year-old daughter was taken from her by US authorities after she asked for asylum legally at a port of entry near San Diego. "When the officers separated them, Ms. L could hear her daughter in the next room frantically scream-ing," according to court documents.

The family separation lawsuit was approved as a class action. Miller was frustrated. They weren't getting the results he wanted. Smugglers were advertising their services by telling Central Amer-icans that their children were a free ticket into the United States. Tens of thousands of families were arriving each month, despite the practice of separations. Miller led meeting after meeting with DHS to try to come up with a solution, but officials were hitting a brick wall with the Flores Settlement.[2] Congress refused to pass legislation to allow the prolonged detention of families for the duration of their asylum proceedings. Congress refused to fund a wall without protecting lots of Dreamers. Congress refused to do anything Miller wanted.

In the spring of 2018, Miller got tired of waiting for a miracle. He and Hamilton wrote up a presidential memorandum that forced everyone's hands.[3] They sent it to the secretary of homeland security, the secretary of defense, the attorney general, the secretary of HHS and the secretary of state. It called for an end to catch and release once and for all, citing the executive order issued in January 2017 and demanding reports on progress, including on the construction of new facilities to detain large numbers of families together. Attorney General Jeff Sessions also sent a memo to federal prosecutors, directing them to "adopt immediately a zero-tolerance policy for all offenses referred for prosecution under section 1325(a)." The statute governed first-time illegal entry, a misdemeanor that is rarely prosecuted because it takes resources from more serious trafficking and money-laundering investigations. The memo was telling prosecutors to prioritize those offenses. Doing so would entail incarcerating parents and, by necessity, sending their children to HHS.

Another exodus of Central American asylum seekers was traveling toward the US. "We are asking the government and migration authorities to respect the right to seek asylum," said organizer Irineo Mujica, with the pro-immigrant group Pueblo Sin Fronteras.[4] "Those who request asylum shouldn't be criminalized."

On April 23, Trump tweeted, "I have instructed the Secretary of Homeland Security not to let these large Caravans of people into our Country. It is a disgrace. We are the only Country in the

World so naive! WALL." DHS secretary Kirstjen Nielsen, who had been confirmed to replace acting secretary Elaine Duke, issued a statement saying those who sought asylum legally would have their claims "adjudicated efficiently." Nielsen had worked as chief of staff for General John Kelly when he was homeland security secretary. She lacked experience but was seen as obedient. Nielsen said additional resources were being sent to the border for the influx. Behind closed doors, she was getting pressure to sign a policy memo to trigger the roll-out of separations within DHS. She signed.

The exodus began to arrive on April 29, when dozens of Central Americans and their supporters rallied at the fence on the coast in Tijuana.[5] The sky was dark with low-hanging clouds. The Pacific Ocean roiled to the west. A few men climbed onto the fence and sat on it, feeding fantasies of an "invasion." In the afternoon, two hundred families marched together to the port to ask for asylum. They were confronted by Mexican authorities who told them the port had reached capacity. DHS said the port had become full prior to the arrival of the asylum seekers, who were traveling together. Asked how the port had reached capacity prior to their arrival, Miller's girlfriend Waldman said CBP officials are required to balance resources to review the crossings of people with legal status as well as those of asylum seekers.

The port between San Diego and Tijuana is the busiest in the Western Hemisphere. Every day, close to 100,000 people with dual citizenship or visas commute across the border to work, to visit relatives, to take children to school. Commercial trucks transfer millions of dollars in products. The previous year, the port added lanes as part of a $741 million expansion. The capacity issues were confusing. Soon, an inspector general's report would clarify that Customs and Border Protection had started a practice known as "metering," in which officers decide how many asylum seekers they will accept each morning.[6] Central Americans fleeing persecution faced weeks, even months of waiting before they could speak to a US asylum officer.

On May 7, Sessions came to San Diego on a sunny day. The sky was blue and clear of clouds. The attorney general stood at a podium in front of the Pacific Ocean, his silver hair blowing in the breeze. "It is a beautiful day indeed," he said in his slow Alabama drawl. Behind him, the border fence extended into the royal blue water, its closely spaced steel bars marred with barnacles in the waves. "We're here to send a message to the world," he said. He announced a "zero tolerance" policy. Rather than focusing on serious crimes, DHS officials would prosecute everyone—including families—who crossed the border illegally. "If you are smuggling a child," he said, "then we will prosecute you and that child will be separated from you."

Cartel-related violence had reached record levels in Tijuana. The morgue was so full of bodies that the city had started stacking corpses on the bloodstained floor, drawing flies and creating a stench.[7] Many asylum seekers felt unsafe in Mexico. Miller's restrictions had set up obstacles at the port—the legal path—at the same time as they promised to crack down on anyone who crossed illegally.

As Sessions spoke, a local protester named William Johnson finished the one-and-a-half-mile hike down a dirt path to the remote site. He approached Sessions at the podium. "Get out of here!" he cried into a megaphone. "We don't want you in our country! We don't want you in our state!" Sessions pressed on with his remarks. Johnson shouted, "Are you gonna be separating families—*is that why you're here*? Why are you doing this? Do you have a heart? Do you have a soul? Why? Why do you work for this administration? Do you *want* to enforce these policies? Why do you want to do this?" He was herded away, adding, "You're an evil evil evil man!"

Sessions offered to take questions. I asked if asylum seekers would be prosecuted under zero tolerance. The Immigration and Nationality Act states that people have the right to seek asylum in the United States regardless of how they entered the country. He said yes, they would be prosecuted as well. Kate Morrissey of the *San Diego Union-Tribune* said, "You are the third high-ranking official from this administration to come to the Southern California border in the last three weeks. Why was it necessary to be here to talk about this today and how much is that costing taxpayers for all of those trips?" Sessions replied, "Well, the illegal flow of immigrants into the country *is* costing us a good deal—we want to see those numbers go down."

The press conference airbrushed a months-long family separation practice, rebranding it as a law enforcement strategy. But it would backfire. HHS officials had not requested enough additional bed space. CNN, Fox and NBC showed children crying in cramped CBP detention facilities amid backups at the border stations, just as the ORR career official Commander Jonathan White had warned. NBC's Jacob Soboroff told the world that kids were being kept in "cages." Former first lady Laura Bush called the zero-tolerance policy "cruel" and "immoral," comparing new tent cities and converted box stores to the Japanese internment camps.[8]

Illegal border crossings surged. During a conference call that month, Miller blamed the skyrocketing apprehensions on liberal "loopholes."[9] As examples of loopholes, he cited the Trafficking Victims Protection Reauthorization Act (TVPRA), a bill signed into law by a bipartisan Congress in 2008 to protect migrant children from trafficking.

More than twenty-seven hundred children were taken from their parents under the zero-tolerance policy, which was unprecedented. Nearly five hundred parents were deported to Central America without their children. The administration had no plan for reuniting them. No centralized database existed to match separated children in ORR custody with parents in DHS custody, let alone deported parents. ORR had been created for unaccompanied minors—not children separated from parents by US authorities. "The intention was for these children to be irretrievable," says a senior government official with knowledge of the plans.[10] "Not in every case, but in enough cases to frighten people . . . [it was] cruelty for cruelty's sake—for the performance of cruelty."

Kevin McAleenan, who was CBP commissioner at the time, asked the chief of the Border Patrol not to separate children under the age of five from their mothers and fathers. (He would later be derided by Trump as an "Obama guy," as he had supported Obama's campaign.)[11] With kind blue eyes and an austere presence, McAleenan understood the contradictions and complexities of the border better than most people. He had served under the Obama and Bush administrations and believed that the United States had limited options due to federal court decisions; he agreed to a zero-tolerance policy. But he couldn't endorse separations of children that young. McAleenan was married to a woman from El Salvador and had children of his own. About a hundred children under age five were separated anyway.

On May 16, Miller joined Trump at a roundtable in the cabinet room to remind people of the alleged dangers of migrants. Attorney General Jeff Sessions, acting ICE director Thomas Homan, border mayors and sheriffs were present. Trump described California's sanctuary laws as "deadly." Miller turned to Trump and told him, "Everything you're doing every day is saving so many lives all across this country, and it's just an endless honor to be a part of it." Trump said, "Thank you, Stephen. That's great. A great job you do, too."

San Diego County Board supervisor Kristin Gaspar was seated beside Miller. She said a twenty-seven-year-old had been "gunned down by an illegal immigrant who had previously been deported." Miller shook his head in evident dismay. Gaspar said San Diego had become a "great place to commit a crime" because of its proximity to Mexico. In fact, FBI statistics the year before had showed that San Diego was the safest American big city in terms of homicides.[12]

"Mexico does nothing for us," Trump said in disgust. "They do nothing for us."

A sheriff mentioned MS-13. Trump said, "We have people coming into the country, or trying to come in. We're stopping a lot of them. You wouldn't believe how bad these people are. These aren't people, these are *animals*."

The *New York Times*, NPR and other outlets were criticized for reporting that Trump had referred to some migrants as "animals." Senior editor Tyler O'Neil of PJ Media called it "a malicious lie." Although Trump made no mention of MS-13 in his comment, for O'Neil it was obvious that he had been referring to MS-13. In a world dominated by white male storytellers, it was easier to imagine good intentions in Trump than to imagine the consequences of his words for the groups he was demonizing. Storytellers went to work again with the whitewashing.

TRUMP STILL DIDN'T HAVE MONEY for his border wall. Desperate, Miller got to work advocating an immigration reform bill he could stomach. The proposal would give more than a million Dreamers a pathway to citizenship and $25 billion for Trump's wall. But it would also curb family migration and end the diversity visa lottery, which provides fifty thousand green cards to people in countries with low immigration to the US. Miller tried to bring allies on board. He had a meeting with Breitbart staffers. They weren't convinced.[13] The amnesty for Dreamers was too generous. The conversation devolved into angry shouting. Lawmakers rejected the bill in a 121–301 vote. More than a hundred Republicans voted against it, as did all Democrats.

Miller's ally Francis Cissna had been confirmed as director of Citizenship and Immigration Services. The agency soon removed the phrase "a nation of immigrants" from its mission statement, which had existed since 2005. Cissna told asylum officers and senior officials, "I am here to right everything that has been wrong," according to a senior official who left the agency after taking issue with the approach.[14] Cissna created a task force to strip people of citizenship, and announced the agency was closing its overseas offices. USCIS began requiring more in-person interviews for certain applications and increased the reasons for which officers could reject applications. The rejection rate jumped by more than a third during Trump's first year in office. Wait times doubled for immigrants seeking citizenship, and the rate of naturalization reached a record low in 2019.[15] People began to call the changes "Trump's invisible wall."

Miller pushed Cissna to issue a regulation that would make it harder for "public charges" to receive green cards. "Public charges" are migrants likely to be a burden on the government, using services such as public housing assistance and food stamps. The Immigration and Nationality Act (INA) of 1965 already bars public charges from getting green cards. But Miller wanted to make it harder for low-income migrants to gain legal status. It was one of his primary obsessions. He bragged that he had been fighting welfare abuse since he was a teenager.[16]

During a meeting in the White House Situation Room, Miller shouted at officials. "You ought to be working on this regulation all day every day! It should be the first thought you have when you wake up. And it should be the last thought you have before you go to bed. And sometimes you shouldn't go to bed!"[17] Miller got angry about how long it was taking. On June 8, he emailed Cissna, asking, "where are we on regs? Public charge? Asylum? Etc."[18]

Miller sent a separate email to him, cc'ing Office of Management and Budget director Mick Mulvaney and DHS chief of staff Chad Wolf. It read: "Francis—the timeline on public charge is unacceptable. The public charge reg has been in the works for a year and a half. This is time we don't have. I don't care what you need to do to finish it on time. You run an agency of 20,000 people. It's an embarrassment that we've been here for 18 months and USCIS hasn't published a single major reg." While Cissna and Miller shared goals, Cissna approached the task from a government official's perspective. He wasn't going to risk violating the Administrative Procedure Act, which governs the process for new regulations. For Cissna—the son of a Peruvian immigrant—the changes he was implementing were about enforcing the law and decreasing abuse of the immigration system.

Miller grew anxious. He thought the public charge rule would be socially transformative and that all of the administration's previous failures would be offset by its passage; Cissna, one of his staunchest allies, was starting to look like the Deep State. Miller later told his friend Matthew Boyle at Breitbart, "One of the gravest threats that we face today—and I can't emphasize this enough—to our republican form of government is the unelected Deep State." He compared the Deep State to "parasites feeding off the nation, feeding off its wealth, feeding off its vitality."

Miller pushed cabinet officials and the Domestic Policy Council to find a way to empower states to block undocumented children from enrolling in public schools.[19] He wanted to bring the most controversial component of Prop 187, the California measure ruled unconstitutional in his childhood, back from the dead.

HAMILTON HAD MOVED FROM DHS to the Department of Justice (DOJ). On June 11, 2018, Attorney General Sessions ordered US immigration courts to stop granting asylum to victims of domestic and gang violence—the two most common reasons for which Central Americans come. With Hamilton's help, he set up new credible fear-screening standards, which govern when asylum officers can refer cases to an immigration judge for a full hearing. Asylum seekers who are found to have a well-founded fear of persecution due to race, religion, nationality, membership in a particular social group or political opinion are allowed to continue to the next step of the asylum process.

Hamilton sought to remove domestic and gang violence victims from qualifying under the "particular social group" category. Sarah Owings, who argued against Hamilton when he was a trial attorney in Atlanta, recalls that Hamilton was passionate about winning cases against domestic violence victims. "He does not believe that people should be able to get asylum based on domestic violence," Owings says.[20] "He thought that's what the police are there for, not our government . . . He didn't understand or recognize or want to recognize the way domestic violence works in different cultures and how the whole system, the police, the courts, everything works to sort of reinforce that dynamic."

A few months later, a federal judge struck down Sessions's decision. Judge Emmet Sullivan said his heightened credible fear-screening standards were "arbitrary" and "capricious," violating laws created by Congress. He ordered that all victims of domestic and gang violence who had been deported be returned to the United States and given new credible fear screenings.

Photographs of migrant children in overcrowded Customs and Border Protection holding cells known as *hieleras*, freezers, continued to spark outrage. Aura Bogado, an investigative journalist for Reveal, exposed the fact that detained migrant children were being injected with psychotropic drugs and subjected to other abuses by independent contractors for the US, according to court documents. On June 18, ProPublica published nearly eight minutes of heart-breaking audio of migrant children sobbing and asking for their parents inside a Customs and Border Protection facility. Within hours, the audio was on CNN, MSNBC, social media. The Central American kids repeatedly called out "mami" and "papi." A border agent said, facetiously, "Well, we have an orchestra here. What we're missing is a conductor."

While Miller was a top advocate of family separations, the administration knew better than to make him its public face. Secretary Nielsen found herself defending the zero-tolerance policy in the White House briefing room, bombarded with questions. She insisted that the government was separating only "alien children" whose parents broke the law—a false claim, as evidenced by the ACLU lawsuit and countless separations at the ports. "DHS is not separating families legitimately seeking asylum at ports of entry," Nielsen said, a lie or a misunderstanding.

Olivia Nuzzi of *New York* magazine started playing the Pro-Publica recording of the children crying. "How is this not child abuse?" another reporter asked. "Be more specific, please," Nielsen replied. "Enforcing the law?" She insisted that zero tolerance was about law and order, not cruelty or deterrence.

Protestors shamed Nielsen while she ate dinner at a Mexican restaurant on June 20.[21] "How dare you spend your evening here eating dinner when you're complicit?" Nielsen stared at her food, still as a statue as the protesters crowded around her and chanted: "Shame! Shame! Shame!"

White nationalists and other members of the far right took to social media to celebrate the sinister policy. Gavin McInnes, founder of the male chauvinist group Proud Boys, told his viewers, "I wish Trump was separating more families."

Sessions gave a speech in Fort Wayne, Indiana, attributing family separations to the will of God. "I would cite you to the Apostle Paul and his clear and wise command in Romans 13 to obey the laws of government," he said, quoting from the Bible as evangelical and other religious groups publicly condemned the policy. "Because God has ordained the government for his purposes."

Faced with the public outcry, Trump relented on June 20. He signed an executive order stating that the administration's policy was to maintain family unity. "We're going to keep the families together," Trump said. But he deflected blame, framing his remarks so he could later deny he'd ever backed separations: "I didn't like the sight, or the feeling, of families being separated. It's a problem that's gone on for many years as you know, through many administrations, and we're working very hard."

The next year, as election season kicked in, he falsely claimed over and over that Obama was to blame for family separations and that it was he—Trump—who ended them. It was an outrageous but effective lie. Obama's administration limited separations to when child safety was in question or when there was doubt about the familial relationship. Trump had issued executive orders and policy memos that launched the systematic separation of children from their parents to end catch and release, regardless of child welfare. But Trump blamed Obama. And his base believed him. At a re-election rally in Orlando the next summer, dozens of his fans said as much. Wendy de la Cerda, a Nicaraguan immigrant who entered the US legally, wears a red MAGA hat. She stands outside the Amway Center with thousands of people in a line that snakes through caution tape and barricades. "Separating kids started in the last administration," she says, adding that the media unfairly vilifies Trump. A white man named Brandon Craig agrees, "It's been going on since Obama's presidency."

People at the rally are devoted to Trump. Many have been following Miller, too. Patrick Bergy, a veteran, says of the advisor, "One hundred years from now, his work will be studied, just like the great writers of the past." There are no protesters at the rally.

The campaign has prohibited them from entering the outdoor area by the Amway entrance. A chipper female recording repeatedly instructs fans to notify law enforcement of the location of protesters "by holding a rally sign over your head and chanting 'Trump, Trump, Trump.' Encourage others around you to do the same until officers can remove the protestor from the rally."

The Proud Boys, a men's rights group, are in the crowd. Some of them wear tactical gear and carry knives. "I'm a proud Western chauvinist who refuses to apologize for creating the modern world!" cries one, face red, through a loudspeaker. "I am a proud boy!" Some people chant, "Build that wall! Build that wall!"

CHAPTER FIFTEEN

"PANDORA'S BOX"

"WE CANNOT ALLOW ALL OF these people to invade our Country," Trump tweeted in June 2018. Central American families continued to arrive at the US-Mexico border by the thousands, despite the zero-tolerance policy. On June 26, a federal judge in San Diego granted the ACLU's request for a preliminary injunction on family separations in the Ms. L case. Dana Sabraw ruled that all children under age five had to be reunited with their parents within two weeks, and that children between the ages of five and eighteen had to be reunited within a month.

He criticized the administration for implementing separations without any process in place to reunite them. "Money, important documents, and automobiles, to name a few, are routinely catalogued, stored, tracked. . . . The unfortunate reality is that under the present system migrant children are not accounted for with the same efficiency and accuracy as property," Sabraw wrote.

ORR's deputy director Jonathan White was put in charge of reunifying the separated children. Commander White, whose warnings about separations had been repeatedly ignored, went to work cleaning up the mess. He was assigned to lead the reunification efforts under the Office of the Assistant Secretary for Preparedness and Response (ASPR), a division of HHS for emergencies and disasters. He created an interagency plan to find out which children had been separated and to locate the parents—including hundreds that had been deported back to Central America without their children.

Declarations he filed in court reveal that Commander White fought to overcome countless obstacles that Miller and his allies had failed to consider or care about in rolling out the family separation practice. For example, the ACLU had difficulty finding deported parents whose children the US government still had in its custody. HHS and DHS dug up their phone numbers. Commander White wrote: "Many parents are appropriately apprehensive about speaking with strangers about their child who is in the U.S. This is particularly true in the Central American Northern Triangle, where there is extensive fraud and extortion of parents by individuals requesting funds to facilitate the child's travel in the U.S. or the child's continued safety." His solution was to have ORR case managers broker three-way calls with parents and the ACLU. He wrote, "ORR shelter case managers may likely be able, on the basis of their years of specialized experience working with this population, to engage some parents who may be reluctant to speak."

Dozens of HHS personnel scoured each of the agency's case files for roughly twelve thousand in-custody children for clues of separation, such as a child's own assertions. Commander White had each grantee at ORR's shelters provide lists of the children they had reason to believe were separated while also collecting records from DHS. Once the agency had a list of potentially separated children—thousands of them—ORR had to locate their parents and determine if it was safe to reunify them. Some wanted their children to stay in the US out of fear that they would be killed in

Central America. The ASPR reunification management team had fifty people working in the HHS Secretary's Operations Center (SOC), a command center operating twenty-four hours a day while officials evaluated whether reunification was possible and appropriate in every case, and finally, implemented it as quickly and safely as possible. Commander White dispatched about 115 personnel to the field to interview parents, and 140 contractors to help with the physical process of reunifying families.

An HHS official learned Miller had been communicating directly with ORR's director, Scott Lloyd, the anti-abortion activist.[1] The official says Lloyd allowed Miller to impose his agenda on ORR with little regard for child welfare. "He was more interested in making Stephen Miller happy and the idea of making the president happy than he was in looking out for his program," says the official, who adds that he cut off communication between Lloyd and the White House after discovering that Lloyd was communicating directly with Miller and not adequately representing or advocating for ORR program operations.

Lloyd disputes this characterization of his relationship with Miller, saying his decisions were reflective of his own desires and the desires of many in the White House.[2] But as the reunification process kicked into gear, Lloyd got in trouble with HHS secretary Alex Azar for failing to promptly produce a list of potentially separated children under age five. "I thought he was going to fire me there, to be honest, but I'm not the only person I've seen in that situation," Lloyd says, adding that he had misunderstood the assignment. "He can get very testy."

Miller was distraught. He thought family separations were necessary. But the crying children had proved too much for Trump. Miller was heckled in public spaces. Protesters gathered at his City-Center condo complex, calling him an "evil man" and "dangerous."

Miller inserted himself into meetings and conference calls about the reunification effort. He advised officials to err on the side of not putting families back together, especially if there was any evidence of criminality or "gang affiliation." During a call about messaging, one HHS official suggested highlighting the positive care children receive at ORR. Miller pushed back, saying it would encourage more of the young people to come.[3] When officials talked about assuring the public that the United States was no longer separating families, Miller's girlfriend, Waldman, said the agencies should use less definitive language; perhaps they would start separations again with another policy. An HHS official was taken aback and argued that no, from now on, HHS would not accept randomly separated children.

During a later National Security Council phone call, Miller suggested repackaging separations as a "binary choice" policy, in which parents would be presented with two options: stay in detention with your children indefinitely or accept separation. The HHS official reiterated that ORR would not accept more children separated for reasons other than child safety—period. If DHS showed up at ORR facilities with children separated for any other reason, ORR would not accept them. "And if a CNN camera happens to be there, then that's on you," said the official.[4]

On July 10, the Salvadoran father separated from his toddler, Jose Fuentes, was released from the Otay Mesa detention facility and reunited with his son. They had been apart for eight months. Mateo's mother, Olivia Caceres, had crossed the border with their four-year-old son, Andree, a few weeks after Fuentes and the toddler were separated by US authorities. They were released on parole. She fought for months to get Mateo back from the government. "I felt like a stranger trying to adopt my own son," she said. Mateo seemed a different child: easily spooked, easily moved to tears. He did not appear to recognize his father.

Rabbi Neil Comess-Daniels of Beth Shir Shalom, a synagogue

Miller's family attended when he was a boy, gave a sermon denouncing Miller. "From the Jewish perspective, the parent-child relationship is sacrosanct. Disrupting it is cruel. Mr. Miller, the policy you helped to conceive and put into practice is cruel."

During his first year in office, Trump recognized Jerusalem as the capital of Israel—a blow to Palestinians and a favor to Prime Minister Benjamin Netanyahu. Trump ended US financial assistance to Palestine and closed the Palestine Liberation Organization's office in Washington. The moves were criticized by many American Jews. "We watch in horror as Netanyahu, with President Trump's encouragement, leads Israel on a path to estrangement and destruction," wrote Dana Milbank in the *Washington Post*. It's unclear what role Miller played in those decisions. But if his university writings are any indication, he fully backed them.

MILLER'S UNCLE DAVID GLOSSER WAS compelled to action again. He wrote an article for *Politico*, calling out his nephew as a "hypocrite."[5] He wrote, "Let me tell you a story about Stephen Miller and chain migration." He told the story of their ancestors arriving in America a few years before nativists closed US borders to millions of Jewish refugees who were then massacred. "I would encourage Stephen to ask himself if the chanting, torch-bearing Nazis of Charlottesville, whose support his boss seems to court so cavalierly, do not envision a similar fate for him."

He condemned the administration for parading the grieving families of people hurt by migrants, "just as the early Nazis dredged up Jewish criminals to frighten and enrage their political base to justify persecution of all Jews." He reminded readers that nearly all Americans come from immigrants. "Immigration reform is a complex issue that will require compassion and wisdom to bring the nation to a just solution, but the politicians who have based their political and professional identity on ethnic demonization and exclusion cannot be trusted to do so."

He wasn't the only relative appalled. Miller's uncle Bill Glosser was videotaped in Johnstown before he died, describing his nephew as "an asshole" and "a pompous jerk."[6] Patti Glosser, Miriam's cousin, says Miller "needs to be punished for crimes against humanity."[7]

She no longer speaks with Miller's mother, with whom she was once very close. "I can't tell you how painful this is to me," she says. "It just breaks my heart that he has caused this division. We just can't believe this is a person from our family that is doing this. I just don't understand it. I don't understand Miriam and Michael . . . I still love my cousin Miriam. Miriam is very smart. Very bright. But I think somebody's taken over her brain."

She recalls that one time she was sitting with Miriam at her house in Santa Monica, telling her about a conversation she'd had with her children. "And she looked at me and she said, 'you said that to your kids?' And I said, 'well of course I said that to my kids. I can say anything I want to my kids. They don't have to like what I say, I don't tell them what to do, but I can say what I like to my kids' . . . and she said, 'I can't do that with my kids.' That made me realize that maybe there isn't anything she can do, you know, even if she wanted to. I don't think she wants to. Because I think they enjoy all the perks that go along with their son being in the White House, and all the things they get invited to, and the hobnobbing, and for Michael I'm sure that's a big friggin deal."

Patti has friends who are in the country without immigration status, "some of the finest, nicest people." She fears ICE is going to collect them. "When we were kids, we wondered, 'Why didn't people fight back [against Hitler]? How did they convince people to hate like that?' And now I see exactly how they did it. It's lies . . . you're taking people's Aryan side of them, that prejudice which would never come out, and you've opened Pandora's box. You've let it out. And I don't think we're going to slam that box shut very fast. I think it's gonna be very hard to slam shut."

IN OCTOBER 2018, TRUMP WAS still railing against an alleged invasion at the border. He wanted a wall. He still didn't have funding from Congress. Trump tweeted: "I must, in the strongest of terms, ask Mexico to stop this onslaught—and if unable to do so I will call up the U.S. Military and CLOSE OUR SOUTHERN BORDER!" He deployed thousands of troops to the border.

Defense secretary Jim Mattis told the president that the troops could only play a support role to DHS, helping build tent cities and fortifying the fence with barbed wire. They could not detain migrants. According to *New York Times* reporters Michael D. Shear and Julie Hirschfeld Davis, Trump wondered aloud about shooting them in the legs.[8]

Miller and his allies believed in the power of messaging. But that month, when a white terrorist stormed the Tree of Life synagogue in Pittsburgh echoing their language about an invasion, the administration denied a role. The shooter wrote on social media that HIAS, which Miller was targeting alongside other refugee resettlement organizations, "likes to bring invaders in that kill our people. I can't sit by and watch my people get slaughtered. Screw your optics, I'm going in." He killed eleven people. Two days later, Trump parroted the terrorist's language, suggesting that the US would use force against the migrants: "This is an invasion of our Country and our Military is waiting for you!" he tweeted.

A fanatical fifty-six-year-old Trump fan, Cesar Sayoc, mailed sixteen explosive devices to top Democratic politicians and media figures, including Obama, Hillary Clinton and the billionaire liberal philanthropist George Soros. None exploded. Sayoc lived in a van decorated with Trump stickers and decals showing Trump's critics with red targets over their faces. On social media, he shared conspiracies about the Clinton Foundation and illegal immigration. Trump was "everything he wanted to be," according to court documents. He was "self-made, successful, and a 'playboy.' " He pleaded guilty to mailing the explosive devices.

Republicans lost control of the House to Democrats. The midterm elections ushered in one of the most diverse groups of politicians in history, including a very popular young congresswoman, Alexandria Ocasio-Cortez of New York. Miller was nervous again. "We need points on the board!" he demanded in interagency meetings he chaired.[9] He urged Cissna and his team to finish the public charge rule, berating his old ally for his slow pace. He wanted to know why more than ninety percent of families seeking asylum were passing their credible fear interviews. Miller believed the interviews were being conducted by bleeding hearts. He urged them to "tighten up."[10] Someone countered that the laws for credible fear were written by Congress. Miller insisted that the officers were doing a terrible job. "Enough. Enough. Stand down!" Cissna said.

Miller was tired of everybody making excuses. "People are dying!" he reminded people in meetings. There was a level of urgency he felt that he demanded of others. He began to plot a purge of officials. Rumors circulated that he was considering getting rid of Cissna, arguably the most effective vessel for his agenda. Sessions resigned as attorney general at Trump's request. ORR's Scott Lloyd was transferred out of his leadership position to a post at the HHS Center for Faith and Opportunity Initiatives. A court had blocked Lloyd's practice of interfering with migrant girls' abortion requests, as well as other moves targeting teenagers.

Meanwhile, one of the largest exoduses of Central Americans was en route to the United States, starting with just over a hundred people and swelling to around five thousand. They had self-organized this time, spurred by word of mouth and false rumors of an open border. Separately, smugglers were telling families that upon entry, they would be given *permisos,* or permission slips to stay in the country indefinitely. (In fact, they would be given notices to appear in immigration court.) Trump threatened to close the border, despite aides telling him—again—that it would be extremely painful economically due to a number of cross-border supply chains in aerospace, medical devices, agriculture and more. He promised to revoke aid to Central America and tear up renegotiations of the North American Free Trade Agreement if Mexican and Central American authorities didn't stop the group. "The assault on our country at our Southern Border, including the Criminal elements and DRUGS pouring in, is far more important to me," Trump tweeted.

At the border with Guatemala, Mexican federal police blocked the exodus at a bridge over the Rio Suchiate. Pueblo Sin Fronteras sent volunteers to save anyone who might jump or fall into the river. They foresaw that some would risk their lives to get around the blockade. Many jumped and were rescued on rafts. Federal police deployed tear gas and rubber bullets. One young Honduran man, twenty-six-year-old Henry Díaz, was shot in the head and died.[11]

When they arrived in Tijuana, hundreds of people from Central America slept on the beach in an affluent coastal neighborhood adjacent to the border. They cradled their children, frightened in this foreign place, confused about what was happening in the United States. The asylum seekers were met with hostility by groups of locals. Some Mexicans wore red baseball camps that said "Make Tijuana Great Again." They threw stones and hurled racial epithets at them.[12]

The asylum seekers improvised waiting lists in tattered notebooks, in response to metering at the ports. Long lines of families formed every morning on the Mexican side of the San Ysidro Port of Entry, waiting to add their names. They took turns reading off of it. The number of names was selected each day by US officials, who told Mexican officials, who told the asylum seekers.

Mexican authorities opened a sports complex to house Central Americans in tents near the city's red light district. Tijuana's migrant shelters were overwhelmed. Two teenage boys waiting to ask for asylum were strangled and killed during an apparent robbery. Left-wing activists from across the US traveled to Tijuana. They visited the camp and encouraged the Central Americans to storm the border, passing out flyers that read in Spanish: "Open the border or we'll shut it down! All of us must be allowed to enter!"[13]

The handouts informed migrants of their right to seek asylum regardless of whether they entered the US through a port or by jumping the fence. They were written in the first-person plural, as if by the Central Americans themselves, but were in fact a product of By Any Means Necessary, a US-based left-wing group. "Getting across the border by any means necessary is absolutely the right thing to do," said the group's national chair, Shanta Driver.[14] "We urge and encourage people to take mass action."

Attorney Erika Pinheiro said the strategy fed Trump's invasion narrative. "That is not solidarity," she said. "That's exploitation. They're exploiting migrants to make a political point."

On November 25, hundreds of Central Americans marched to the border. They marched for different reasons. Some were trying to raise awareness about their plight. Others were looking for an opening. US and Mexican authorities shut down the San Ysidro Port of Entry in both directions. Binational residents found themselves stuck on either side. Millions of dollars in daily commercial exchange screeched to a halt. As the marching asylum seekers approached the fence, Border Patrol fired tear gas. Some men threw stones. Maria Meza, from Honduras, was photographed running from the chemical plumes with her two daughters trailing behind her.

Back at the camp, false rumors spread. The specter of a child who allegedly died during the incident—a death that did not occur—haunted the crowds. They passed around spent tear gas canisters, marveling at the show of force by a country they had thought was a safe haven. Dozens headed back to Central America. A Honduran woman named Maria del Carmen Mejía said, "Instead of letting the president kill my kids, better to have them die in hunger in Honduras."[15]

The power of stories was evident in the push and pull of the exodus. Deterrence worked. But it came at a great cost. Lives were lost. Children were traumatized. Many of the asylum seekers from Central America had heard the US was receiving people with open arms. Others knew it would be difficult and were determined to wait. Maria Edwina Perez, cradling her three-year-old son, feared an unruly minority would give all asylum seekers a bad name. "If [Trump] doesn't want the men to enter, he should let the women enter," she said.[16] After a day of heavy rains, the camp in the sports facility flooded. People's clothes and blankets floated in the muddy water that rose in and around people's tents. The families were forced out. Tijuana opened up an abandoned concert hall on the outskirts of the city—far from the border, where the improvised asylum waiting list was read every morning.

Karen Perez, a thirty-two-year-old Nicaraguan who traveled with the exodus and her four children, was at the new camp after the clash. After putting her name in the notebook, she was told someone would send her a text message when it was her turn to cross. She put her faith in the process. In her tent, she kept her chin up as she wiped tears from her face. Perez was afraid. She was being harassed by strange men, but she did not want to leave the camp because of the violence outside. "Sometimes I get hopeless, thinking I'll say yes to the people telling me to jump [the fence]—but no. What am I, crazy?" she said. "I'm not crazy. I'm going to wait."[17]

The following month, a Guatemalan man named Nery Caal crossed through the desert with his seven-year-old daughter, Jakelin. They belonged to the indigenous Maya Q'eqchi' group in Raxruha, where deforestation for palm-oil plantations has pushed farmers like him off their land. The oil extracted from palm fruit is used in ice cream, lipstick and detergents, sold to US-headquartered multinational corporations. The father and daughter turned themselves in to Border Patrol. Jakelin developed a fever. She began vomiting and having seizures. Border Patrol agents tried to save her as she was flown to a hospital in El Paso. She died.

MILLER APPEARED ON CBS'S *FACE the Nation* to discuss Jakelin's death. Host Margaret Brennan asked him who bore responsibility. "The loss of that precious life is horrifying," Miller said, licking his lips. Then he leaned forward and stuck out a hand. "Smuggling organizations profit off of death and misery! They are vicious, vile organizations!" Brennan interrupted, "Border Patrol, though, says it wasn't adequately equipped to deal with the record number of families coming across. Why aren't they?" Miller blamed "left-wing activist judicial rulings."

Nielsen was in diplomatic talks with Guatemala's interior minister Enrique Degenhart about how to address the influx of families. But Trump was still obsessed with his wall. In addition to the obstacle of the Flores Settlement, the administration faced another challenge: shaky international relations. Trump's rhetoric made it difficult to negotiate with leaders abroad who might otherwise want to help the US by beefing up their own border security measures.

Trump met with Nancy Pelosi and Chuck Schumer in the Oval Office and said he would be "proud" to shut down the government for wall funding. Congress refused to give the president the much lower figure of $5 billion he was now demanding. Trump refused to sign their spending bill. The government went into a partial shut-down. Again and again, he demanded funding. The Democrats did not budge. Democrats had supported border barriers for decades, but now they were fiercely against them. The wall had become synonymous with Trump, and thus, it was politically radioactive. Politics had become more than ever a sinister game with lives in play.

On New Year's Day, a group of about 150 mostly Central American asylum seekers approached the fence, hoping to climb over and turn themselves in to Border Patrol, bypassing the long lines. They were accompanied by left-wing activists who had brought milk of magnesia in case tear gas was fired. As the crowd quietly lifted children over the fence, the agents deployed tear gas, smoke and pepper spray. Waldman, Miller's girlfriend, called them "a violent mob." [18]

The shutdown continued. It became the longest in American history. Michael Steele, the former Republican National Committee chairman, said Trump was putting the working class "through hell for nothing," as the wall had no validity on Capitol Hill. Trump relented as criticism mounted. The shutdown ended on January 25, after thirty-four full days. Trump gave Congress until February 15 to come up with a border wall funding solution.

Miller took the lead crafting Trump's State of the Union speech, invoking Gerald and Sharon David, burglarized and fatally shot in Reno, Nevada, by a person who was in the country without legal permission. [19] On February 15, Trump declared a national emergency for wall funding. It was an act of desperation, as Congress had not budged in the allotted time. The administration began to dismantle billions of dollars in military construction projects for his wall.

THE ADMINISTRATION LAUNCHED A PROGRAM deceptively called Migrant Protection Protocols. More accurately called the Stay in Mexico program, it meant asylum seekers who passed credible fear interviews in the US were sent back to Mexico to await their hearings. It was something Miller had been dreaming about since he had come across lines in the Immigration and Nationality Act (INA) that caught his eye. Section 235(b)(2)(C) said, "In the case of an alien described in subparagraph (A) who is arriving on land (whether or not at a designated port of arrival) from a foreign territory contiguous to the United States, the Attorney General may return the alien to that territory pending a proceeding." The subparagraph (A) referred to "an alien who is an applicant for admission."

Miller saw it as a tool—the US could turn Central American families away by sending them back to Mexico. In January 2017, Miller had laid the groundwork for Stay in Mexico in one of his first executive orders. Released a few days before the so-called Muslim ban that distracted the world, it had read, "Return to Territory. The Secretary shall take appropriate action, consistent with the requirements of section 1232 of title 8, United States Code, to ensure that aliens described in section 235(b)(2)(C) of the INA (8 U.S.C. 1225(b)(2)(C)) are returned to the territory from which they came pending a formal removal proceeding."

Finally, following years of planning, Trump launched the Stay in Mexico program in early 2019. The American Civil Liberties Union sued. Migrant advocates argued asylum seekers were not safe in Mexico, and that section 235(b)(2)(C) did not apply to asylum seekers. They said the program violated international law and the 1951 United Nations Convention on Refugees "nonrefoulement" principle, which prohibits countries—including the US—from returning refugees to a place where they have a credible fear of persecution based on race, religion, nationality, membership in a social group or political opinion.

The judge granted a preliminary injunction, but an appeals court allowed the program to resume. Tens of thousands of asylum seekers were sent back to Mexico. In June 2019, the union for asylum officers in DHS's Citizenship and Immigration Services filed an amicus brief supporting the ACLU lawsuit. Asylum officers such as Doug Stephens resigned in protest.[20] "I was asked to do work that I believed to be illegal and immoral," he said. "Ultimately I had to voice my dissent and quit." The program thwarted the ability of US lawyers to provide representation to asylum seekers. Some Customs and Border Protection officers were writing *domicilio conocido,* or "known address," on asylum seekers' paperwork instead of legally required addresses, precluding their ability to be informed of changes to their court dates.[21] If they missed a hearing, many had their asylum cases closed in absentia.

Vilma Mendoza, a twenty-year-old Guatemalan woman who entered the United States on July 4 seeking asylum, was one of those returned under the policy.[22] Desperate, she tried to sneak back across by entering an irrigation canal in El Paso. She drowned.

CHAPTER SIXTEEN

"OUT OF LOVE"

MILLER PUSHED TO END BIRTHRIGHT citizenship, which he called "frankly ridiculous."[1] At the G-7 Summit in France, Miller chuckled at a reporter's mention that it was enshrined in the Fourteenth Amendment. "Many constitutional scholars would wholeheartedly disagree with that. Most Americans think it is crazy," he said, referring to those who refer to the US-born children of migrants pejoratively as "anchor babies." He continued to fight for renewed separations of migrant children from parents under the "binary choice" policy. John Feeley, former US ambassador to Panama who resigned because he felt Trump's policies "warped and betrayed" American values, compared Miller's proposal to "Sophie's Choice."[2] The phrase came from the 1979 William Styron novel in which a woman must decide which of her two children to send to a Nazi death camp and which to send to a forced labor camp.

Contrary to popular perception, however, family separations had never stopped. In September 2018, public records in San Diego County showed that dozens of asylum seekers had been separated at ports of entry since the injunction against separations was filed in federal court.³ In 2019, the ACLU reported that more than nine hundred families, including babies, had been separated since then. The injunction was not being enforced. Parents were having their children taken away for reasons as minor as a dirty diaper.⁴ One father was separated from his four-year-old son because he could not clearly answer agents' questions, due to a speech impediment.

Federal judge Dana Sabraw expanded the Ms. L case to include potentially thousands more parents and children. In a court filing, the government admitted that finding all of them may not be "within the realm of the possible." And DHS officers were still taking children from parents at the border. ORR's Commander White repeatedly told Congress that if lawmakers wanted family separations to stop, they needed to act. "There is nothing in law which either precludes arbitrary separation or defines the terms for separations," he said, slowly and clearly during a House subcommittee hearing in February 2019.⁵ He repeated: "There is no specification in law from you all in Congress about the permissible grounds for separating a child from a parent. And I would submit that if you want to see that, that's on y'all."

As of the writing of this book, there has been no legislation passed in Congress to clarify when it is permissible for DHS to separate families. California senator Dianne Feinstein introduced a bill—Keep Families Together Act—ordering that children be separated only if they are being trafficked, abused, or if there is strong evidence that there is no familial relationship. But Republicans haven't signed on. An April 2019 memo for Customs and Border Protection agents showed officials can continue to separate families at ports for a number of reasons, including "At the Request of ICE/ERO."⁶ The agency that has been led by Miller's Enforcement and Removal Operations allies is allowed to tell officers at ports of entry to separate asylum seekers who have broken no laws whatsoever.

At the end of March, DHS secretary Nielsen traveled to Europe for a weeklong trip to meet with leaders on counterterrorism and election security. Miller was not happy. Apprehensions had reached their highest levels in more than a decade, from tens of thousands a month to more than a hundred thousand a month. After a day in Britain, Nielsen promptly returned to the US.[7] Trump was again threatening to close the border, panicking binational commercial suppliers. He blamed Democrats for the surge in illegal crossings. In Calexico, a two-mile stretch of fencing had been replaced by his administration. He traveled there and stood in front of the slatted thirty-foot-high fence, praising it with Nielsen at his side as his photos were taken.

Nielsen's job as secretary of DHS was to protect homeland security on all fronts. DHS consists of twenty-two agencies, including the Federal Emergency Management Agency (FEMA), the Secret Service and the Coast Guard. Miller, with his single-minded focus on immigration, was pushing for her to funnel all of her attention on the US-Mexico border. "Under President Trump, the Department of Homeland Security has become the Department of Border Enforcement," says David Lapan, a former DHS official in the Trump administration and retired Marine colonel.[8]

DHS is supposed to help with disaster recovery and protect America against cyberattacks, terrorism and trafficking through airports and ports of entry. Juliette Kayyem, assistant secretary for intergovernmental affairs at DHS under the Obama administration, says Miller's laser focus on the border explains why the US is still vulnerable to election interference and why the US response to Hurricane Maria in Puerto Rico—killing more than three thousand people—was so weak.[9] "He turned the department into an immigration tool," she says.

John Cohen, a homeland security intelligence and counterterrorism expert who worked under Bush and Obama, says Trump has "every right" to be frustrated about the situation at the border. "But his frustration shouldn't be focused on Democrats or the Justice Department—it should be focused on Stephen Miller," Cohen said.

Miller convinced Trump that the record-high apprehensions were the fault of feeble leaders at DHS. He orchestrated an unprecedented purge of the department. Nielsen resigned as DHS secretary. Cissna, at the helm of US Citizenship and Immigration Services, was sacked. Ron Vitiello, a top CBP official selected to lead ICE, had his nomination pulled. Kevin McAleenan, the CBP commissioner who had asked his officers not to separate children younger than five, was named acting DHS secretary in Nielsen's place; he was seen as an "Obama guy," but his knowledge of border enforcement was undeniable; perhaps he'd get some results, which they desperately needed. Ken Cuccinelli, Virginia's attorney general, was named acting director of USCIS where Cissna had been. The USCIS union leader Danielle Spooner said Cuccinelli's leadership role at the agency "spells the end of legal immigration as it currently exists."[10]

Immigration hardliners were becoming upset with Miller, too. Miller had gotten rid of Cissna, who had done much to restrict legal immigration. The far right media personality Ann Coulter, who had once gushed about Miller, became convinced the senior advisor was more interested in maintaining singular control over immigration than in actually solving the problem. She wondered why he wasn't hiring other "immigration patriots," saying, "He wants to be the only one, he wants the full credit. And he wants Trump to *only* check with him."[11]

Trump announced that he was cutting hundreds of millions of dollars in aid to El Salvador, Guatemala and Honduras. While many in the White House had warned him against this—saying it would worsen conditions in those countries and fuel another exodus— Miller encouraged Trump's tougher instincts. On April 17, the chairman of the House Oversight Committee asked Miller to testify "because it appears that you are one of the primary moving forces behind some of the most significant—and in my view, troubling— immigration policies coming out of the Trump White House." The White House refused to make him available.[12]

THAT MONTH, A WHITE TERRORIST opened fire at a synagogue in Poway, California, with a semi-automatic rifle. He killed one woman and injured three others before his weapon malfunctioned. A nine-page manifesto that authorities believe belongs to him claims he was inspired by the Tree of Life synagogue shooter and that he wanted to exterminate Jews before they could "doom" the white race. Trump said: "We forcefully condemn the evil of anti-Semitism and hate."

Trump promised to get to the bottom of where all the hate was coming from, then proceeded to hatemonger about Democrats plotting to steal people's guns, and falsely accused them of supporting the execution of babies during late-term abortions. "The baby is born, the mother meets with the doctor. They take care of the baby. They wrap the baby beautifully," Trump said, gesturing as if he were cradling an infant. "Then the doctor and mother determine whether or not they will execute the baby."

Trump escalated his war of words against Mexico, threatening tariffs if the country didn't stop Central Americans at its own southern border. Oscar Alberto Martinez Ramirez, Tania Vanessa Avalos and their nearly two-year-old daughter, Valeria, arrived at the border city of Matamoros from El Salvador in June, oblivious to all this. They walked along the banks of the Rio Grande. Oscar waded into the water with Valeria straddling his back, tucked under his black shirt. He told her to hold on tight. Tania, Valeria's mother, watched as they swam. Oscar approached the northern bank. Dropping his daughter on the shore, he swam back for his wife. Seeing her father leave, Valeria dropped back into the river. As he rushed to save her, the roiling river pulled them away. Their bodies were found the next morning. A photograph showed them facedown in the green water by some reeds, Valeria's small body still tucked inside her father's T-shirt, her arm draped over his neck.

Politicians pointed fingers at one another. America's Voice and Voto Latino launched a campaign to get Miller fired. They circulated a statement. "Unfortunately, decrying Miller's racist viewpoints in the media will only ingratiate him to his boss," they said. "The most effective, proven way to turn Donald Trump against Miller is to amplify the message that Miller is the one in charge of immigration . . . Trump is ruled by his ego, and his actions are meant to protect his ego and shore up his status as the most important person in the world . . . We believe that by uniting around the message that Stephen Miller is setting immigration policy, we can raise Miller's visibility and make Trump insecure enough that he fires Miller or benches him."

Miller's long-awaited public charge rule went through, making it easier for the United States to deny green cards to immigrants who use public assistance. The regulation did not penalize people for seeking benefits on behalf of a family member, such as American children. Still, families began to dis-enroll their children from a range of public benefits out of fear that they'd be penalized. Most immigrants who use public benefits do so for their US-citizen children. The headline in Breitbart was breathless: "Trump Ending Welfare-Dependent Immigration, Saving Taxpayers Billions." Federal judges issued nationwide preliminary injunctions against it.

Miller kept pushing for a termination of the Flores Settlement, which limits how long migrant children can be detained. Conditions in detention were worsening amid the backlog. Migrants were denied soap and toothbrushes amid lice and flu outbreaks. In a case appealing a 2017 ruling that the administration had violated the Flores Settlement by failing to provide children access to basic toiletries and sleeping conditions, an attorney for the administration argued that migrant children don't need soap. Meanwhile, DHS published new regulations gutting the settlement and forging a path toward months-long or even years-long detention.

McAleenan tried a different approach. He hoped to stop the influx of families through diplomacy. A former DHS official says of McAleenan, "[He's] different from these other characters . . . He understands the long-term solution is resolving the push factors." (Push factors are the conditions of poverty and violence in Central America that push families north.)

McAleenan knew that aid—which Trump had cut off—was a part of resolving the push factors. But neither Miller nor Trump was a fan of sending money to Central America. Perhaps, by delivering results on apprehensions, McAleenan could convince them to reinstate the aid.

Early on in his post as acting secretary, he clashed with Miller. In May, Miller asked Trump to install Mark Morgan to head CBP. Morgan was a gray-haired Fox News personality who had been courting Trump's approval by bashing migrants on TV. He had a few months of Border Patrol experience and was already under consideration to lead ICE. Like Miller, Morgan was obsessed with MS-13. He once led an FBI "Hispanic gang task force" in Los Angeles that focused on MS-13. "When the president referred to them as animals, I absolutely said, that is correct," Morgan said. He claimed he could tell who would become a gang member just by looking the teenager in the eyes.[13]

McAleenan threatened to resign if Morgan was put at the helm of CBP. Miller hesitated.[14] In early May, Morgan was named head of ICE. He pushed for a mass roundup of migrant families in the US. On June 17, Trump tweeted, "Next week ICE will begin the process of removing the millions of illegal aliens who have illicitly found their way into the United States."

McAleenan pushed back. He said it would derail negotiations with Democrats on a $4.6 billion emergency aid package for the border, ruining their chances of stemming the influx. The roundup was canceled, and the aid package went through. Suddenly, conservative media began attacking McAleenan, quoting anonymous officials saying the operation had been called off because McAleenan had leaked news of it to the press to "sabotage" it, endangering the lives of ICE officers.[15] (Trump had tweeted about the operation before it was reported.) Brandon Judd, the Border Patrol union head, repeated the false claims, saying McAleenan "put the public at risk" and that he was "anti-Trump."[16] Miller convinced Trump to put Morgan at the head of CBP after all, against McAleenan's wishes. But McAleenan did not resign. He was in the middle of important negotiations with Central American officials.

In July, Miller sat with McAleenan at a long conference table in the Eisenhower Executive Office Building. They were meeting with Guatemalan leaders in an official capacity, but Miller dressed colorfully, with a bright navy blue suit and a banana-yellow tie covered in blue polka dots.[17] Miller leaned forward, listening intently as McAleenan spoke with Guatemala's interior minister Enrique Degenhart. McAleenan and Degenhart were discussing an asylum cooperation agreement. Mexico had significantly ramped up border enforcement operations along its southern border and agreed to accept asylum seekers returned under the Stay in Mexico policy. But the Trump administration wanted Central America's cooperation as well.

Despite intense opposition at home, Guatemala's president Jimmy Morales, a former comedian facing corruption charges, agreed to cooperate under threat of sanctions. Guatemala, with the world's sixth-highest rate of chronic malnutrition but a recent drop in homicides, would be recognized as a safe third country for asylum seekers. Degenhart and McAleenan ironed out the details as Miller sat with them.

In the coming weeks, DHS signed similar asylum cooperation agreements with Honduras and El Salvador. The accords gave the US authority to turn away people from the most unsafe countries in the region, as well as to ship them back to Central America. About seventy-five percent of people who arrive at the US border seeking asylum are from those countries.[18] None has a fully functioning asylum system.

Miller had another idea: denying asylum to anyone who passes through a third country en route to the US—in other words, nearly everyone from Central America. In July, the Department of Justice and the Department of Homeland Security issued a rule making those people ineligible. In combination with the asylum cooperation agreements, it effectively ended asylum at the US-Mexico border for Central Americans.[19]

ON JULY 21, MILLER PUT on the same colorful outfit he wore earlier in the month while meeting with Guatemalan officials and McAleenan. He planned to go on Fox News and defend his boss. Trump was in trouble again. He had urged four minority congresswomen known as the Squad to "go back" to their countries, echoing teenage Miller. He targeted Alexandria Ocasio-Cortez of New York, Ilhan Omar of Minnesota, Rashida Tlaib of Michigan and Ayanna S. Pressley of Massachusetts. Only Omar, an American refugee from Somalia, was born outside of the US. "Why don't they go back and help fix the totally broken and crime infested places from which they came," Trump had tweeted. The comment was widely denounced as racist.

Miller was thinking about MS-13 again. Twenty-two members had recently been indicted in Los Angeles for a string of grisly murders, including carving out a rival's heart. With names like Desastre, Delito, Conejo and Chaos, they had captured his imagination. He sat down with Fox News host Chris Wallace. The network played clips of Trump targeting Muslims, Mexicans and Barack Obama. "That's not protecting the American people—that is playing the race card," Wallace said. "I couldn't disagree more," Miller said, spreading his hands and keeping his voice casual, "I mean, let's take for example the issue of the recent indictment that we saw of twenty-two MS-13 gang members in California."

Wallace was ready. "We're not talking about hardened criminals," he said, interrupting him. But the distraction was enough. Miller had reminded the American public about MS-13 once more. Wallace pressed Miller about Trump's comments, noting that Miller had helped craft some of them. Miller deflected, saying the congresswomen had been critical of the US and deserved to be criticized. Wallace noted, "Mr. Trump has been as critical of this country as anything the squad has ever said."

Miller said the congresswomen's criticism came from a place of hate, while Trump's criticism was made "out of love." He said Trump wanted to preserve "Western civilization," whereas Ocasio-Cortez wanted to turn the US into Venezuela. (Ocasio-Cortez has never said she wants to turn the US into Venezuela.)

The next month, Israeli prime minister Netanyahu blocked two of the congresswomen—Omar and Tlaib—from carrying out a planned trip to Israel, under intense pressure from Trump. The decision stunned onlookers across the world. Trump had convinced a foreign government to take action against two American citizens whose only crime was disagreeing with him.

MEANWHILE, MILLER'S OLD FRIEND BANNON was planning a spectacle. At the end of July, he held a symposium at a half-mile stretch of privately funded border fencing near El Paso. Far-right leaders and social media influencers traveled there to pose in front of the barriers while hate-mongering about an alleged invasion of "illegal aliens" who were a "fiscal drain" on the US. The event was live-streamed against a carefully designed backdrop: a green war truck with a US flag was parked beside the brown steel of the wall. "Quiet on the set!" Bannon repeatedly cried.

Kris Kobach, the former Kansas secretary of state and Miller ally, told tens of thousands of viewers across the US and dozens of people in attendance that it was important for them to act against the alleged invaders. "The battle of Fort McHenry, which our 'Star-Spangled Banner' is about—was that won only by George Washington's professional soldiers? No. It was the private citizens, the farmers of Maryland who held the line against the British," he said.

Kobach asked the audience if they were offended by the term "illegal alien." They laughed and shouted "No!" Border Patrol and ICE union leaders Brandon Judd and Chris Crane were at the wall event. Crane was unhappy. Despite helping Miller with the ICE union endorsement, Miller had let him down. Crane had wanted every ICE officer to be able to carry a Taser in the field while arresting migrants in their neighborhoods. "The issuance of Tasers to ICE Officers was a matter that I raised directly with Stephen Bannon and Stephen Miller. Now that ICE has finally created a Taser policy, it unfortunately gives each Program Office the ability to deny their ICE Officers Taser equipment," he wrote in a public letter to Trump. Crane said he had tried in vain to communicate with Trump repeatedly. "ICE managers laugh and claim that 'Trump used you and threw you away like trash when he was done with you.' "[20]

Brandon Judd, the BP union chief, was in a better mood. A Latin-American woman did his makeup by the stage. Sure, Miller hadn't been able to get *everything* they wanted done. But he had done his best, and the administration was on the right track in his view. Judd admires Miller's strong personality, his ability to give and take. He says, "If anybody wants to say that he's not an Alpha personality, they're wrong. He absolutely has an Alpha personality."[21]

Bannon offered to drive me back to my hotel. As we rode together, he brought up Miller's recent appearance on Fox News, referring to him affectionately as an "evil robot."

Bannon's right-wing influencers cleared out of El Paso. A few days later, a twenty-one-year-old white terrorist drove ten hours from Allen, Texas, to the border town. A hate-filled manifesto conjuring a "Hispanic invasion of Texas" went up on 8chan; authorities believed it belonged to Patrick Crusius. It invoked a "cultural and ethnic replacement." It read, "America is rotting from the inside out." In 2014, Trump had said in an interview Miller liked and shared, "Our whole country is rotting."[22] Like Tanton, the hate manifesto's author expressed environmental concerns. He blamed US corporations for "shamelessly overharvesting resources" with the help of foreign workers. But, he wrote, he couldn't bring himself to kill his "fellow Americans." Instead, he'd target the ones whose interior lives he found it difficult to imagine—the ones he believed were taking American jobs and American welfare.

The author correctly pointed out that his philosophy predated Trump's rise. "White Americans must start to take the offensive," said the Santa Monica High School hate letter read in 1991. "We must come to the defense of our heritage," Miller wrote in 2005.[23] "This is just the beginning of the fight for America and Europe," Crusius allegedly wrote in 2019, and strode into an El Paso Walmart crowded with Mexican Americans. The white terrorist pulled out his assault rifle, the screams and sobs unmoving to him because the other voices were so loud.

He murdered twenty-two people.

FOR THE FIRST TIME SINCE the early months of Trump's presidency, apprehensions plummeted. McAleenan's negotiations with US lawmakers and Central American authorities had worked.[24] Border officials apprehended about 104,000 people in June. By July, the number had dropped to about 82,000. It fell in August to 63,000, to 52,500 in September. By October, it was 45,000.[25] That month, McAleenan convinced Trump to reverse his decision to revoke aid to Central America. He also resigned as he had threatened to do. He cited personal and family reasons. Miller remained at Trump's side, plotting more political attacks on migrants. The ban on public education for their children was still an option. So was ending birthright citizenship for some of their babies. He planned to advocate for embedding ICE agents within the refugee agency for migrant children, ORR, to better target their relatives for deportation.[26] There was the possibility of sending migrants to Guantánamo Bay. There were plans to add Nigeria and five other mostly African countries to the travel ban. But for a moment, Miller let himself get carried away by something else. In the fall, Miller got engaged to his girlfriend, Waldman. She was fanatical and hardworking, like him. She had moved out of her position as a press secretary at DHS and was now press secretary for Vice President Mike Pence.

Miller's grandfather Izzy, when he was alive, had warned against intermarriage, saying reproducing outside of the faith was "almost like helping Hitler with his job of destroying the Jewish people," according to an interview Izzy gave the Johnstown Area Heritage Association. Jewish fears of annihilation are a response to real historical trauma. Neo-Nazis have appropriated Jewish terminology, in the same way the far right has appropriated the language of civil rights. But white genocide is not real. It's a myth perpetuated by Neo-Nazis—who blame the Jews.

Shortly after proposing marriage to Waldman, Miller stood with her in front of a tree wrapped with strings of light that glowed like a fairy tale. Waldman rested her left hand on Miller's chest, showcasing her engagement ring. They both grinned; handsome and happy.

Several days later, the Southern Poverty Law Center began publishing stories about hundreds of emails obtained from former Breitbart editor Katie McHugh, who had renounced the far right.[27] She had been fired from Breitbart in 2017, allegedly for anti-Muslim tweets after Bannon left the blog for the White House. She was the blogger who had regularly published racist tweets such as " 'Slaves' built the country much as cows 'built' McDonald's," while being praised by Breitbart leaders. McHugh's emails showed Miller directing her, among other things, to a white nationalist website that promotes the white genocide theory. They showed Miller endorsing white supremacist and overtly racist literature. Democrats and Jewish groups called for his resignation, labeling him a white nationalist. The White House attacked the SPLC in a statement, saying it was "an utterly discredited, far-left smear organization." Miller defended his emails, saying, "There's nothing wrong in anything I said, unless being proud to be American and standing up for American citizens is a crime." With signature deflection, he said people referring to him as a white nationalist were "anti-Semitic."[28]

I meet McHugh, the woman who leaked the emails, at a café in California. She is short, dark haired with blue eyes. Her phone rings repeatedly with calls from major news organizations seeking her take. She says the emails speak for themselves. "He radicalized me," McHugh says of Miller.[29] She says she was traumatized imagining the crimes of minorities, and that white nationalists such as Miller took advantage of her trauma by pushing her toward racist pseudoscience suggesting that people of color are innately more violent than white people. "He should resign, and I think he should come to terms with his conscience," she says. "I would suggest he do the same thing I did: say, 'I was wrong.' He should think about what he has wrecked." McHugh compares her descent into white nationalism to wading into a pool of water; it wasn't until she was fully immersed that she felt the hatred all around, a lack of oxygen. She saw the murder of Heather Heyer in Charlottesville and realized she had to get out.

She says it's dangerous for Miller to be in power. She knows. She saw the hate from the inside. "The risk is that more people will die," she says.

Calls for Miller's resignation mounted. Trump attended Miller's wedding at the Trump International Hotel in DC on February 16.

An Elvis impersonator performed, but it was the president who stole the show. He praised Miller. "We're doing more than any president, any administration has ever done in the first three years," he said, "and we've had help from people in this room."

Miller stood a few footsteps away with his new bride at his side, grinning. Trump teased his senior advisor for celebrating his wedding on President's Day weekend. He said he told people to "break Steve's ass" and to tell Miller that Trump was "very busy" and might not make it. "Did you hear that message? Did they say that?" Trump asked, turning to Miller.

Yes sir," Miller said, laughing. Katie Waldman curled her arm around Miller's and smiled at him as his eyes remained fixed on Trump.

You thought it was about fifty-fifty at best, right?" Trump said, watching his senior advisor. Miller affirmed the estimate. Trump spread his arms wide, as if unveiling the size of his affection for Miller. "It was about one hundred percent. I just didn't want to tell you."

Trump wouldn't have missed Miller's special day. He was like a son to him—a son who'd helped win him unprecedented power, and vice versa. They would always be there for each other.

AUTHOR'S NOTE

Hatemonger is based on more than 150 interviews, more than 100 of them directly acquainted with Miller as friends, family or colleagues. It draws on hundreds of pages of court records, email correspondence and other documents. Fact-checkers combed through the content to verify accuracy, including quotes, specific facts and more. Neither the White House nor Stephen Miller responded to repeated requests for comment over the course of several months.

I attributed quotations and thoughts to characters when (a) they were stated directly to me by the characters, (b) they were recalled to me by sources who were firsthand participants in conversations with those characters and whose accounts could be verified by other sources, and (c) when I found them directly in court documents and other records. Several sources requested anonymity, saying they feared retaliation from Miller or the administration. I used pseudonyms for two characters to protect their identities for reasons stated within the text. The book pulls from nearly a decade of reporting from the border, Mexico and Central America.

ACKNOWLEDGMENTS

The team at William Morrow played a critical role in bringing *Hatemonger* into being, especially my editor Mauro DiPreta, who conceived of the idea in the first place. Vedika Khanna, Maureen Cole, Kayleigh George, Ben Steinberg, Liate Stehlik, Pamela Barricklow, Aryana Hendrawan also deserve credit. David R. Patterson of Stuart Krichevsky Literary Agency was a top-notch advocate, as always, with Aemilia Phillips's help. Thank you to my KPBS family for nurturing my coverage and for the extended leave. Thank you to Scott Horsley at NPR and Paul Kane at the *Washington Post* for crash courses in key subjects. I appreciate the support from my team at One World, which published my first book, *Crux: A Cross-Border Memoir*.

My fact-checkers, Tekendra Parmar and Chris Gelardi, were exhaustive and impressive in their review of the manuscript. Disinformation warfare in the digital age makes fact-checking work more crucial than ever. While Stephen Miller did not respond to my inquiries, I am grateful to all of the reporters with whom he did speak, such as McKay Coppins of *The Atlantic,* Nick Miroff and Josh Dawsey of the *Washington Post,* Julia Ioffe of *Politico Magazine* and Michael D. Shear and Julie Hirschfeld Davis of the *New York Times*. Their stories provided important bread crumbs and insights. The journalists Jonathan Blitzer, Dan Diamond, Hannah Levintova, Rosie Gray, Elaina Plott, Eliane Johnson, Aura Bogado, Karla Zabludovsky, Adolfo Flores, Rob Eschman, Rebekah Entralgo, Jason Leopold, Hannah Drier and Olivia Nuzzi did exceptional work digging into the administration's actions and some provided generous advice.

In recent years, national immigration coverage has benefited immensely from the hard work of local journalists at the US-Mexico border, many of whose stories are often overlooked or used without due credit by Washington- and New York–based outlets. A beat of this magnitude at a historical turning point requires a team effort, and among those who shared in the gargantuan task are Reynaldo Leaños Jr. at Texas Public Radio; Kate Morrissey, Gustavo Solis, Wendy Fry and Sandra Dibble of the *San Diego Union-Tribune*; Maya Srikrishnan of the Voice of San Diego; Alfredo Corchado and Dianne Solis at the *Dallas Morning News*; Angela Kocherga at the *Albuquerque Journal*; Max Rivlin-Nadler at KPBS; Aaron Montes at the *El Paso Times*; Kate Linthicum and Esmeralda Bermudez at the *Los Angeles Times*; Valerie Gonzalez at KRGV; freelance photojournalist Verónica Gabriela Cárdenas in McAllen, Texas; and more.

My sources, especially those who took risks to speak, have my deepest gratitude. A special thanks to Richard Burkert of the Johnstown Area Heritage Association for his extensive help during my visit to Johnstown, as well as to Renee Steinig, Sarton Weinraub, Anna Fiorino, Quinn Owen and Michael Kirk for their research assistance. Daniel Denvir's book, *All-American Nativism,* opened my eyes to the way in which the bipartisan dichotomy between "legal" and "illegal" immigration has been used to target non-white migrants as a whole.

Kim Freda at Oregon Public Broadcasting helped me follow the paper trail. Rich Marosi and Ruben Navarette provided invaluable mentorship. My friends—you know who you are—and the women in my family encouraged me, as always, to take the leap with caution and conscience.

NOTES

PROLOGUE

1. Michael Edison Hayden, "Stephen Miller's Affinity for White Nationalism Revealed in Leaked Emails," Southern Poverty Law Center, November 12, 2019. https://www.splcenter.org/hatewatch/2019/11/12/stephen-millers -affinity-white-nationalism-revealed-leaked-emails.
2. Stephen Miller, "Justice," *The Chronicle,* Duke University, November 7, 2005. https://www.dukechronicle.com/article/2005/11/justice.
3. Rush Limbaugh, *The Way Things Ought to Be* (New York: Pocket Books, 1992).
4. Dan Morain and Mark Gladstone, "Racist Verse Stirs Up Anger in Assembly," *Los Angeles Times,* May 19, 1993. https://www.latimes.com/archives /la-xpm-1993-05-19-mn-37021-story.html.
5. Sharon Bernstein, "Network of Rightists Recruited by Activist," *Los Angeles Times,* April 12, 1993. https://www.latimes.com/archives/la-xpm-1993 -04-12-me-22079-story.html.
6. Rebecca Solnit, "The Ideology of Isolation," *Harper's Magazine,* July 2016. https://harpers.org/archive/2016/07/the-ideology-of-isolation/.

CHAPTER ONE "BROWN ANIMALS"

1. William A. Henry III, "Beyond the Melting Pot," *Time,* April 9, 1990. http://content.time.com/time/covers/0,16641,19900409,00.html.
2. B. Drummond Ayres Jr., "Down 5 Years, California's Economy Shows Signs of Regaining Its Glitter," *New York Times*, December 19, 1995. https:// www.nytimes.com/1995/12/19/us/down-for-5-years-california-economy -shows-signs-of-regaining-itsglitter.html.
3. Daniel M. Weintraub, "Wilson Sues U.S. Over Immigrants' 'Invasion,' " *Los Angeles Times,* September 23, 1994. https://www.latimes.com/archives /la-xpm-1994-09-23-mn-42037-story.html.
4. Pete Wilson 1994 campaign ad on illegal immigration. https://www.you tube.com/watch?v=lLIzzs2HHgY.
5. Julio Moran, "Latinos Seek Wider Probe of Hate Letter," *Los Angeles Times*, July 25, 1991. https://www.latimes.com/archives/la-xpm-1991-07-25-we -507-story.html.
6. Barbara Koh, "Hate Letters Spur Students to Focus on Race Relations," *Los Angeles Times*, May 24, 1991. https://www.latimes.com/archives/la-xpm -1991-05-24-me-2207-story.html.
7. Author interview with Oscar de la Torre, in 2019.
8. Public Records Request, City of Santa Monica, Reference #R003191 -051219.
9. Santa Monica High School did not respond to author's requests for comment.

10. Dan Morain and Mark Gladstone, "Racist Verse Stirs Anger in Assembly," *Los Angeles Times,* May 19, 1993.
11. Rodolfo F. Acuña, *Anything But Mexican: Chicanos in Contemporary Los Angeles* (Brooklyn, NY: Haymarket Series, Verso, 1996).
12. Alan C. Miller, "Outcry Against Immigration Is Loud in Valley," *Los Angeles Times*, August 1, 1993. https://www.latimes.com/archives/la-xpm-1993 -08-01-mn-19196-story.html.
13. Michael Connelly, David Freed and Sonia Nazario, "Southland Is Ripe Turf for White Hate Groups," *Los Angeles Times*, July 25, 1993. https://www .latimes.com/archives/la-xpm-1993-07-25-mn-16832-story.html.
14. Jeff Greenfield, "Trump Is Pat Buchanan with Better Timing," *Politico Magazine*, September/October 2016. https://www.politico.com/magazine /story/2016/09/donald-trump-pat-buchanan-republican-america-first-na tivist-214221.
15. Author interview with Pete Nuñez, in 2019.
16. Stephen Miller, "Attack on the Secularist Scrooges," *The Chronicle,* Duke University, December 5, 2005. https://www.dukechronicle.com/arti cle/2005/12/attack-secularist-scrooges.
17. McKay Coppins, "Trump's Right-Hand Troll," *The Atlantic,* May 28, 2018. https://www.theatlantic.com/politics/archive/2018/05/stephen-miller -trump-adviser/561317/.
18. Rush Limbaugh, *The Way Things Ought to Be* (New York: Pocket Books, 1992).
19. Court documents, *Michael D. Miller v. Stern, Neubauer, Greenwald & Pauly, etc., et al.,* Superior Court of the State of California for the County of Los Angeles.
20. Ibid.
21. Author interview with David Stern, in 2019.
22. Court documents, *William Miller v. Cordary, Inc.,* Superior Court of the State of California for the County of Los Angeles.
23. Court documents, *Flatiron Property Corp., Inc., v. Cordary, Inc.,* Superior Court of the State of California for the County of Los Angeles.
24. Author interview with David Glosser, in 2019.
25. Author interview with Taylor Brinckerhoff, in 2019.
26. Facebook page for "California Villages in Valley Village." https://www .facebook.com/pg/ValleyVillage11/about/?ref=page_internal.
27. Yelp page for "California Villages." https://www.yelp.com/biz/california -villages-valley-village.
28. Benjamin Svetkey, "Stephen Miller's Third-Grade Teacher: He Was a 'Loner' and Ate Glue," *Hollywood Reporter,* October 10, 2018. https://www .hollywoodreporter.com/news/stephen-millers-third-grade-teacher-tells -all-1150549
29. John F. Muller, "I Sat on the Other Side of Stephen Miller's First Wall," *Politico Magazine,* June 22, 2018. https://www.politico.com/magazine /story/2018/06/22/i-sat-on-the-other-side-of-stephen-millers-first -wall-218886.
30. Author interview with Jason Islas, in 2019.

31. Juan Rivera, Scott Whiteford and Manuel Chavez, eds., *NAFTA and the Campesinos* (Scranton, PA: University of Scranton Press, 2009).
32. Jean Guerrero, "Illegal Crop Is Swapped for Legal One," *Wall Street Journal*, March 10, 2011. https://www.wsj.com/articles/SB10001424052748704623404576187264138169734.
33. Jason De Leon and Michael Wells, *The Land of Open Graves: Living and Dying on the Migrant Trail* (Oakland: University of California Press, 2015).
34. Yael Zárate, "70 años, 70 datos (y mitos) de Carlos Salinas de Gortari," *El Universal*, November 4, 2018. https://www.eluniversal.com.mx/nacion/sociedad/70-anos-70-datos-y-mitos-de-carlos-salinas-de-gortari.
35. Ibid.
36. Emails shared by neighbor Kathy Seal.
37. Author's confidential interview with a nearby resident, in 2019.
38. Author interviews with Gladys Quispe, in 2019.
39. *False Patriots: The Threat of Antigovernment Extremists* (Darby, PA: DIANE Publishing, 1996). https://www.google.com/books/edition/False_Patriots/zN_vAlq4eUcC?hl=en&gbpv=1&pg=PP1&printsec=frontcover.
40. Coppins, "Trump's Right-Hand Troll."
41. Santa Monica High School Yearbook, 2003.
42. Author interview with Taylor Brinckerhoff, in 2019.
43. Court documents, *William Miller v. Cordary, Inc.,* Superior Court of the State of California for the County of Los Angeles.
44. Court documents, *Flatiron Property Corp., Inc., v. Cordary, Inc.,* Superior Court of the State of California for the County of Los Angeles.
45. Author's confidential interview with a participant in the class, in 2019.
46. Author interview with two participants in the class, Sophie Goldstein and David Ginsburg, in 2019.
47. The Jay C. Miller and Freya B. Miller Trust, Superior Court of the State of California for the County of Los Angeles.
48. Francine Orr, *Los Angeles Times,* photograph on page A16, May 19, 2003.
49. Author interviews with Miller, Glosser family members and friends, in 2019.

CHAPTER TWO "RIDICULOUS LIBERAL ELITE"

1. Federal Election Commission data.
2. Mark E. Kahn, *Middle Class Radicalism in Santa Monica* (Philadelphia: Temple University Press, 1988).
3. "Santa Monica by the Sea," Real Estate Pamphlet, Santa Monica History Museum.
4. Paul Ciotti, "Socialism . . . on the Street Where You Live," *Reason*, April 1981. https://reason.com/1981/04/01/socialismon-the-street-where-y/.
5. Tracy Wilkinson, "Death Threats and Long Waiting Lists," *Los Angeles Times*, April 29, 1989. https://www.latimes.com/archives/la-xpm-1989-04-29-mn-1659-story.html.
6. Ibid.
7. The Hebrew Union College–Jewish Institute of Religion press release, October 18, 2013.

8. Author interview with Chris Harding, in 2019.

9. Author interview with Bob Wolfe, in 2019.

10. Author interview with Paul Grossman, in 2019.

11. Inglewood High School yearbook, 1968.

12. The Academy of Magical Arts, Inc. membership archives.

13. The Magic Castle, The Academy of Magical Arts, Dress Code & Rules. http://www.magiccastle.com/visiting/.

14. Author interview with Sharon Rifelli, in 2019.

15. Lesley Kennedy, "Most Immigrants Arriving at Ellis Island in 1907 Were Processed in a Few Hours," History, June 21, 2018; updated March 7, 2019. https://www.history.com/news/immigrants-ellis-island-short-processing -time.

16. Nison Miller naturalization documents, courtesy of genealogist Renee Stern Steinig.

17. Freya Baker Miller obituary, *Los Angeles Times,* February 3, 2015. https://www.legacy.com/obituaries/latimes/obituary.aspx?n=freya -miller&pid=174041987&fhid=12214.

18. Author interview with Margie Strimling, in 2019.

19. Ronald Reagan, "A Time for Choosing," October 27, 1964. https://www .youtube.com/watch?v=qXBswFfh6AY.

20. *Stanford Lawyer*, Celebration Issue 10, no. 2 (Fall 1975), page 28.

21. *Stanford Lawyer* 10, no. 1 (Winter 1975), page 30.

22. Biography of Miriam Miller, Yonezawa-Miller Company, LLC, https://ymcllc .com/management-team/.

23. Author interview with David Glosser, in 2019.

24. Author interview with Michael Hirschfeld, in 2019.

25. John H. Bunzel, *New Force on the Left: Tom Hayden and the Campaign Against Corporate America* (Stanford, CA: Hoover Institution Press, 1983).

26. Tom Hayden, "Things Come Around in the Mideast," Truthdig, July 18, 2006. https://www.truthdig.com/articles/tom-hayden-things-come-around -in-the-mideast/.

27. Court documents, *Michael D. Miller vs. Stern, Neubauer, Greenwald & Pauly, etc., et al.,* Superior Court of the State of California for the County of Los Angeles.

28. Author interview with David Ellenson, in 2019.

29. Author interview with David Glosser, in 2019.

30. Author interview with Richard Burkert, in 2019.

31. Ruth Glosser, "A Precious Legacy," Johnstown Area Heritage Association, 1998.

32. Ibid.

33. Ewa Morawska, *Insecure Prosperity: Small-Town Jews in Industrial America, 1890–1940* (Princeton: Princeton University Press, 1999).

34. *Generations* by the Johnstown Area Heritage Association.

35. David McCullough, *The Johnstown Flood* (New York: Simon & Schuster, 1987).

36. Glosser, "A Precious Legacy."

37. David Glosser, "Lessons for Trump from Johnstown History," *Tribune-*

Democrat Facebook page, October 28, 2016. https://ko-kr.facebook.com
/TribuneDemocrat/posts/1271660039530911.

38. Morawska, *Insecure Prosperity: Small-Town Jews in Industrial America.*

39. Author interview with Richard Burkert, in 2019.

40. Robert Jeschonek, *Long Live Glosser's* (Johnstown, PA: Pie Press, 2014).

41. Ibid.

42. Westmont Hilltop Senior High School yearbook (Johnstown, PA, Class of 1966).

43. Author interview with Jack Roscetti, in 2019.

CHAPTER THREE "SPEAK ONLY ENGLISH"

1. Los Angeles County Assessor Records.

2. *The Samohi,* February 14, 2003.

3. Interview with an individual who was friends with Miller for more than a decade, conducted in confidence by the author in 2019 and corroborated by photographs.

4. Stephen Miller, "Santa Monica High's Multicultural Fistfights," Frontpage magazine.com, July 19, 2005. https://archive.amren.com/news/2005/07 /santa_monica_hi.

5. Author interview with Maria Vivanco, in 2019.

6. McKay Coppins, "Trump's Right-Hand Troll," *The Atlantic,* May 28, 2018. https://www.theatlantic.com/politics/archive/2018/05/stephen-miller -trump-adviser/561317/.

7. Lisa Mascaro, "How a liberal Santa Monica high school produced a top Trump advisor and speechwriter," *Los Angeles Times,* January 17, 2017. https://www.latimes.com/politics/la-na-pol-trump-speechwriter-santa monica-20170117-story.html.

8. Author's confidential interview with a teacher at Santa Monica High School, in 2019.

9. John L. Mitchell, "Larry Knows Best," *Los Angeles Times,* May 31, 1998. https:// www.latimes.com/archives/la-xpm-1998-may-31-tm-54962-story.html.

10. Larry Elder, *The Ten Things You Can't Say in America* (New York: St. Martin's Griffin, 2001).

11. McKay Coppins, "Trump's Right-Hand Troll," *The Atlantic,* May 28, 2018. https://www.theatlantic.com/politics/archive/2018/05/stephen-miller -trump-adviser/561317/.

12. Author interview with Kesha Ram, in 2019.

13. Stephen Miller, "Santa Monica High's Multicultural Fistfights," Frontpage magazine.com, July 19, 2005. https://archive.amren.com/news/2005/07 /santa_monica_hi.

14. Author interview with Julia Brownley, in 2019.

15. Author interview with Jenness Hartley, in 2019

16. Author' confidential interview with a classmate, in 2019.

17. Bernard Lewis, "License to Kill: Usama bin Ladin's Declaration of Jihad," *Foreign Affairs,* November/December 1998. https://www.foreignaffairs

.com/articles/saudi-arabia/1998-11-01/license-kill-usama-bin-ladins-dec
laration-jihad.

18. Author interview with Sarton Weinraub, in 2019.

19. Author interview with Ben Tarzynski, in 2019.

20. Author interview with Jenness Hartley, in 2019.

21. Author interview with Larry Elder, in 2019.

22. Author interview with Adrian Karimi, in 2019.

23. Wil S. Hylton, "Down the Breitbart Hole," *New York Times Magazine,* August 16, 2017. https://www.nytimes.com/2017/08/16/magazine/breitbart
-alt-right-steve-bannon.html.

24. Larry Elder, *The Ten Things You Can't Say in America* (New York: St. Martin's Griffin, 2001).

CHAPTER FOUR "PICK UP MY TRASH"

1. Noah Kulwin, "Watch: Young Stephen Miller jokes 'torture is a celebration of life,' " Vice News, May 30, 2017. https://www.vice.com/en_us/article
/9kdvby/stephen-miller-torture-video-iraq.

2. Author interview with Nick Silverman, in 2019.

3. Steve Miller, "How I Changed My Left-Wing High School," Frontpage magazine.com, July 8, 2003. http://www.psaf.org/archive/2004/August
/ChangedLeftWingHS.html.

4. Stephen Miller, "Political Correctness Out of Control," "Letters to the Editor," The LookOut, March 27, 2002. https://www.surfsantamonica.com
/ssm_site/the_lookout/letters/Letters-2002/MARCH_2002/03_27
_2002_Political_Correctness_Out_of_Control.htm.

5. Fernando Peinado, "Exclusive: The high school speech by Stephen Miller that offended students, got him thrown off stage," Univision News, February 13, 2017. https://www.univision.com/univision-news/politics/exclu
sive-the-high-school-speech-by-stephen-miller-that-offended-students
-and-got-him-thrown-off-stage.

6. Author interview with Coleen Armstrong-Yamamura, in 2019.

7. Author's confidential interview with teacher, in 2019.

8. Author interview with Rachel Greenberg, in 2019.

9. Author interviews with David Horowitz, in 2019.

10. Sharon Bernstein, "Network of Rightists Recruited by Activist," *Los Angeles Times*, April 12, 1993. https://www.latimes.com/archives/la-xpm-1993
-04-12-me-22079-story.html.

11. Steve Miller, "The Politics of a High School Education," Frontpagemaga zine.com, November 18, 2002. http://www.psaf.org/archive/2004/August
/PoliticsOfHighSchool.html.

12. Miller, "How I Changed My Left-Wing High School."

13. Author interviews with David Horowitz, in 2019.

14. David Horowitz, *The Black Book of the American Left* (New York: Encounter Books, 2013).

15. David Horowitz, *Hating Whitey and Other Progressive Causes* (Ashland, OR: Blackstone Publishing, 2013).

16. Stephen Miller, "Santa Monica High's Multicultural Fistfights," Frontpage magazine.com, July 19, 2005. https://archive.amren.com/news/2005/07/santa_monica_hi.

17. Preston Ni, "7 Stages of Gaslighting in a Relationship," *Psychology Today*, April 30, 2017. https://www.psychologytoday.com/us/blog/communication-success/201704/7-stages-gaslighting-in-relationship.

18. Eric Beerbohm and Ryan Davis, "Gaslighting Citizens," Harvard University, 2018. https://scholar.harvard.edu/files/beerbohm/files/eb_rd_gaslighting_citizens_apsa_2018_v1_1_0.pdf.

19. Front page of the *Los Angeles Times*, August 23, 1985.

20. Joseph B. Frazier, "Authorities Study Cause of Spy Plane Crash in El Salvador," Associated Press, August 24, 1985.

21. Denise Gellene, "Lear Siegler Puts Several of Its Businesses Up for Sale," *Los Angeles Times*, February 19, 1989. https://www.latimes.com/archives/la-xpm-1987-02-19-fi-4177-story.html.

22. Mark Danner, "The Truth of El Mozote," *The New Yorker,* December 6, 1993. https://www.newyorker.com/magazine/1993/12/06/the-truth-of-el-mozote.

23. Ibid.

24. Ibid.

25. Court documents, *Pico Neighborhood Association vs. City of Santa Monica*, Superior Court of the State of California for the County of Los Angeles.

26. Francine Orr, *Los Angeles Times*, photograph on page A16, May 19, 2003.

27. Erika Hayasaki, "2 Rs Left in High School," *Los Angeles Times*, May 19, 2003. https://www.latimes.com/archives/la-xpm-2003-may-19-me-term19-story.html.

CHAPTER FIVE "THERE IS NO PALESTINE"

1. Buzz Bissinger, "Duke Lacrosse Case," *Vanity Fair's Schools for Scandal* (New York: Simon & Schuster, 2017).

2. Author interview with Michael Parker Ayers, in 2019.

3. Author's confidential interview with classmate, in 2019.

4. Author's confidential interview with classmate, in 2019.

5. Author's confidential interview with classmate, in 2019.

6. Author interview with Sean Hou, in 2019.

7. Author interview with Amy Terwilleger, in 2019.

8. Author interview with Alec Macaulay, in 2019.

9. Author's confidential interview with classmate, in 2019.

10. Author interview with Aaron Thomas Johnson, in 2019.

11. Author interview with Rebecca Suffness, in 2019.

12. Author's confidential interviews with three classmates, in 2019.

13. Paul Lewis, "U.N. Repeals Its '75 Resolution Equating Zionism with Racism," *New York Times*, December 17, 1991. https://www.nytimes.com/1991/12/17/world/un-repeals-its-75-resolution-equating-zionism-with-racism.html.

14. Dana Milbank, "America's Jews Are Watching Israel in Horror," *Washing-*

ton Post, September 21, 2018. https://www.washingtonpost.com/opinions/israel-is-driving-jewish-america-farther-and-farther-away/2018/09/21/de2716f8-bdbb-11e8-8792-78719177250f_story.html.

15. Author interview with Yehuda Kurtzer, in 2019.

16. Stephen Miller, "FREEP Duke: Terrorists Call for US Intifada and Actively Recruit Future Terrorists on Campus," Freerepublic.com, November 10, 2004. http://www.freerepublic.com/focus/f-news/1278354/posts.

17. John F. Burness, "University Denounces Bogus Message Seeking to Discredit Palestine Solidarity Movement," Duke University, October 13, 2004. https://today.duke.edu/showcase/mmedia/features/psm/bogusmessage.html.

18. Author interview with John Burness, in 2019

19. Stephen Miller, "Duke's Weekend of Terror," Discoverthenetworks.com, November 2005. http://www.discoverthenetworks.com/Articles/Duke.htm.

20. Stephen Miller, "Santa Monica High's Multicultural Fistfights," Frontpagemagazine.com, July 19, 2005. https://archive.amren.com/news/2005/07/santa_monica_hi.

21. Joaquin Vega, "Police Memo Details Encounter with Board Member on Samohi Campus," *Santa Monica Mirror*, April 27, 2006. https://smmirror.com/2005/04/police-memo-details-encounter-with-board-member-on-samohi-campus/.

22. Author interview with Katie McHugh, in 2019.

23. "News from the Front," Center for the Study of Popular Culture, Academic Freedom Conference, Center for the Study of Popular Culture, www.frontpagemag.com (May 2006).

24. Stephen Miller, "Welcome to Leftist University," *The Chronicle*, Duke University, September 5, 2005.

25. Stephen Miller, "Tricky Extrapolations," *The Chronicle*, Duke University, October 26, 2005.

26. Stephen Miller, "Paranoia," *The Chronicle*, Duke University, September 25, 2006.

27. Author interview with Ben Shapiro, in 2019.

28. Stephen Miller, "Justice," *The Chronicle*, Duke University, November 8, 2005.

29. Stephen Miller, "Sorry Feminists," *The Chronicle*, Duke University, November 11, 2005.

30. Stephen Miller, "Attack of the Secularist Scrooges," *The Chronicle*, Duke University, December 6, 2005.

31. Stephen Miller, "A Smoker's Plea," *The Chronicle*, Duke University, April 9, 2007.

32. Stephen Miller, "Hollywood and the Culture War," *The Chronicle*, Duke University, January 11, 2006.

33. Stephen Miller, "Unpatriotic Dissent," *The Chronicle*, Duke University, February 8, 2006.

34. Stephen Miller, "Farewell," *The Chronicle*, Duke University, April 23, 2007.

35. Stephen Miller, "America: The Forgotten Campus Culture," *The Chronicle*, Duke University, November 20, 2006.
36. Miller, "Farewell."
37. Miller, "America: The Forgotten Campus Culture."

CHAPTER SIX "CUT THEIR SKIN"

1. Author interview with David Horowitz, in 2019.
2. Terrorism Awareness Project, Wayback Machine, Internet Archive, Archive.org.
3. "The Alt-Right Is Killing People," Southern Poverty Law Center, February 5, 2018. https://www.splcenter.org/20180205/alt-right-killing-people.
4. Author interview with Richard Spencer, 2019.
5. Richard Bertrand Spencer, Southern Poverty Law Center. https://www.splcenter.org/fighting-hate/extremist-files/individual/richard-bertrand-spencer-0.
6. Graeme Wood, "His Kampf," *The Atlantic,* June 2017. https://www.theatlantic.com/magazine/archive/2017/06/his-kampf/524505/.
7. Author interview with Richard Spencer, in 2019.
8. Josh Harkinson, "Trump's Newest Senior Adviser Seen as a White Nationalist Ally," *Mother Jones*, December 14, 2016. https://www.motherjones.com/politics/2016/12/trumps-newest-senior-adviser-seen-ally-white-nationalists/.
9. *The Chronicle*, Duke University, March 26, 2007. https://issuu.com/dukechronicleprintarchives/docs/the_chronicle_2007-03-26_sm.
10. Author interview with Peter Laufer, in 2019.
11. Author interview with Peter Brimelow, in 2019.
12. Adele M. Stan, "White Supremacist Peter Brimelow Invited to White House Advisor Kudlow's Birthday Party," Right Wing Watch, August 21, 2018. https://www.rightwingwatch.org/post/white-supremacist-peter-brimelow-invited-to-white-house-advisor-kudlows-birthday-party/.
13. Michael Edison Hayden, "Stephen Miller's Affinity for White Nationalism Revealed in Leaked Emails," Southern Poverty Law Center, November 12, 2019. https://www.splcenter.org/hatewatch/2019/11/12/stephen-millers-affinity-white-nationalism-revealed-leaked-emails.
14. Jason Kessler, "Yes, Virginia (Dare), There Is Such a Thing as White Genocide," VDARE.com, December 24, 2016.
15. Author interview with David Bitner, in 2019.
16. Julia Ioffe, "The Believer," *Politico Magazine*, June 27, 2016. https://www.politico.com/magazine/story/2016/06/stephen-miller-donald-trump-2016-policy-adviser-jeff-sessions-213992.
17. Stephen Miller, "Remembering 9/11," Freerepublic.com, September 26, 2006. https://www.freerepublic.com/focus/f-news/1708418/posts.
18. Author interview with Elliott Wolf, in 2019.
19. William D. Cohan, *The Price of Silence: The Duke Lacrosse Scandal, the Power of the Elite, and the Corruption of Our Great Universities* (New York: Scribner, 2015).

20. Bootie Cosgrove-Mather, "The Devils at Duke," CBS News, April 6, 2006. https://www.cbsnews.com/news/the-devils-at-duke/.

21. Cohan, *The Price of Silence.*

22. Rachel Smolkin, "Justice Delayed," *American Journalism Review* Archive, August/September 2007. https://ajrarchive.org/Article.asp?id=4379&id=4379.

23. Reverend Jesse L. Jackson Sr., "Duke: Horror and Truth," Tribune Media Services, April 13, 2007. https://www.kfvs12.com/story/6366245/jesse-jackson-article/.

24. Cohan, *The Price of Silence.*

25. Rick Lyman, "New Strain on Duke's Ties with Durham," *New York Times,* March 31, 2006. https://www.nytimes.com/2006/03/31/us/new-strain-on-dukes-ties-with-durham.html.

26. William D. Cohan, "How Stephen Miller Rode White Rage from Duke's Campus to Trump's West Wing," *Vanity Fair,* May 30, 2017. https://www.vanityfair.com/news/2017/05/stephen-miller-duke-donald-trump.

27. Stephen Miller, "Prejudice," *The Chronicle,* Duke University, April 12, 2006.

28. Author interview with Alex Rosenberg, in 2019.

29. Cohan, *The Price of Silence.*

30. "President Brodhead Speaks on Lacrosse Situation at Alumni Reunion," Duke Today, April 22, 2006. https://today.duke.edu/2006/04/rhb_alumni.html.

31. M. Shadee Malaklou, "An Open Letter to Duke University's Class of 2007, About Your Open Letter to Stephen Miller," Counterpunch.org, March 24, 2017. https://www.counterpunch.org/2017/03/24/an-open-letter-to-duke-universitys-class-of-2007-about-your-open-letter-to-stephen-miller/.

32. Duke University Class of 2007, "Open Letter to Stephen Miller." https://docs.google.com/forms/d/e/1FAIpQLSf9JDRbGYhkAEMJ3hFlypzanVEi9lFEYQfDXD1XX3g_3RInDw/viewform.

CHAPTER SEVEN "OUR WHOLE COUNTRY IS ROTTING"

1. Author's confidential interview with a friend of Stephen Miller, in 2019.

2. Lisa Makson, "Islamo-Fascism Week Spotlights Terrorism," Newsmax, October 23, 2007. https://www.newsmax.com/Newsfront/islamofascism-week/2007/10/23/id/321973/.

3. Author interview with David Horowitz, in 2019.

4. Tom Scheck, "Bachmann doesn't like McCain or global warming," MPR Newshoax, March 17, 2008. https://www.mprnews.org/story/capitol-view/2008/03/bachmann_doesnt.

5. Emily Heil, "Stephen Miller blasted a reporter as 'cosmopolitan.' But he lives in a $1 million CityCenter condo," *Washington Post,* August 7, 2017. https://www.washingtonpost.com/news/reliable-source/wp/2017/08/07/stephen-miller-blasted-a-reporter-as-cosmopolitan-but-he-lives-in-a-1-million-citycenter-condo/.

6. Rosemount Newsroom, "Drivers ask: Who is behind the wheel?" River

towns.net, March 5, 2008. https://www.rivertowns.net/news/1078312
-drivers-ask-who-behind-wheel.

7. Alex Nowrasteh, "Illegal Immigrants and Crime—Assessing the Evidence,"
Cato Institute, March 4, 2019. https://www.cato.org/blog/illegal-immi
grants-crime-assessing-evidence.

8. Pat Doyle, "Thursday: Bachmann, Tinklenberg air it out," *Star Tribune*, October 18, 2008. http://www.startribune.com/thursday-bachmann-tinklen
berg-air-it-out/31145584/.

9. Author interview with David Horowitz, in 2019.

10. Rachael Revesz, "Jeff Sessions, Donald Trump's new attorney general, said
the Ku Klux Klan 'was OK until I found out they smoked pot,' " *Independent,* November 18, 2016. https://www.independent.co.uk/news/world
/americas/jeff-sessions-attorney-general-marijuana-justice-department-anti
-drug-laws-a7425511.html.

11. Amber Phillips, "That time the Senate denied Jeff Sessions a federal judgeship over accusations of racism," *Washington Post,* January 10, 2017. https://
www.washingtonpost.com/news/the-fix/wp/2016/11/18/that-time-the
-senate-denied-jeff-sessions-a-federal-judgeship-over-accusations-of-rac
ism/.

12. Author interview with Pete Nuñez, in 2019.

13. Author interview with John Stanton, in 2019.

14. Matt Flegenheimer, "Stephen Miller, the Powerful Survivor on the President's Right Flank," *New York Times*, October 9, 2017. https://www.ny
times.com/2017/10/09/us/politics/stephen-miller-trump-white-house
.html.

15. Ronald Radosh, "Steve Bannon, Trump's Top Guy, Told Me He Was a
Leninist," Daily Beast, August 22, 2016. https://www.thedailybeast.com
/steve-bannon-trumps-top-guy-told-me-he-was-a-leninist.

16. Julia Ioffe, "The Believer," *Politico Magazine*, June 27, 2016. https://politico
.com/magazine/story/2016/06/stephen-miller-donald-trump-2016-policy
-adviser-jeff-sessions-213992.

17. Chris Roberts, "The Brutal Reality of Black on White Crime," American
Renaissance, July 27, 2019. https://www.amren.com/news/2019/11/black
-on-white-crime-racism-murder-rape/.

18. Author interview with David Horowitz, in 2019.

19. David Horowitz, "American Conservatism: An Argument with the Racial
Right," Frontpagemagazine.com, August 27, 2002. http://www.freerepublic
.com/focus/news/740659/posts.

20. Author's confidential interview with former Senate aide, in 2019.

21. Glenn Kessler, "A misleading chart on 'welfare' spending," *Washington Post*,
February 21, 2013. https://www.washingtonpost.com/blogs/fact-checker
/post/a-misleading-chart-on-welfare-spending/2013/02/20/1b40bcde
-7ba4-11e2-82e8-61a46c2cde3d_blog.html.

22. The National Academies of Sciences, Engineering and Medicine, https://
www.nap.edu/catalog/23550/the-economic-and-fiscal-consequences
-of-immigration.

23. Author's confidential interview with former Senate staffer, in 2019.

24. Ioffe, "The Believer."
25. Author's confidential interviews with former Senate aides, in 2019.
26. Kelly Cohen, "DACA has been in Jeff Sessions' sights for some time," *Washington Examiner*, September 11, 2017. https://www.washingtonexaminer .com/daca-has-been-in-jeff-sessions-sights-for-some-time.
27. Jean Guerrero, "Tijuana Migrants Hide in Tunnels as Police Raids Get Deadly," KPBS, January 28, 2016. https://www.kpbs.org/news/2016 /jan/28/tijuana-migrants-hide-tunnels-police-raids-get-dea/.
28. Christie Thompson and Anna Flagg, "Who is ICE Deporting?" Marshall Project, September 26, 2016. https://www.themarshallproject.org /2016/09/26/who-is-ice-deporting.
29. Nicholas Kulish and Mike McIntire, "Why an Heiress Spent Her Fortune Trying to Keep Immigrants Out," *New York Times*, August 14, 2019. https:// www.nytimes.com/2019/08/14/us/anti-immigration-cordelia-scaife-may .html.
30. Eli Clifton, "Meet an Islamophobia Network Funder: Richard Scaife," ThinkProgress, August 29, 2011. https://thinkprogress.org/meet-an-islam ophobia-network-funder-richard-scaife-14a9d2cbfae0/.
31. Nicholas Kulish, "Dr. John Tanton, Quiet Catalyst in Anti-Immigration Drive, Dies at 85," *New York Times*, July 18, 2019. https://www.nytimes .com/2019/07/18/us/john-tanton-dead.html.
32. Carly Goodman, "John Tanton has died. He made America less open to immigrants—and more open to Trump," *Washington Post*, July 19, 2019. https://www.washingtonpost.com/outlook/2019/07/18/john-tanton-has -died-how-he-made-america-less-open-immigrants-more-open-trump/.
33. Humberto Sanchez, "Did FAIR Action Violate Law?" *Roll Call*, July 30, 2012. https://www.rollcall.com/news/Did-FAIR-Action-Violate-Law-216 570-1.html.
34. Author interview with Steve Camarota, in 2019.
35. Mark Krikorian, "How labeling my organization a hate group shuts down public debate," *Washington Post*, March 17, 2017. https://www .washingtonpost.com/opinions/how-labeling-my-organization-a-hate -group-shuts-down-public-debate/2017/03/17/656ab9c8-0812-11e7 -93dc-00f9bdd74ed1_story.html.
36. Peter Beinart, "The GOP Fails Its Empathy Test," *The Atlantic*, June 29, 2015. https://www.theatlantic.com/politics/archive/2015/06/-empathy-gop -presidential-race-2016-/397115/.
37. Jennifer Rubin, "GOP autopsy report goes bold," *Washington Post*, March 18, 2013. https://www.washingtonpost.com/blogs/right-turn/wp /2013/03/18/gop-autopsy-report-goes-bold/.
38. Garance Franke-Ruta, "What You Need to Read in the RNC Election-Autopsy Report," *The Atlantic*, March 18, 2013. https://www.theatlantic.com /politics/archive/2013/03/what-you-need-to-read-in-the-rnc-election -autopsy-report/274112/.
39. Sean Trende, "The Case of the Missing White Voters," RealClearPolitics, November 8, 2012. https://www.realclearpolitics.com/articles/2012/11/08 /the_case_of_the_missing_white_voters_116106.html.

40. Emails shared by David Horowitz with the author in 2019.
41. Stephen Miller, Breitbart News Saturday, February 27, 2016. https://soundcloud.com/breitbart/breitbart-news-saturday-stephen-miller-february-26-2016.
42. Stephen Miller, Breitbart News Daily, April 6, 2016. https://www.breitbart.com/radio/2016/04/06/stephen-miller-trump-won-on-the-issues-republican-party-donor-class-has-lost/.
43. Author interview with Mark Krikorian, in 2019.
44. Author interview with Katie McHugh, in 2019.
45. Author's confidential interview with former Senate staffer, in 2019.
46. Emails shared by David Horowitz with the author in 2019.
47. Matt Hansen and Kate Linthicum, "Murrieta protestors turn back Border Patrol detainees," *Los Angeles Times*, July 1, 2014. https://www.latimes.com/local/la-me-murrieta-immigrants-20140702-story.html.
48. Matt Flegenheimer, "Stephen Miller, the Powerful Survivor on the President's Right Flank," *New York Times*, October 9, 2017. https://www.nytimes.com/2017/10/09/us/politics/stephen-miller-trump-white-house.html.

CHAPTER EIGHT "I WANT TO HATE"

1. Jonathan Greenberg, "Saving face," *Washington Post*, June 14, 2019. https://www.washingtonpost.com/news/posteverything/wp/2019/06/14/feature/how-donald-trump-silenced-the-people-who-could-expose-his-business-failures/.
2. Tony Schwartz, "I wrote 'The Art of the Deal' with Trump. His self-sabotage is rooted in his past," *Washington Post*, May 16, 2017. https://www.washingtonpost.com/posteverything/wp/2017/05/16/i-wrote-the-art-of-the-deal-with-trump-his-self-sabotage-is-rooted-in-his-past/.
3. Michael Kranish, "Trump pressured his alcoholic brother about his career. Now he says he has regrets," *Washington Post*, August 8, 2019. https://www.washingtonpost.com/politics/trump-pressured-his-alcoholic-brother-about-his-career-now-he-has-regrets-/2019/08/07/58ec2d70-b216-11e9-8f6c-7828e68cb15f_story.html.
4. Jason Horowitz, "For Donald Trump, Lessons from a Brother's Suffering," *New York Times*, January 2, 2016. https://www.nytimes.com/2016/01/03/us/politics/for-donald-trump-lessons-from-a-brothers-suffering.html.
5. Charles V. Bagli, "A Trump Empire Built on Inside Connections and $885 Million in Tax Breaks," *New York Times*, September 17, 2016. https://www.nytimes.com/2016/09/18/nyregion/donald-trump-tax-breaks-real-estate.html.
6. John O'Donnell and James Rutherford, *Trumped! The Inside Story of the Real Donald Trump* (New York: Simon & Schuster, 1991).
7. Patrick Radden Keef, "How Mark Burnett Resurrected Donald Trump as an Icon of American Business Success," *The New Yorker*, December 27, 2018. https://www.newyorker.com/magazine/2019/01/07/how-mark-burnett-resurrected-donald-trump-as-an-icon-of-american-success.

8. Jean Guerrero, "Investors in Donald Trump's Failed Mexico Resort Speak Out," KPBS, July 14, 2016. https://www.kpbs.org/news/2016/jul/14/investors-trumps-failed-mexico-resort-speak-out/.

9. Emily Heil, "Stephen Miller blasted a reporter as 'cosmopolitan.' But he lives in a $1 million CityCenter condo," Washington Post, August 7, 2017.

10. Author interview with Robert Carey, in 2019.

11. Author interview with Cecilia Muñoz, in 2019.

12. Jonathan Blitzer, "A Trump Official Behind the End of DACA Explains Himself," The New Yorker, November 10, 2017. https://www.newyorker.com/news/news-desk/trump-official-behind-the-end-of-daca-explains-himself.

13. Mario Trujillo, "Tech cranks up pressure on Obama for immigration order," The Hill, November 9, 2014. https://thehill.com/policy/technology/223391-tech-cranks-up-pressure-on-obama-for-immigration-order.

14. Julia Ioffe, "The Believer," Politico Magazine, June 27, 2016. https://www.politico.com/magazine/story/2016/06/stephen-miller-donald-trump-2016-policy-adviser-jeff-sessions-213992.

15. Nick Miroff and Josh Dawsey, "The Adviser Who Scripts Trump's Immigration Policy," Washington Post, August 17, 2019. https://www.washingtonpost.com/graphics/2019/politics/stephen-miller-trump-immigration/.

16. Julie Hirschfeld Davis and Michael D. Shear, Border Wars (New York: Simon & Schuster, 2019).

17. Author interview with Sam Nunberg, in 2019.

18. Corey Lewandowski speech, Symposium at the Wall, July 2019. https://www.youtube.com/watch?v=T_xPDpI7W0g&list=PLdhephwzoqJBYiKvd8NNmwdil86P_ZDRl&index=10&t=0s.

19. Author interviews with Katie McHugh, in 2019.

20. Ibid.

21. Rosie Gray, "A Former Alt-Right Member's Message: Get Out While You Still Can," Buzzfeed News, May 1, 2019. https://www.buzzfeednews.com/article/rosiegray/katie-mchugh.

22. Ibid.

23. Lloyd Grove, "How Breitbart Unleashes Hate Mobs to Threaten, Dox, and Troll Trump Critics," Daily Beast, March 1, 2016. https://www.thedailybeast.com/breitbart-news-helped-trump-win-under-steve-bannon-it-might-also-help-him-lose.

24. Michael Edison Hayden, "Stephen Miller's Affinity for White Nationalism Revealed in Leaked Emails," Southern Poverty Law Center, November 12, 2019.

25. Julia Hahn, " 'Camp of the Saints' Seen Mirrored in Pope's Message," Breitbart, September 24, 2015. https://www.breitbart.com/politics/2015/09/24/camp-saints-seen-mirrored-popes-message/.

26. Ben Mathis-Lilley, "Bannon, Adviser Behind Travel Ban, Is Fan of Novel About Feces-Eating, Dark-Skinned Immigrants Destroying White Society," Slate, March 6, 2017. https://slate.com/news-and-politics/2017/03/steve-bannon-and-the-camp-of-the-saints.html.

27. McKay Coppins, "Trump's Right-Hand Troll," The Atlantic, May 28, 2018.

https://www.theatlantic.com/politics/archive/2018/05/stephen-miller
-trump-adviser/561317/.

28. Eli Stokols, "Sen. Jeff Sessions Endorses Trump," *Politico Magazine*, February 28, 2016. https://www.politico.com/story/2016/02/sen-jeff-sessions
-endorses-trump-219939.

29. Paul Jay, "Trump's Senior Policy Advisor Defends Curbing Immigration," The Real News Network, February 10, 2016. https://therealnews.com/stories
/smiller0209.

CHAPTER NINE "NEW DAY IN AMERICA"

1. Author interview with Brandon Judd, in 2019.
2. Brandon Darby and Stephen Miller, Breitbart News Daily, March 23, 2016. https://soundcloud.com/breitbart/breitbart-news-daily-brandon-darby
-stephen-miller-march-23-2016.
3. Ibid.
4. Author's confidential interview with a person familiar with the incident, in 2019.
5. "Female Genital Mutilation/Cutting," Government Accountability Office, June 2016. https://www.gao.gov/assets/680/678098.pdf.
6. Author interview with Maha Hussein, in 2019.
7. Author's confidential interview with friend of Stephen Miller, in 2019.
8. Caroline May, "Trump Senior Policy Advisor: Trade an Issue of 'National Security,'" February 12, 2016. https://www.breitbart.com/pol
itics/2016/02/12/trump-senior-policy-advisor-trade-is-a-national-security
-issue/.
9. Stephen Miller and Steve Bannon, "Breitbart News Saturday: Stephen Miller," Breitbart News Daily, February 26, 2016. https://soundcloud.com
/breitbart/breitbart-news-saturday-stephen-miller-february-26-2016.
10. Stephen Miller and Steve Bannon, "Breitbart News Daily: Stephen Miller," Breitbart News Daily, March 9, 2016. https://soundcloud.com/breitbart
/breitbart-news-daily-stephen-miller-march-9-2016.
11. Ibid.
12. Stephen Miller and Steve Bannon, "Breitbart News Saturday: Stephen Miller," Breitbart News Daily, April 6, 2016; Dan Riehl, "Stephen Miller: Trump 'Won on the Isssues' the Republican 'Donor Class Has Lost,'" Breitbart, April 6, 2016. https://www.breitbart.com/radio/2016/04/06/stephen
-miller-trump-won-on-the-issues-republican-party-donor-class-has-lost/.
13. Stephen Miller and Steve Bannon, Breitbart News Daily, April 14, 2016. John Hayward, "Stephen Miller: Cruz 'Double Agent Delegates' Disenfrancise Voters," April 14, 2016. https://www.breitbart.com/radio/2016/04/14
/stephen-miller-ted-cruz-disenfranchisement-candidate-loses-people-vote/.
14. Stephen Miller and Steve Bannon, "Breitbart News Saturday: Stephen Miller," Breitbart News Daily, February 26, 2016. https://soundcloud.com
/breitbart/breitbart-news-saturday-stephen-miller-february-26-2016.
15. Emails shared with the author by David Horowitz in 2019.
16. Emails shared with the author by Larry Elder in 2019.

CHAPTER TEN "WE LOVE DEFEATING THOSE PEOPLE"

1. Emails shared with the author by David Horowitz in 2019.
2. Ibid.
3. Author interview with Talessia Martin, in 2019.
4. Jean Guerrero, "Death at the Border," KPBS, December 13, 2016. https://www.kpbs.org/news/death-at-the-border/.
5. Ibid.
6. Rebecca Shabad, "Donald Trump: Immigrants are pouring into the U.S. so they can vote," CBS News, October 7, 2016. https://www.cbsnews.com/news/donald-trump-immigrants-being-let-in-so-they-can-vote/.
7. Erik Stokols and Madeline Conway, "Trump hosts surprise panel with Bill Clinton's accusers," *Politico Magazine*, October 9, 2016. https://www.politico.com/story/2016/10/donald-trump-bill-clinton-accusers-229441.
8. Author interview with Larry Elder, in 2019.
9. Julia Hahn, "Criminal Aliens Sexually Assault 70,000 American Women— But Paul Ryan Targets Trump," Breitbart, October 13, 2016. http://www.5tjt.com/criminal-aliens-sexually-assault-70000-american-women-but-paul-ryan-targets-trump/.
10. Emails shared with the author by David Glosser in 2019.
11. Author interview with Jack Roscetti, in 2019.
12. Author interview with Kassidi Heavner, in 2019.
13. Author interview with Jamie Mitchell, in 2019.
14. *New York Times* Presidential Forecast, October 18, 2016. http://www.nytimes.com/newsgraphics/2016/10/18/presidential-forecast-updates/newsletter.html.
15. Robert Farley, "Trump's Bogus Voter Fraud Claims," Factcheck.org, October 19, 2016. https://www.factcheck.org/2016/10/trumps-bogus-voter-fraud-claims/.
16. Author interview with Bob Maupin, in 2016, for KPBS.
17. Robert O'Harrow Jr. and Shawn Boburg, "How a 'shadow' universe of charities joined with political warriors to fuel Trump's Rise," *Washington Post*, June 3, 2017. https://www.washingtonpost.com/investigations/how-a-shadow-universe-of-charities-joined-with-political-warriors-to-fuel-trumps-rise/2017/06/03/ff5626ac-3a77-11e7-a058-ddbb23c75d82_story.html.
18. Ibid.
19. Ibid.
20. Miranda Blue, "Sessions Defends 'Brilliant' David Horowitz in Confirmation Hearing," RightWingWatch, January 10, 2017. https://www.rightwingwatch.org/post/sessions-defends-brilliant-david-horowitz-in-confirmation-hearing/.
21. Jason Zegerle, "How America Got to 'Zero Tolerance' on Immigration: The Inside Story," *New York Times*, July 16, 2019. https://www.nytimes.com/2019/07/16/magazine/immigration-department-of-homeland-security.html.
22. Author interview with Kris Kobach, in 2019.
23. Zack Ford, "Leaked Trump transition doc flagged 'white supremacy'

concerns for Kris Kobach," ThinkProgress, June 24, 2019. https://think
progress.org/leaked-trump-vetting-docs-kris-kobach-white-supremacist
-laura-ingraham-transphobic-429b4d2993c8/.

24. Jonathan Shorman, "Kobach: 'Rule of law prevents ethnic cleansing in
America but Obama breaks laws,' *Topeka Capital-Journal*, November 20,
2014. https://www.cjonline.com/article/20141120/NEWS/311209738.

25. Author's confidential interview with transition official, in 2019.

26. Author's confidential interview with observer of ceremony, in 2019.

27. Author interview with Cecilia Muñoz, in 2019.

CHAPTER ELEVEN "AMERICAN CARNAGE"

1. James Fallows, " 'American Carnage': The Trump Era Begins," *The Atlantic*,
January 20, 2017. https://www.theatlantic.com/politics/archive/2017/01
/american-carnage-the-trump-era-begins/513971/.

2. Ed Pilkington, " 'American carnage': Donald Trump's vision casts shadow
over day of pageantry," *The Guardian*, January 21, 2017. https://www
.theguardian.com/world/2017/jan/20/donald-trump-transition-of-power
-president-first-speech.

3. Matt O'Brien, Spencer Raley, Robert Law and Sarah Rehberg, "Immigration Priorities for the 2017 Presidential Transition Team," Federation for
American Immigration Reform, November 2016. https://www.fairus.org
/sites/default/files/2017-08/FAIR_2017TransitionDocument.pdf.

4. Author's confidential interview with former DHS official, in 2019.

5. Author interview with David Lapan, in 2019.

6. Alice Speri, "Top Trump Official John Kelly Ordered ICE to Portray Immigrants as Criminals to Justify Raids," The Intercept, October 16, 2017.
https://theintercept.com/2017/10/16/top-trump-official-john-kelly-or
dered-ice-to-portray-immigrants-as-criminals-to-justify-raids/.

7. Fernando Peinado and Anna Spelman, "The undocumented heroes never
mentioned by Donald Trump," Univision, March 10, 2017. https://www
.univision.com/univision-news/immigration/the-undocumented-he
roes-never-mentioned-by-donald-trump.

8. Elizabeth Grieco, "Newsroom employees are less diverse than U.S. workers overall," Pew Research Center, November 2, 2018. https://www.pewre
search.org/fact-tank/2018/11/02/newsroom-employees-are-less-diverse
-than-u-s-workers-overall/.

9. Hayley C. Cuccinello, "World's Highest Paid Authors 2018," *Forbes*, December 11, 2018. https://www.forbes.com/sites/hayleycuccinello/2018/12/11
/worlds-highest-paid-authors-2018-michael-wolff/#3b77c0112517.

10. Stacy L. Smith, Marc Choueiti, Angel Choi and Katherine Piper, "Inclusion in
the Director's Chair," University of Southern California, January 2019. http://
assets.uscannenberg.org/docs/inclusion-in-the-directors-chair-2019.pdf.

11. Doris Truong, "AP Stylebook update: It's OK to call something racist
when it's racist," Poynter, March 29, 2019. https://www.poynter.org/report
ing-editing/2019/ap-stylebook-update-its-ok-to-call-something-racist
-when-its-racist/.

12. "Executive Order: Border Security and Immigration Enforcement Improvements," President Donald J. Trump, January 25, 2017. https://www.whitehouse.gov/presidential-actions/executive-order-border-security-immigration-enforcement-improvements/.

13. "Executive Order Protecting the Nation from Foreign Terrorist Entry into the United States," President Donald J. Trump, January 27, 2017. https://www.whitehouse.gov/presidential-actions/executive-order-protecting-nation-foreign-terrorist-entry-united-states/.

14. Stephen Miller and Steve Bannon, "Trump 'Won on the Issues' the Republican 'Donor Class Has Lost,'" Breitbart News Daily, April 6, 2016. https://www.breitbart.com/radio/2016/04/06/stephen-miller-trump-won-on-the-issues-republican-party-donor-class-has-lost/.

15. Matt Stevens, "First Travel Ban Order Left Officials Confused, Documents Show," New York Times, October 2, 2017. https://www.nytimes.com/2017/10/02/us/trump-travel-ban.html.

16. Hameed Darweesh, "I risked my life for the U.S. Army in Iraq. But when I came here, I was nearly sent back," Washington Post, February 10, 2017. https://www.washingtonpost.com/posteverything/wp/2017/02/10/i-worked-for-the-u-s-army-in-iraq-but-when-i-landed-in-america-i-was-detained/.

17. Pamela Engel, "Trump's immigration ban doesn't include the country most of the 9/11 hijackers came from," "Business Insider," (New York) Daily News, January 30, 2017. https://www.nydailynews.com/news/politics/trump-muslim-ban-excludes-countries-linked-businesses-article-1.2957956.

18. Michael Wolff, Fire and Fury: Inside the Trump White House (New York: Henry Holt, 2018).

19. Nick Miroff and Josh Dawsey, "The Adviser Who Scripts Trump's Immigration Policy," Washington Post, August 17, 2019. https://www.washingtonpost.com/graphics/2019/politics/stephen-miller-trump-immigration/.

20. Jason Zengerle, "How America Got 'Zero Tolerance' on Immigration," New York Times, July 16, 2019. https://www.nytimes.com/2019/07/16/magazine/immigration-department-of-homeland-security.html.

21. Michael D. Shear and Julie Hirschfeld Davis, "Stoking Fears, Trump Defied Bureaucracy to Advance Immigration Agenda," New York Times, December 23, 2017. https://www.nytimes.com/2017/12/23/us/politics/trump-immigration.html.

22. McKay Coppins, "Trump's Right-Hand Troll," The Atlantic, May 28, 2018. https://www.theatlantic.com/politics/archive/2018/05/stephen-miller-trump-adviser/561317/.

23. Author's confidential interview with former State Department official, in 2019.

24. Author interview with James Nealon, in 2019.

25. Salvador Rizzo, "How many migrants show up for immigration court hearings?," Washington Post, June 26, 2019. https://www.washingtonpost.com/politics/2019/06/26/how-many-migrants-show-up-immigration-court-hearings/.

26. John Kelly, "Implementing the President's Border Security and Immigration

Enforcement Improvements Policies," Department of Homeland Security memo, February 20, 2017. https://www.dhs.gov/sites/default/files/publica tions/17_0220_S1_Implementing-the-Presidents-Border-Security-Immi gration-Enforcement-Improvement-Policies.pdf.

27. Matthew Albence, "Implementing the President's Border Security and Interior Immigration Enforcement Policies," US Immigration and Customs Enforcement memo, February 21, 2017. https://www.documentcloud.org /documents/3889695-doc00801320170630123624.html.

28. Rory Carroll, " 'It's life and death': Border crossings continue despite the Trump effect," *The Guardian,* May 1, 2017. https://www.theguardian.com /us-news/2017/may/01/us-border-asylum-seekers-trump-effect.

29. Author interview with Michael Anton, in 2019.

30. Gabriel Sherman, " 'I Have Power': Is Steve Bannon Running for President?" *Vanity Fair,* December 21, 2017. https://www.vanityfair.com /news/2017/12/bannon-for-president-trump-kushner-ivanka.

31. Josh Dawsey and Eliana Johnson, "Trump's got a new favorite Steve," *Politico Magazine*, April 13, 2017. https://www.politico.com/story/2017/04 /stephen-miller-white-house-trump-237216.

32. Michael Goodwin, "Trump won't definitively say he still backs Bannon," *New York Post*, April 11, 2017. https://r-login.wordpress.com /remote-login.php?action=auth&host=nypost.com&id=56757 169&back=https%3A%2F%2Fnypost.com%2F2017%2F04%2F11%2F trump-wont-definitively-say-he-still-backs-bannon%2F&h=.

33. Cliff Sims, *Team of Vipers: My 500 Extraordinary Days in the Trump White House* (New York: Thomas Dunne Books, 2019).

34. Ibid.

35. Author interviews with Scott Lloyd, in 2019.

36. Hannah Levintova, "The Trump Official Overseeing Girls' Health Care Once Wrote He Couldn't 'Support Abortion for Any Reason,' " *Mother Jones*, August 22, 2018. https://www.motherjones.com/politics/2018/08 /scott-lloyd-essay-orr-pregnant-migrants-abortion/.

37. Ibid.

38. *Azar v. Garza*, 584 U.S. US Supreme Court. https://supreme.justia.com /cases/federal/us/584/17-654/.

39. Ibid.

40. Author's confidential interview with former ORR official, in 2019.

41. "Unaccompanied Children: Agency Efforts to Reunify Children Separated from Parents at the Border," Government Accountability Office, October 9, 2018. https://www.gao.gov/reports/GAO-19-163/.

42. Dan Diamond, "Former Trump refugee director says he never warned higher-ups about family separations," *Politico Magazine*, February 26, 2019. https:// www.politico.com/story/2019/02/26/scott-lloyd-migrant-family-separa tions-1216323.

43. *L.V.M, a minor, by and through his next friend Edith Esmeralda Mejia de Galindo, on his own behalf and on behalf of others similarly situated v. Scott Lloyd, Jonathan White, Steven Wagner, Alex Azar, Elcy Valdez, Jeremy Kohomban.* https:// www.nyclu.org/sites/default/files/field_documents/ecf_1_class_action

_complaint_and_petition_for_a_writ_of_habeas_corpus_2018-02-16_0
0062143xb2d9a.pdf.

44. Ibid.

45. Author's confidential interview with former ORR official, in 2019.

46. Hannah Dreier, "He Drew His School Mascot—and ICE Labeled Him a Gang Member," ProPublica, December 27, 2018. https://features.propublica.org/ms-13-immigrant-students/huntington-school-deportations-ice-honduras/.

47. *Guardian* staff and agencies, "Trump says acting cabinet members give him 'more flexibility,'" *The Guardian,* January 6, 2019. https://www.theguardian.com/us-news/2019/jan/06/trump-acting-cabinet-members-give-him-more-flexibility.

48. Jonathan Blitzer, "A Trump Official Behind the End of Daca Explains Himself," *The New Yorker,* November 10, 2017. https://www.newyorker.com/news/news-desk/trump-official-behind-the-end-of-daca-explains-himself.

49. "In migrant caravans, safety in numbers and no smuggling fees," Associated Press, October 26, 2018. https://www.staradvertiser.com/2018/10/26/breaking-news/in-migrant-caravan-safety-in-numbers-and-no-smuggling-fees/.

50. Author interviews with Jose Fuentes and Olivia Caceres for KPBS, in 2017. https://www.kpbs.org/news/2017/dec/13/father-fleeing-violence-struggles-reunion-1-year-o/.

51. Author interview with Jose Fuentes in detention for KPBS, in 2017. https://www.pbs.org/newshour/show/migrant-seeking-asylum-says-his-toddler-was-taken-away-at-the-u-s-border.

CHAPTER TWELVE "COSMOPOLITAN BIAS"

1. Author's confidential interview with meeting participant, in 2019.

2. Julie Hirschfeld Davis and Michael D. Shear, *Border Wars: Inside Trump's Assault on Immigration* (New York: Simon & Schuster, 2019).

3. "Review of Allegations of Politicized and Other Improper Personnel Practices in the Bureau of International Organization Affairs," Office of Inspector General, State Department, August 2019.

4. Julie Hirschfeld Davis and Somini Sengupta, "Trump Administration Rejects Study Showing Positive Impact of Refugees," *New York Times,* September 18, 2017. https://www.nytimes.com/2017/09/18/us/politics/refugees-revenue-cost-report-trump.html.

5. Eliana Johnson, Michael Crowley and Shane Goldmacher, "New NSC chief pushed Trump to moderate his language on terrorism," *Politico,* February 28, 2017. https://www.politico.com/story/2017/02/mcmaster-trump-terrorism-speech-23547.

6. Davis and Shear, *Border Wars.*

7. Gregory Korte, "Trump signs order cutting refugee quota to lowest level since 1980," *USA Today,* September 29, 2017. https://www.usatoday.com

/story/news/politics/2017/09/29/trump-set-cut-refugee-quota-lowest
-level-since-1980/713463001/.

8. Author's confidential interviews with two people familiar with the matter, in 2019.

9. Author's confidential interviews with two people present in the meeting, in 2019.

10. Michelle Kosinski, "Exclusive: Trump appointee guts UN document on racism, says leaders don't have duty to condemn hate speech," CNN, June 29, 2018. https://www.cnn.com/2018/06/29/politics/veprek-state-dept-un
-racism/index.html.

11. Molly McKew, "Did Russia Affect the 2016 Election? It's Now Undeniable," *Wired*, February 16, 2018. https://www.wired.com/story/did-russia
-affect-the-2016-election-its-now-undeniable/.

12. Peter Baker, Michael S. Schmidt and Maggie Haberman, "Citing Recusal, Trump Says He Wouldn't Have Hired Sessions," *New York Times*, July 19, 2017. https://www.nytimes.com/2017/07/19/us/politics/trump-interview
-sessions-russia.html.

13. Special Counsel Robert S. Mueller III, "Report on the Investigation into Russian Interference in the 2016 Presidential Election," March 2019. https://
www.justice.gov/storage/report.pdf.

14. Michael D. Shear and Zolan Kanno-Youngs, "White House Considered Releasing Migrants in 'Sanctuary Cities,'" *New York Times,* April 11, 2019. https://www.nytimes.com/2019/04/11/us/politics/sanctuary-cities
-trump.html.

15. Gabby Orr and Andrew Restuccia, "How Stephen Miller made immigration personal," *Politico Magazine*, April 22, 2019. https://www.politico.com
/story/2019/04/22/stephen-miller-immigration-trump-1284287.

16. David Rogers, "Trump's Immigration Crackdown Hits Vietnam," *Politico Magazine*, August 14, 2017. https://www.politico.com/story/2017/08/14
/trump-immigration-crackdown-vietnam-241564.

17. Bob Woodward, *Fear: Trump in the White House* (New York: Simon & Schuster, 2018).

18. Jeff Sessions press releases during Obama's implementation of DACA. http://finder.cox.net/main?ParticipantID=96e687opkbv4scrood8k84drs
6gw5duf&FailedURI=http%3A%2F%2Fwww.sessions.senate.gov%2F
public%2Findex.cfm%2Fnews-releases%3FID%3DF14E2E92-944C-FC
56-330D-B17E70665661&FailureMode=1&Implementation=&AddIn
Type=4&Version=pywr1.0&ClientLocation=us.

19. Rebekah Entralgo, "Stephen Miller attacks Statue of Liberty poem, echoing popular white nationalist talking point," ThinkProgress, August 2, 2017. https://thinkprogress.org/stephen-miller-attacks-statue-of-liberty-poem
-echoing-popular-white-nationalist-talking-point-f90c2ae0be48/.

20. Andrew Anglin, "Jews and Anti-Semites Torn on Stephen Miller," June 26, 2018. https://dailystormer.name/jews-torn-on-stephen-miller/.

CHAPTER THIRTEEN "WHITE LIVES MATTER"

1. Janet Reitman, "U.S. Law Enforcement Failed to See the Threat of White Nationalism. Now They Don't Know How to Stop It," *New York Times Magazine,* November 3, 2018. https://www.nytimes.com/2018/11/03/mag azine/FBI-charlottesville-white-nationalism-far-right.html.

2. "ADL Report: White Supremacist Murders More than Doubled in 2017," Anti-Defamation League, January 17, 2018. https://www.adl.org/news /press-releases/adl-report-white-supremacist-murders-more-than-dou bled-in-2017.

3. Olivia Nuzzi, "Trump Always Had the Power to Ruin Bannon, But His Chief Strategist Didn't See It," "Intelligencer," *New York*, January 10, 2018. http://nymag.com/intelligencer/2018/01/steve-bannon-never-saw-it -coming.html.

4. Michael Wolff, *Fire and Fury: Inside the Trump White House* (New York: Henry Holt, 2018).

5. Emails obtained by the author in 2019 from Senator Jeff Merkley's office.

6. Michael Edison Hayden, "Stephen Miller's Affinity for White Nationalism Revealed in Leaked Emails," Southern Poverty Law Center, November 12, 2019.

7. Author interview with Peter Vincent, in 2019.

8. Sebastian Rotella, Tim Golden and ProPublica, "Human Smugglers Are Thriving Under Trump," *The Atlantic*, February 21, 2019. https://www .theatlantic.com/politics/archive/2019/02/human-smugglers-thrive-under -trumps-zero-tolerance/583051/.

9. Jason Buch, "ICE Criminal Investigators Ask to be Distanced from Detentions, Deportations in Letter to Kirstjen Nielsen," *Texas Observer*, June 27, 2018. https://www.texasobserver.org/ice-hsi-letter-kirstjen-nielsen-criminal -civil-deportation-zero-tolerance/.

10. A. C. Thompson, "Inside the Secret Border Patrol Facebook Group Where Agents Joke About Migrant Deaths and Post Sexist Memes," ProPublica, July 1, 2019. https://www.propublica.org/article/secret-border-patrol-face book-group-agents-joke-about-migrant-deaths-post-sexist-memes.

11. Mitra Ebadolahi, "CBP Fails to Discredit Our Report on Abuse of Immi- grant Kids," American Civil Liberties Union, May 31, 2018. https://www .aclu.org/blog/immigrants-rights/ice-and-border-patrol-abuses/cbp-fails -discredit-our-report-abuse-immigrant.

12. Jean Guerrero, "Government Report Shows Border Wall Designs Can Be Broken," KPBS, September 17, 2018. https://www.kpbs.org/news/2018 /sep/17/government-report-shows-border-wall-designs-broken/.

13. Bob Woodward, *Fear: Trump in the White House* (New York: Simon & Schus- ter, 2018).

14. Ibid.

15. Ellen Cranley, "Everything we know about Mike Pence's press secretary Ka- tie Waldman—who is reportedly engaged to Trump advisor Stephen Miller," Business Insider, November 15, 2019. https://www.businessinsider.com/katie -waldman-mike-pence-new-press-secretary-stephen-miller-2019-9.

16. Jordain Carney, "Graham blasts Homeland Security statement as 'poison-ous,'" *The Hill*, February 15, 2018. https://thehill.com/blogs/floor-action/senate/374032-graham-blasts-homeland-security-statement-as-poisonous.

CHAPTER FOURTEEN "THESE ARE *ANIMALS*"

1. Emails exchanged with Katie Waldman by the author in 2018.
2. Author's confidential interview with DHS official, in 2019.
3. Ibid.
4. "Remnants of Mexico migrant caravan closer to US border," Associated Press, April 23, 2018. https://apnews.com/7ade41f45a7b44169427a7bb1cffb40f/Remnants-of-Mexico-migrant-caravan-closer-to-US-border.
5. Jean Guerrero, "Caravan of Central Americans and supporters arrive at U.S.-Mexico border fence," Facebook Live, KPBS. https://www.facebook.com/KPBSSanDiego/videos/10155709626756748/.
6. "Initial Observations Regarding Family Separation Issues Under the Zero Tolerance Policy," Office of the Inspector General, Department of Homeland Security, September 27, 2018. https://www.oig.dhs.gov/sites/default/files/assets/2018-10/OIG-18-84-Sep18.pdf.
7. Sandra Dibble, "Tijuana medical examiner's office threatened with shut-down," *San Diego Union-Tribune*, December 13, 2017. https://www.sandiegouniontribune.com/news/border-baja-california/sd-me-tijuana-medical-examiner-20171212-story.html.
8. Laura Bush, "Separating children from their parents at the border 'breaks my heart,'" *Washington Post*, June 17, 2018. https://www.washingtonpost.com/opinions/laura-bush-separating-children-from-their-parents-at-the-border-breaks-my-heart/2018/06/17/f2df517a-7287-11e8-9780-b1dd6a09b549_story.html.
9. Conference Call with White House Officials on Immigration, May 29, 2018. https://www.c-span.org/video/?446289-1/radio-conference-call-white-house-officials-immigration.
10. Author's confidential interview with government official, in 2019.
11. Ana Giaritelli, "Trump DHS Secretary McAleenan gave solely to Democrats for years, filings show," *Washington Examiner*, June 24, 2019. https://www.washingtonexaminer.com/news/trump-dhs-secretary-mcaleenan-gave-to-solely-democrats-for-years-fec-filings-show.
12. Dan Plante, "New FBI report names San Diego safest big city in America," KUSI News, September 27, 2018. https://www.kusi.com/new-fbi-report-names-san-diego-safest-big-city-in-america/.
13. Ashley Parker and Josh Dawsey, "Stephen Miller: Immigration agitator and White House survivor," *Washington Post*, January 21, 2018. https://www.washingtonpost.com/politics/stephen-miller-immigration-agitator-and-white-house-survivor/2018/01/21/7a1f7778-fcae-11e7-b832-8c26844b74fb_story.htm.
14. Author's confidential interview with former USCIS official, in 2019.
15. Miriam Jordan, "Wait Times for Citizenship Have Doubled in the Last

Two Years," *New York Times*, February 21, 2019. https://www.nytimes
.com/2019/02/21/us/immigrant-citizenship-naturalization.html.

16. Julie Hirschfeld Davis and Michael D. Shear, *Border Wars: Inside Trump's Assault on Immigration* (New York: Simon & Schuster, 2019).

17. Eileen Sullivan and Michael D. Shear, "Trump Sees an Obstacle to Getting His Way on Immigration: His Own Officials," *New York Times*, April 14, 2019. https://www.nytimes.com/2019/04/14/us/politics/trump-immigra tion-stephen-miller.html.

18. Ted Hesson, "Emails show Stephen Miller pressed hard to limit green cards," *Politico Magazine*, August 2, 2019. https://www.politico.com/story /2019/08/02/stephen-miller-green-card-immigration-1630406.

19. Eric Lutz, "Stephen Miller's Anti-Immigrant Plan Deemed Too Racist to Be Legal," *Vanity Fair*, August 19, 2019. https://www .vanityfair.com/news/2019/08/stephen-millers-ban-immigrant-chil dren-public-school-racist.

20. Author interview with Sarah Owings, in 2018.

21. Meagan Flynn, "Kirstjen Nielsen heckled by protestors at Mexican restaurant. Other diners applauded them," *Washington Post*, June 20, 2018. https:// www.washingtonpost.com/news/morning-mix/wp/2018/06/20/kirstjen -nielsen-heckled-by-protesters-at-mexican-restaurant-if-kids-dont-eat-in -peace-you-dont-eat-in-peace/.

CHAPTER FIFTEEN "PANDORA'S BOX"

1. Author's confidential interview with former HHS official, in 2019.

2. Author interviews with Scott Lloyd, in 2019.

3. Author's confidential interviews with sources on the call, in 2019.

4. Ibid.

5. David Glosser, "Stephen Miller Is an Immigration Hypocrite. I Know Because I'm His Uncle," *Politico Magazine*, August 13, 2018. https://www .politico.com/magazine/story/2018/08/13/stephen-miller-is-an-immigra tion-hypocrite-i-know-because-im-his-uncle-219351.

6. Kevin Huffman Facebook Page, https://www.facebook.com/100005 622728535/posts/879882865542463/.

7. Author interview with Patti Glosser, in 2019.

8. Julie Hirschfeld Davis and Michael D. Shear, *Border Wars: Inside Trump's Assault on Immigration* (New York: Simon & Schuster, 2019).

9. Author's confidential interview with participant in the meeting, in 2019.

10. Eileen Sullivan and Michael D. Shear, "Trump Sees an Obstacle to Getting His Way on Immigration: His Own Officials," *New York Times*, April 14, 2019. https://www.nytimes.com/2019/04/14/us/politics/trump-immigra tion-stephen-miller.html.

11. Jeff Abbott and Sandra Cuffe, "Honduran killed in border crackdown on migrant caravan," Al-Jazeera, October 29, 2018. https://www.aljazeera .com/news/2018/10/honduran-killed-mexican-border-crackdown-mi grant-caravan-181029130957107.html.

12. Leah McDonald, " 'Go home!': Residents in an upscale Tijuana neighbor-

hood throw rocks at the migrant caravan and order them out of Mexico while US troops put MORE barbed wire up to stop hundreds arriving at the border from climbing the wall," DailyMail.com, November 15, 2018. https://www.dailymail.co.uk/news/article-6396159/Residents-upscale-Tijuana -neighborhood-throw-rocks-migrant-caravan.html.

13. Jean Guerrero, "Radical American Activists Flock to Migrants Caravan in Tijuana," KPBS, January 16, 2019. https://www.kpbs.org/news/2019 /jan/16/radical-american-activists-flock-migrant-caravan-t/.

14. Ibid.

15. Jean Guerrero, "False Rumors in Tijuana Motivate Some Migrants to Turn Back," KPBS, November 28, 2018. https://www.kpbs.org/news/2018 /nov/28/false-rumors-fuel-some-migrant-decisions-give-amer/.

16. Jean Guerrero, "Mothers in Migrant Caravan Fear Unruly Men Will Ruin Chance at Asylum," KPBS, November 23, 2018. https://www.kpbs.org /news/2018/nov/23/mothers-migrant-caravan-fear-unruly-men-will-ruin-/.

17. Jean Guerrero, "Radical American Activists Flock to Migrant Caravan in Tijuana," KPBS, January 16, 2019. https://www.kpbs.org/news/2019 /jan/16/radical-american-activists-flock-migrant-caravan-t/.

18. Email received by the author from Katie Waldman in 2019.

19. Jacqueline Alemany, "Power Up: Trump's State of the Union address was Stephen Miller's speech, too," *Washington Post*, February 6, 2019. https://www .washingtonpost.com/news/powerpost/paloma/powerup/2019/02/06 /powerup-trump-s-state-of-the-union-address-was-stephen-miller-s -speech-too/5c59f35f1b326b66eb09862a/.

20. Doug Stephens, "Why I Quit My Job Carrying Out Trump's Immigration Policies," *New York Times*, November 20, 2019. https://www.nytimes .com/2019/11/20/opinion/trump-asylum-remain-mexico-policy.html.

21. Kate Morrissey, "San Diego Immigration Court 'Overwhelmed' by Remain in Mexico cases," *San Diego Union-Tribune*, June 3, 2019. https://www.sandie gouniontribune.com/news/immigration/story/2019-05-31/san-diego -immigration-court-overwhelmed-by-remain-in-mexico-cases.

22. Angel Canales and Caroline Linton, "Asylum seeker dies trying to re-enter U.S. after she was sent to Mexico," *CBS News*, August 2, 2019. https:// www.cbsnews.com/news/migrant-drownings-el-paso-asylum-seeker-dies -trying-to-re-enter-us-after-she-was-sent-to-mexico/.

CHAPTER SIXTEEN "OUT OF LOVE"

1. John Roberts, "White House senior policy advisor: Trump shows a great wisdom on China no other president has ever shown," Fox News, August 25, 2019. https://video.foxnews.com/v/6076932181001/#sp=show-clips.

2. John Feeley, "Stephen Miller and 'Sophie's Choice': History Repeats Itself," Univision, April 9, 2019. https://www.univision.com/univision-news /opinion/stephen-miller-and-sophies-choice-history-repeats-itself.

3. Jean Guerrero, "US Still Separating Families at Border When Children Are US Citizens," KPBS, September 26, 2018. https://www.kpbs.org /news/2018/sep/26/us-is-still-separating-families-border/.

4. Elliot Spagat and Astrid Galvan, "ACLU: 911 children split at border since 2018 court order," Associated Press, July 31, 2019. https://apnews.com /ba5a05e6a7f14b6b898d75712dee1f6b.

5. Jonathan White, "Migrant Family Separation Policy," House Energy and Commerce Subcommittee, February 7, 2019. https://www.c-span.org /video/?457545-1/gao-hhs-officials-testify-migrant-family-separation -policy.

6. A memo obtained by the author in confidence in 2019.

7. Jason Zengerle, "How America Got 'Zero Tolerance' on Immigration," *New York Times*, July 16, 2019. https://www.nytimes.com/2019/07/16/magazine /immigration-department-of-homeland-security.html.

8. Author interview with David Lapan, in 2019.

9. Author interview with Juliette Kayyem, in 2019.

10. Devan Cole and Geneva Sands, "Union chief blasts Trump pick to lead citizenship agency, says signals 'end of legal immigration,' " CNN, May 27, 2019. https://www.cnn.com/2019/05/27/politics/danielle-spooner-ken-cuccinelli-uscis/index.html.

11. Ann Coulter on PBS *Frontline*, "Zero Tolerance," October 22, 2019. https:// www.youtube.com/watch?v=VXOFHr6tGMQ.

12. Colby Itkwowitz and Rachael Bade, "White House Rejects Democrats' Call for Stephen Miller to Testify on Immigration," *Washington Post*, April 24, 2019. https://www.washingtonpost.com/politics/white -house-rejects-democrats-call-for-stephen-miller-to-testify-on-immi gration/2019/04/24/02b47740-66fe-11e9-8985-4cf30147bdca_story .html.

13. Ted Hesson, "Trump's pick for ICE director: I can tell which migrant children will become gang members by looking into their eyes," *Politico Magazine*, May 16, 2019. https://www.politico.com/story/2019/05/16/mark -morgan-eyes-ice-director-1449570.

14. Nick Miroff and Josh Dawsey, "Acting secretary blocked Miller's bid for another DHS shake-up," *Washington Post*, May 18, 2019. https://www .washingtonpost.com/national/acting-secretary-blocked-stephen-millers -bid-for-another-dhs-shakeup/2019/05/17/20608bf6-78e4-11e9-b3f5 -5673edf2d127_story.html.

15. Anna Giaritelli, "Officials accuse DHS chief Kevin McAleenan of leaking ICE raids plan to sabotage operation," *Washington Examiner*, June 22, 2019. https://www.washingtonexaminer.com/news/officials-accuse-dhs-chief -kevin-mcaleenan-of-leaking-ice-raids-plan-to-sabotage-operation.

16. Brandon Judd, "Acting DHS chief McAleenan's refusal to do his job puts law enforcement and Americans at risk," Fox News, June 24, 2019. https:// www.foxnews.com/opinion/brandon-judd-dhs-kevin-mcaleenan-ice-anti -trump.amp?__twitter_impression=true.

17. Photographs posted by DHS secretary Kevin McAleenan on Twitter.

18. Alex Nowrasteh, "1.3 Percent of All Central Americans in the Northern Triangle Were Apprehended by Border Patrol This Fiscal Year—So Far," Cato Institute, June 7, 2019. https://www.cato.org/blog/13-percent-all-central -americans-northern-triangle-were-apprehended-border-patrol-fiscal-year.

19. Jonathan Blitzer, "Does Asylum Have a Future at the Border?" *The New Yorker,* October 3, 2019. https://www.newyorker.com/news/daily-comment/does-asylum-have-a-future-at-the-southern-border.

20. Chris Crane, Public Letter to Trump, November 13, 2017. https://www.scribd.com/document/364452909/ICE-Letter-to-President-Trump.

21. Author interview with Brandon Judd, in 2019.

22. Matthew Boyle, "Donald Trump: Cantor's Defeat Shows 'Everybody' in Congress Is Vulnerable If They Support Amnesty," Breitbart, June 12, 2014. http://www.breitbart.com/big-government/2014/06/12/donald-trump-cantor-s-defeat-shows-everybody-in-congress-is-vulnerable-if-they-support-amnesty/.

23. Stephen Miller, "America: the forgotten campus culture," *The Chronicle,* Duke University, November 19, 2006. https://www.dukechronicle.com/article/2006/11/america-forgotten-campus-culture.

24. Nick Miroff, "Acting homeland security chief frustrated and isolated—even as he delivers what Trump wants at the border," *Washington Post,* October 1, 2019. https://www.washingtonpost.com/immigration/acting-homeland-security-chief-frustrated-and-isolated—even-as-he-delivers-what-trump-wants-at-the-border/2019/10/01/b62e740c-e3ad-11e9-b403-f738899982d2_story.html.

25. CBP official data, "Southern Border Migration FY 2019." https://www.cbp.gov/newsroom/stats/sw-border-migration.

26. Nick Miroff, "Under secret Stephen Miller plan, ICE to use data on migrant children to expand deportation efforts," *Washington Post,* December 20, 2019. https://www.washingtonpost.com/immigration/under-secret-stephen-miller-plan-ice-to-use-data-on-migrant-children-to-expand-deportation-efforts/2019/12/20/36975b34-22a8-11ea-bed5-880264cc91a9_story.html.

27. Michael Edison Hayden, "Stephen Miller's Affinity for White Nationalism Revealed in Leaked Emails," Southern Poverty Law Center, November 12, 2019.

28. Trish Regan Primetime Team, "Stephen Miller: Democrats 'traffic in lies, hatred and yes, racism," Fox Business, December 20, 2019. https://www.foxbusiness.com/politics/stephen-miller-democrats-lies-hatred-racism.

29. Author interviews with Katie McHugh, in 2019.

INDEX